Sole

in the

Solemn Duty
in the Old Guard

*From Arlington National Cemetery
to the Pentagon on 9/11
in America's Oldest Regiment*

MARK JOSEPH MONGILUTZ

McFarland & Company, Inc., Publishers
Jefferson, North Carolina

Library of Congress Cataloguing-in-Publication Data

Names: Mongilutz, Mark Joseph, author.
Title: Solemn Duty in the Old Guard : From Arlington National
    Cemetery to the Pentagon on 9/11 in America's Oldest Regiment /
    Mark Joseph Mongilutz.
Description: Jefferson, North Carolina : McFarland & Company, Inc.,
    Publishers, 2018 | Includes index.
Identifiers: LCCN 2018033392 | ISBN 9781476672212 (softcover :
    acid free paper) ∞
Subjects: LCSH: United States. Army. Infantry Regiment, 3rd—
    History—21st century. | Arlington National Cemetery (Arlington,
    Va.)—History—21st century. | September 11 Terrorist Attacks,
    2001. | Pentagon (Va.)—History—21st century.
Classification: LCC UA29 3d .M66 2018 | DDC 356/.1130973—dc23
LC record available at https://lccn.loc.gov/2018033392

British Library Cataloguing data are available

ISBN (print) 978-1-4766-7221-2
ISBN (ebook) 978-1-4766-3179-0

Front cover image of members of The Old Guard Caisson
Platoon and Casket Team escort a casket into Section 60
of Arlington National Cemetery for burial service on
October 26, 2011 (Joint Base Myer-Henderson Hall)

Printed in the United States of America

McFarland & Company, Inc., Publishers
  Box 611, Jefferson, North Carolina 28640
  www.mcfarlandpub.com

Table of Contents

Author's Note

I never kept my military orders. I rarely keep documentation of any sort. However, it became apparent while authoring the pages herein that a few of my official orders would have been helpful in zeroing in on precise arrival/departure dates. I welcome any verifiable corrections to the record, should those of you more inclined to harbor paperwork elect to provide them.

Preface

This work is dedicated to the men and women of the United States Armed Forces, a collection of distinctive military services of which I was, in some small way, a part for several years. Were I to dedicate the first one-hundred pages of this book to a written celebration and extolling of the magnificence so routinely achieved by America's brilliant military, I would ultimately find myself exceeding that limit tenfold, tenfold, and tenfold still again. To this day, to this moment, to this very heartbeat, I am impossibly humbled to have stood in those hallowed and storied ranks of The Old Guard—even if the significance was often lost upon me at the time.

There is no question of it: for my every success in uniform, I fell decidedly short in some other way. My service was an ongoing lesson in humility, a tapestry of error that I labored mightily to adorn with the occasional triumph. On balance, I cannot say with any certainty that mine was as noble, dignified, and worthy an Army enlistment as I would like for it to have been. But the U.S. Army is a staggeringly effective institution; it can more than bear the burden of a young soldier not quite mature enough to be worthy of it, but too stubborn and fearful of failure to quit. My sincere, and lasting, and heartfelt thanks to every officer, non-commissioned officer, and fellow grunt (ceremonial and otherwise) who gave shape to my potential, who afforded my shortfalls their graceful patience, and who entrusted me with responsibility for which my capability was often just barely commensurate. I am in your debt for the remainder of my days.

Tone and theme will flexibly shift a bit from page to page and chapter to chapter throughout this work. It is a memoir, and my writing is, to that end, accordingly conversational and accessible. I will provide a glimpse into the challenges endured by a wholly unprepared and bookish Infantry (11B) recruit, a quick look at Airborne School, and a close examination of my nearly four years' time with the 3rd United States Infantry (The Old Guard). The last of these will see me covering everything from routine burials (I was a casket bearer) and endless Summerall Field parades, to the horrors of

September 11, 2001 as experienced in surreal fashion by the Army's only active duty Washington, D.C.–based infantry unit.

And there will be anecdotes. Plenty of anecdotes. As these are almost invariably supplied in service to humorous storytelling, many might be correctly regarded as rather embarrassing by their star and supporting casts. Where necessary, names have been politely changed, physical descriptions and identities otherwise protected. I am not spared where the sheepishness factor is concerned, and my own mistakes, failings, and occasional foolishness will be on full display. Rest assured, my own name will not be changed, nor my identity protected. It will be laid bare for a gentle reckoning.

Aside from several comedic exaggerations and numerous imperfect recollections, what I have written is as true an account of the tale I have sought to tell as my memory and writing capacity can between them yield.

Enjoy.

Overview of
Military Terminology

Enlisted Ranks

E-1—Private (abbreviation: PV1)

E-2—Private (abbreviation: PV2)

E-3—Private First Class (abbreviation: PFC)

E-4—Specialist (abbreviation: SPC) ("Spec4")

E-5—Sergeant (abbreviation: SGT) (idiom: Buck Sergeant)

E-6—Staff Sergeant (abbreviation: SSG) (note: "staff" is not applied to this rank in spoken transactions; they are referred to as "Sergeant")

E-7—Sergeant First Class (abbreviation: SFC)

E-8—Master Sergeant/First Sergeant (abbreviations: MSG/1SG); ("Top")

E-9*—Sergeant Major/Command Sergeant Major (abbreviations: SGM/CSM)

The Sergeant Major of the Army—its most senior enlisted member—is also an E-9, though in a "First Amongst Equals" sort of capacity, as the rank of E-10 does not exist.

Officer Ranks

O-1—Second Lieutenant (abbreviation: LT)

O-2—First Lieutenant (abbreviation: LT)

O-3—Captain (abbreviation: CPT)

O-4—Major (MJR)

O-5—Lieutenant Colonel (abbreviation: LTC)

O-6—Colonel (abbreviation: COL)

O-7—Brigadier General (abbreviation: Brig. Gen.)

O-8—Major General (abbreviation: MG)

O-9—Lieutenant General (abbreviation LTG)

O-10—General

O-11—General of the Army

Warrant Officer Ranks

W-1—Warrant Officer

W-2—Chief Warrant Officer (abbreviation: CW2)

W-3—Chief Warrant Officer (abbreviation: CW3)

W-4—Chief Warrant Officer (abbreviation: CW4)

W-5—Master Warrant Officer (abbreviation: CW5) (idiom: "Oh, so *you're* the one.")

Common Terms, Acronyms and Esoteric Military Jargon

AIT—Advanced Individual Training (MOS-specific and follows the standard basic training period)

ANC—Arlington National Cemetery

APFT—Army Physical Fitness Test

BDUs—Battle Dress Uniform (the standard camouflage top/trousers worn during the duty day, for field training exercises, and in military theaters of operation; available in various prints and color schemes)

BRM—Basic Rifle Marksmanship

Caisson Platoon—An Old Guard specialty platoon charged with conveying casketed remains to their final resting place via horse-drawn caisson. The animals' welfare (exercise, feeding, grooming) also falls to these men.

Class A Uniform—Formal attire generally reserved for important occasions (required for official DA photographs; not unique to The Old Guard)

Class B Uniform—Mid-level formal attire (often worn during ceremony rehearsals and in instances for which dress blues would be impractical or unnecessary; not unique to The Old Guard)

Colors—These select marchers are charged with showcasing the National Colors (American Flag) as well as the Organizational/Branch Colors.

Conmy Hall—Fort Myer's indoor parade/ceremony facility (used during inclement weather and for smaller scale events; often used for push-up/sit-up portion of APFT during winter months)

CONUS—Continental United States

CQ—Charge of Quarters (company-level desk duty spanning 24 hours' time and consisting of an E-5/Sergeant + a lower-enlisted runner)

Degree Four—An enlisted soldier who, by virtue of joining the service having completed a four-year college degree program, is permitted to bypass paygrades

1–3 and assume the rank of E-4. Such soldiers are either mildly smug or pleasantly humble, with few souls occupying the middle ground.

DFAC—Dining Facility (known idiomatically as the "chow hall")

ETS—Expiration Term of Service (orders delivered in advance of one's discharge from the Armed Forces)

Flagged—Administratively forbidden from performing certain professional duties; typically ineligible for favorable actions (awards, passes, etc.) while thusly restricted

GP—General Purpose (used before various nouns)

Grunt—A lower-ranking infantry or combat arms soldier charged with audibly grunting on a semi-regular basis, typically whilst engaged in physically arduous training, missions, work details, et cetera; more precisely, a soldier belonging to any combat arms MOS

HESCO Barrier—Defensive fortification consisting of earth and rock packed densely within a stretch of mesh containment

High-&-Tight—A common alternative to the completely shaven head, this variant sees the soldier maintaining much of their crown hair while forfeiting the sides to a barber's merciless clippers.

Hooah—An Army colloquialism which often stands in for "Yes," "No," "Maybe," "I don't know," "Depends on who's asking," "Definitely," and "Gotcha," provided it is followed by "Sergeant" or "Sir," depending on the situation. Ex. "You boys ready for a long day of road marching?" "Hooah, sir!"

Manual/Standing Manual—Essentially the prescribed ceremonial weapon movements exhibited in crisp fashion by a soldier or formation of soldiers.

MDW—The Military District of Washington (as in, the District of Columbia)

MOS—Military Occupational Specialty (Infantry=11Bravo, for example)

NCO—Non-Commissioned Officer (E-5 through E-9)

NCOIC—Non-Commissioned Officer In Charge (of a given detail, tasking, etc.)

OCONUS—Outside Continental United States

PCS—Permanent Change of Station (these orders precede an official departure for one's next duty station)

POG—Piece of Garbage; disparaging term employed by combat arms soldiers in describing their non-combat arms counterparts

PT—Physical Training, often avoided by turds who are instead engaged in the work of shamming (see below)

PTs—Exercise attire (worn during physical training hours; also worn during the duty day by certain breeds of turd)

P/X—Post Exchange; take your local K-Mart, age it 12 years, then transplant it to a military post

Sham—To strategically avert one's duties, training responsibilities, etc.

Smoke Session—A round of punitive exercise visited upon unruly, disrespectful or otherwise deserving soldiers (see "Turd" below)

SOP—Standard Operating Procedure

TRADOC—United States Army Training and Doctrine Command (administrative command charged with determining how many flutter kicks it takes to produce a qualified 11Bravo; they also oversee dozens of important and impressive military schools across the country)

Turd—The sort of soldier given to shamming; also, a piece of human excrement

Organizational Overview

Field Army—80,000+ soldiers

Corps—Army sub-formation numbering 20,000+ soldiers

Division—Corps sub-formation numbering 10,000–20,000 soldiers

Brigade (Regiment)—Division sub-formation numbering 1,800–3,600 soldiers— The Old Guard existed solely as a regiment for many years, but is now home to a deployable battalion.

Battalion—Brigade sub-formation numbering 300–800 soldiers

Company—Battalion sub-formation numbering 100–140 soldiers

Platoon—Company sub-formation numbering 15–30 soldiers

Squad—Platoon sub-formation numbering 8–12 soldiers

Fire-Team—Squad sub-formation numbering 3–4 soldiers

Soldier—Fire-Team sub-formation numbering 1 soldier

Common Weapon Systems

M4 Carbine—A ubiquitous assault rifle issued throughout the Armed Forces; 5.56x45mm NATO cartridge

M249 (SAW)—A relatively light, gas-operated machine gun, the Squad Automatic Weapon also fires a 5.56x45mm round but typically does so in a belt-feed, fully automatic capacity. Magazine feed is an option, albeit a less reliable one

M240B—Gas-operated machine gun utilizing a belt-feed system and firing a 7.62x51mm NATO cartridge

M203—A 40mm grenade launcher designed specifically to fit beneath the barrel of a compatible assault rifle

M9—A semiautomatic pistol which fires a 9x19mm NATO cartridge. Officers and senior NCOs are typically assigned this weapon in a sidearm capacity. It is also used by the Military Police, with some exceptions

M14—At one point in time, this automatic rifle, which fires a 7.62x51mm NATO cartridge, was standard issue throughout the United States Army and Marine Corps. Though it sees fairly common use in combat zones throughout the world, it is a neutered (firing pin removed) version of the weapon that is used by the 3rd United States Infantry Regiment for ceremonial purposes.

M2 Browning—A massive machine gun which fires the formidable .50 BMG (12.7×99mm NATO), this weapon is designed for use in a vehicle-mounted or fixed position capacity. It is far too heavy to be wielded in any other manner.

Mk 19—A fully automatic grenade launcher. Think on that for a moment.

I

Home, Memories Thereof

"Yeah, just lay in bed."

I don't believe Drill Sergeant Spencer meant any harm when speaking to me in his menacing voice that we (I am including my platoon mates here) would eventually come to cherish ... to some degree. And I often recall the sentence ending with "motherfucker," though that might not have been the *specific* epithet he directed towards me. In truth, I had heard that term thrown about so frequently during the preceding week that it almost invariably materializes in my memory of those days.

"Get the *fuck* up."

My bare feet had already landed on the cold, crappy linoleum bay floor by the time Spencer finished this second verbal broadside, but he nevertheless saw fit to voice it. If his aim had been to command my full attention, he had succeeded handily, a few moments prior, with the violent hurling of a tin trash can (think Oscar T. Grouch) down the bay's wide-open center. This he had done at 0500hrs EST in Fort Benning, Georgia. The intent behind so cruel a wakeup call was precisely that: cruelty. Such measures make good soldiers—kindness less so. There are no safe spaces on Sand Hill. Well, one or two, but we'll get to those. In fact, to go forward, let us first go back.

This all begins in one of two Washingtons, which will be explored to wildly varying degrees in our story of unanticipated travails. And of an accidental soldier.

I was not born in Washington, but it is my home state.

It is.

Whatever thoughts/images of Pennsylvania populate the darkest recesses of my otherwise excellent memory are wholly inaccessible to me. Washington is my home, and always will be.

So, then, to our story's beginning. Washington is a beautiful state to call home, a marvelous place in which to be raised, and a topographical treasure all too hastily dismissed as a rainy shithole by the republic beyond. The mountains are breathtaking; truly, they take one's breath from one's lungs.

Don't believe me?

Do believe me.

The forests possess a splendor all their own. The lakes sparkle brilliantly, the skies teem with thick blueness, the clouds arrest one's vision with their puffy, saturated whiteness. And, yes, rain does fall from the sky. A pittance of a fee to live among remarkable natural beauty, to be sure.

Leaving was difficult. More difficult than I could have imagined. Prior to June of 2000, I had never experienced homesickness. I had never wept for my own bed while staying the night at a friend's house, had never expressed anxiety about an impending road trip, and had never taken proper inventory of the blessings inherent in a Western Washington upbringing. I am not a son of privilege and was wholly unacquainted with the comfort that stems from not having to think about money.

The Army was a sensible move. Even for a natural born writer and life-long storyteller with a penchant for British colloquialisms.

Had I gone straightaway to community or state college, I might have done all right for myself. Maybe. But I had spent much of my K-12 time yearn-ing for something visceral—an outlet, a risk, an adventure. That much was to be expected of a kid who had connected very closely with Greek mythology and Medieval history. That I was perhaps an inch or two higher than 5 feet until high school certainly didn't make exercising my heroic, adventurous, childish ambitions during adolescence an overly realistic proposition. Such fantasies were instead played out imaginatively.

I was always a storyteller, a characteristic which would land me in a bit of trouble during my Army years. To hold an audience's attention with an array of imaginings, exaggerated truths, wholesale myths, and a host of (mostly passable) impressions was innate in me from early on. That this char-acteristic had little to do with my heroic ambitions would not fully dawn upon me until adulthood. We are seldom who we think ourselves to be.

In *Neverending Story* terms, I thought myself an Atreyu; I was more a Bastian.

There is a fantasy card game known as Magic: The Gathering which my closest childhood friends, Geoff and Andy, along with a few acquaintances and peripheral neighborhood kids, played for years on end during our shared adolescence. The game combines elements of strategy and deck formulation with beautiful, inventive storyweaving and overarching gameplay mythology. It was the latter of these that consumed my attention while the others focused on besting one another in duels and team matches.

This had always been the case since I met Geoff in the summer of 1989.

I was walking about Rolling Greens, the residential development where I spent my childhood and early adolescence, and had struck a delicate balance between enjoying the day's sunny beauty and actively enhancing it with imagined fantastical creatures, when a voice bellowed from nearby. The neighborhood is circular and bisected by a paved trail lined by dozens of homes. These all face away from the trail, which is to say their backyards and second-story rear decks all look upon the bisection and all who traverse it. Geoff, who, being a year older, was a grade ahead of me, had been standing atop his own rear deck and spotted me—a kid utterly lost in his own head.

"Hey, you wanna come play *Kid Icarus*?" he asked in a wholly noncommittal tone of voice. It was as though he had called out against his better judgment.

"Me?" I asked, knowing full well there was no one else around.

"It's kind of a stupid game, but you might like it." This, too, is characteristic of my dear friend Geoff. He is profoundly particular about the games he'll spend any significant amount of time.

"Okay." I replied with an inborn enthusiasm and friendliness that would only begin to wane in me many years later.

Making my way to Geoff's front door was a matter of turning left at one of the trail intersections, walking alongside his house for a few paces, making another left into his driveway, and then a final left up to the steps.

Geoff was at the door and invited me in for the first of what must surely have been a thousand visits between that morning and the day of Drill Sergeant Spencer's inventive wakeup call eleven years later. Descending into Geoff's basement, which would eventually become a second home, I saw *Kid Icarus* glowing somewhat shakily on a television set perfectly sized for video gaming … at least by the standards of the day.

"How do you play?" I asked, having only a handful of games at home.

"You'll figure it out. Just keep climbing."

And that really is the game. Ascend, shoot, dodge, ascend, fall, re-ascend, and so on. For those possessing a linear, systematic thought process (have I introduced Geoff yet?), *Kid Icarus* is not impossible to beat; just somewhat difficult, a bit tricky. For those *not* possessing a linear way of thinking, the game is effectively impossible. Geoff realized quickly that I was no match for the array of villains and level tricks working against me in the game. He took over and, at least a half-hour prior to lunch, had beaten a game which I, twenty-seven years later, have yet to overcome.

And so it went for the next decade. Geoff, Andy (who joined us a couple of years later), and I would move from one gaming fixation to the next, despite our differing aims in engaging with fantasy via gameplay. For Geoff, the process was the purpose. He was systemization incarnate and lived to pioneer the most efficient means of conquering a game.

Andy brought to the trio something else entirely. There was a parliamentarian quality to his way of speaking, to his way of interacting with others, to his contributing to in-group settings. Geoff prioritized logic above context; Andy attempted to prioritize both. He was only rarely successful, but proved himself a strong and forceful intellect all the same. He was something of a deciphering agent when the need arose. My hyper-emotional personality often clashed with Geoff's detached indifference—outbursts ensued. It was Andy who would so often translate for us in a given situation. He was, in effect, the group's mediator. He was also a good gamer and provided Geoff with something approaching an equal.

For my part, the games were always about the stories told therein. It made achieving any excellence in their playing almost impossible. I certainly had my moments and could, given the proper motivation, zero in with frightful intensity to either defeat an adversary (Geoff included) or, at bare minimum, fight to a draw. But these were rare circumstances. I was the dreamer of the group and was driven by the idea of one day inhabiting the heroics I had spent so many hours idolizing.

Atreyu > Bastian

In some ways, this was an intuitive and predictable mentality. What I lacked in Geoff's profound capacity for raw logical thought process and Andy's ambassadorial penchant, I made up for in at least two relevant ways. First, I was usually (though not always) more adventurous than either and spent as much time outdoors, bruising and scraping my body in the neighboring woods, as I did indoors engaging in gameplay.

Second, I had developed a certain physicality during my childhood and early teen years which rendered me the "athlete" of the group, by default. I was by no means a big kid, and did not fully develop in terms of height, musculature, or endurance until well into my Army tenure. But time spent climbing, sprinting the neighborhood hills, and weightlifting with a neighborhood World War II veteran and fitness fanatic would impart upon me a grace, a sturdiness, and a strength which eluded many within our group. One among them referred to me as "Master Skywalker" rather frequently, a direct reference to the *Star Wars* protagonist.

As to how much this de facto athletic credibility would later influence my interest in joining the Armed Forces is difficult to know. But it *was* influential. I felt somehow protective of my geekier friends and associates when we made our routine long walks to Fred Meyer, the grocery store where I would eventually work in a bagger/cart pusher capacity. The fact that I probably could not have protected them from any major threat occurred to me often; but I knew I would try. Joining the Army after high school was as much a way of proving myself as it was an exercise in patriotism, in adventurism, in narcissism. I wanted so much to become worthy of the reputation I had come nowhere near rightly earning.

I would ultimately fail.

II

"You're in the motherfucking Army now, motherfucker"

"Well, do you wanna dance?"

There are no words to describe how radically things changed for me in my final year of high school. Well, actually, there are—and here they are.

Ariel Denton (obvious pseudonym) had asked me to dance. It was homecoming. I was there with the classically beautiful Audrey Roman, a knockout redhead with skin like milk and eyes of sapphire. Just a knockout.

Ariel was her own beauty, and she defied any standard arrangement of nouns and adjectives. I had known of her since our junior year but we moved in different circles. She was an ultra-cool skater chick with elfin features and a "Who gives a fuck?" sort of sweetness to her. If I live a hundred more hours, a hundred more years, or a hundred more lifetimes, I will never fully understand what compelled that perfect creature to approach me during Marysville Pilchuck's Fall '99 homecoming dance.

Although, it was not *completely* unexpected.

Don't misunderstand—being asked to dance by Ariel was indeed unexpected, as we had never spoken, took none of the same classes, and shared virtually no common ground (of which we were aware). However, something had occurred in the latter half of my junior year, had gathered momentum over the summer, and was blossoming fully by that September.

As it happens, the moving of heavy weights via muscular exertion yields physiological results which many among the fairer sex find attractive. I had been insanely active during my elementary/middle school years, climbing, sprinting, and lifting grades three through six. And while traces of that activity persisted throughout junior high and well into my sophomore year, I did not engage in anything in the way of sustained, aggressive exercise for the better part of four years' time.

Then I took a job at Fred Meyer.

Then I reacquainted myself with weightlifting.

Then I returned to school for my senior year.

Heads were turning, and in my obliviousness, I was largely unaware of as much for those first couple of weeks. But it was soon impossible to ignore.

This is not to say that I went from a virtual non-entity to dominating the Pilchuck High dating scene. Far from it. But suddenly there was interest, demand, and flirtation. I had put on some shapely muscle, had grown considerably, and had stumbled quite accidentally into an attractive bedhead look which was met with many a hungry glance by girls who literally (literally) would not have known me by name or appearance as little as a year prior. I was bookish, quite devoted to the written word, had done well in a few spelling bees, and made the miscalculation of thinking that broadcasting my vocabulary skills during sophomore English class would win me friends, notoriety, acceptance, or at least one of these. In short, my first two years of high school were a bit of a slog. Factor in the daydreaming and my disinclination towards mathematics, and I was fated for an uphill climb.

I never envied the more conventionally successful students their popularity. I was content with my afterschool activities and quietly hoped that better things awaited me on the other side of my diploma. Besides, I was rarely lonely. If not enjoying the company of my closest friends, I was immersed in literature. There are many worse fates; few (if any) better.

But a fate I long since embraced as one I would endure right up to the end had suddenly been hijacked by favorably complicating factors which sought to politely throw a wrench in the works. And Ariel had asked me to dance.

"Okay." I labored with the might of fifty stevedores to maintain a look of coolness. Oddly enough, I think Geoff was the mental reference for whatever outward appearance I ended up achieving.

And so we danced. I wish to this day that I could recall the song. In truth, I don't think I ever knew it to begin with. Dancing with a pretty girl—and upon her request, rather than the reverse—was enough to send my mind into a tailspin.

Am I dreaming? I know it's a cliché, but seriously, am I dreaming? This is Ariel Denton. She would surely not have asked that I dance with her a year past. Holy shit, we're pulled in to one another still tighter.

The dance had become more intimate than I could handle. It was overwhelming. There was something so paramount in the placement of her hands upon my shoulders. I had worked hard to build those into something strong, into something masculine, into something capable. Those delicate, graceful, elfin hands placed gently upon my shoulders was validating to a degree Ariel could never have known. I played it cool.

And so it went for the remainder of the '99–'00 school year. I was dating, and flirting, and resisting advances, and making my own, and even dealing with the peculiar situation of being pursued (even if playfully) by a Fred Meyer colleague ten years my senior. Oh, yes—I should say, my virginity was that winter rendered forfeit to a seasoned woman of eighteen years. The idea of graduating high school a virgin had seemed so very probable during my adolescence that the alternative almost never occurred to me as a real possibility.

And then it was gone.

I had been invited to her house around Valentine's Day (the weekend prior, I believe), we had messed about in clumsy fashion, and then ... well, you know.

In short, by the time high school graduation was nearing, I was the very definition of confidence. Much of this self-perception was misplaced, as I would soon find out, but that seventeen-year-old kid felt capable of anything. I felt strong, I felt invincible, and I felt worthy of the adventurous path for which I had long yearned. When our local Army recruitment office reached out in April of 2000, they had unknowingly contacted a boy whose psychological profile was ripe for the military's plucking.

Childhood had introduced me to myths and legends which I cherish to this day; early adolescence had juxtaposed my inherent physicality and dreaming penchant with a group whose every pastime inadvertently nurtured the hero's impulse within; and my childhood's closing chapter would vault my self-image onto a plane which was perhaps only partially deserved.

And so I joined up.

I know my recruiter thought he had made a brilliant sale in closing me on a four-year enlistment, and I know he meant his every encouraging word. But it was all of limited relevance. The Army was a channel via which my dreams of heroism might be realized. My swearing of that oath was a foregone conclusion.

If only I had known what awaited me ... and how ill prepared I truly was. Had I elected to join the Air Force, or had I sought out a Military Occupation Specialty (MOS) of the non-combat arms variety, my physical conditioning and ambitious mentality would likely have been equal to or greater than the task. But, for reasons of heroic ambition, I elected to join the Infantry, an MOS for which hastily built-up weightlifting muscle offers essentially no professional advantages.

High school graduation came and went in early-June of 2000. I had been so consumed with romantic forays, with my after-school job, with incessant exercise, and with a palpable feeling of liberation that I had spent perhaps as few as ten days with Geoff and Andy, my brothers. They, being one and two years older, respectively, were both off to college by then, but as we all lived in Marysville, we really should have seen more of one another. The fault rests solely with me; arrogance and self-absorption had overtaken me in grand style. It is the first of many failures for which I harbor deep and lasting regret.

The twelve days which separated graduation from my shipping off to basic training passed in what seemed like the span of three hours' time. I drove around Marysville. I lifted. I ran. I read. I visited friends and family. And then I was gone. Even when I was dropped off at the recruiting station, an office I had walked, bicycled, or driven past three-thousand times since first arriving in Marysville over a decade prior, the reality of leaving home behind had not yet taken firm root in my mind. The drive from Marysville—my beloved Marysville—to Seattle went quickly. The traffic was decent, and I was shaking hands with my recruiter in the parking garage less than an hour later. I made a point of shaking with a degree of force that was, naturally, surplus to necessity. Nascent manhood makes imaginary lions of us all.

Seattle's Military Entrance Processing Station (MEPS) is a dump. That may or not be the case for all MEPS nationwide.

From a lighting perspective, the Seattle MEPS is reminiscent of a mid–1980s thrift store, its walls bring to mind the set of a made-for-television white-collar drama, and the food, well, the food is served by the hotel where we are lodged while awaiting our departure. Draw your own conclusions.

I believe my stay lasted around thirty hours. In fact, I wouldn't be surprised in the least if records of my stay's exact duration are still accessible. The military is pathologically devoted to maintaining certain records; others, however, are left largely up to the individual soldier. My own service record has been inaccurate for years on end. Much of it falls on me, as I am notoriously irresponsible when it comes to maintaining documentation and the like. So, what do you say, Army? Split the difference?

Anyway, back to the early summer of 2000 and the depressing dump that is MEPS. While there, I struck deep, meaningful, and lasting (fun fact: I never again saw anyone from MEPS) friendships with a number of soldiers who were also en route to Fort Benning, Georgia. Though MEPS is far from the "real" Army, faint traces of the shuffling about, the hurrying up in advance of long waits, and the general dehumanization process are certainly underway as one is ordered from one office to the next.

While there is a great deal of paperwork required to transform a free citizen into U.S. Government property, the bottom line is that MEPS exists to consolidate (if not expedite) the process in order that newly minted soldiers, sailors, airmen, guardsmen, and whatever Coast Guard service members call themselves might quickly board their lowest-possible-fare commercial flights to training hubs the nation over.

As mentioned above, my group was bound for Fort Benning, "Home of the Infantry" and an Army relic largely forgotten by Father Time himself.

And while seated in charmless waiting rooms, demoralizing hallways, and eventually in a pleasant Sea-Tac terminal, the group got to know itself rather well.

Oh yes, before I forget, the group was more or less evenly divided between two subgroups of hugely distinctive types. You might be thinking men/women or, if you have never visited Seattle, black/white; but, no. It was neither of these. It was, instead, divided between so-called "Split-Ops" recruits and the, well, I guess just the recruits. I belonged to the latter group. The former consisted of recruits who had completed the initial phase of their basic training process the previous summer, had returned to live out their senior year of high school, and then once again reported to MEPS for round two with Fort Benning the following summer.

Imagine that, if you are able.

Forfeiting your summer vacation in favor of a nine-week Boot Camp ass-kicking, then returning to high school and re-entering the mindset not just of a civilian, but of a high school kid. And if that isn't enough, you must then reactivate a soldier's psychology the following summer after having been braced for that punch to the nutsack for nine months' time.

I found those guys fascinating.

With one in particular, I spoke at great length about what was to come. His name was (is?) Summers, and he was endlessly patient with my endless line of questioning.

"Does it suck?"

"Yeah."

"How much does it suck?"

"A lot."

"What was the punchline of that one story?"

"Oh hell no."

You see, by the midpoint of our five-hour Sea-Tac bivouac, Summers had related one apocryphal story no fewer than a half-dozen times, all at my request. It had to do with an ill-fated private who, after having consumed two canteens of water, was forced to stand at attention for something in the neighborhood of two hours' time. A rather strict, austere drill sergeant was overseeing this round of punishment and repeatedly denied pleas for a latrine break, and they were many. Somewhere around the hour plus point, the drill sergeant detected a pungent aroma. Walking over to where the private stood, the drill sergeant noticed a yellow pool at the man's feet. Realizing what had happened, the drill sergeant looked the man in the eye and said in a voice both soft and hostile, "Oh hell no."

"Hey, Summers. What was the punchl—"

"Oh hell no."

Summers had grown accustomed to my asking to hear the story and was, by the time of our boarding, interrupting my requests with what he knew I wanted to hear. There was another tidbit I rather enjoyed.

"Hey, Summers, what was the drill sergeant's nickname for you?"

"[sigh] Summer Sausage."

"And it's because...?"

"Because I was fat."

"What was the drill sergeant's name?"

"You're not gonna have him. There's like fifty platoons going at once. The odds are impossible."

"I know, I know. But just in case, what is his name?"

"It's Spencer. He might be gone by now. He had already been there for a long time when I was going through basic last summer."

"Okay, I'll keep an eye out."

Two things dominate my mind when recalling this episode of some sixteen summers past. The first is an appropriate degree of embarrassment for what I now realize was terribly immature behavior (I've always been young and old at once). Second is how strangely fitting it was that I should meet a Split-Ops kid who had known the very drill sergeant I would myself meet in just over a week's time.

What followed was a long West Coast to East Coast flight with a stop somewhere in the middle, an airport dinner (my first), and a late-night landing in Atlanta. Our group was gathered up at baggage claim by a civilian driver who loaded us aboard a full-size charter bus and told us to get comfortable.

It was a long enough drive that I had time to think about home. Long enough that I had time to, for once, think about the impulsive decision I had made. Long enough for a trace of doubt to materialize. I remember hoping that our Seattle MEPS group would move through whatever was to come in a cohesive manner of shared misery.

But it wouldn't.

Once we arrived at 30th AG (a martial counterpart to the civilian-friendly MEPS), all hell broke loose and I never spoke another word to Summer Sausage ... er, Summers.

Imagine those hissing and creaking sounds which follow the halting of every charter bus. Like a giant soda can being snapped open, the carbonated air slicing out in snapping fashion. Now imagine those sounds being followed by a verbal barrage along these lines:

Get the fuck off that fucking bus! Your ass fuckin' sleeping? Fuck no! FUCK NO! Get the fuck up, get the fuck up, get the fucking fuck up. Move yo' soft asses, move them soft fuckin' asses. Now get yo' fuckin' bags off that man's bus, motherfucker. NOW! Move, motherfucker. You lookin' at me? You wanna fuck me? *Do You Want To Fuck Me?* No? Then take those faggot ass eyes off me, motherfucker, 'fore I beat that pussy ass of yours. Move that fuckin' ass. Move!

Looking back, it's difficult to know which particular pejorative epithets and foul-mouthed threats were aimed specifically at me. At the time, I was sure it was every one of them. I needn't have been so selfish. There were twenty of us on the bus and none was spared the wrath of that rather animated bunch of non-commissioned officers. They necessarily loathed each and every one of us all the same.

One passage was indeed directed at me specifically, though I don't recall at what point during that verbal onslaught it materialized.

"You're in the motherfucking Army now, motherfucker."

And so I was.

III

Boots, Chutes and Amended Contracts

Our arrival was, by design, a late one. We had not arrived at our official Basic Training barracks, as so many among our MEPS group had imagined. We instead found ourselves at 30th AG, or 30th Adjutant General Reception Battalion.

Sounds nice, doesn't it? Reception.

It was miserable.

And, in truth, it *should* be miserable. Had it been anything else, we would have been psychologically unprepared for what was to come. Namely, Basic Combat/Infantry Training, or One Station Unit Training (OSUT) as we would come to know it.

Now then, having departed from Sea-Tac the day prior around noon, we connected somewhere in the middle (was it Memphis?), landed in Atlanta, and arrived at 30th AG close to midnight. We were then shepherded with considerable urgency and a great deal of cursing (most of it gratuitous) into a large, bench-laden room where we found similarly distressed recruits who were pouring the contents of their luggage onto the floor. We were, of course, expected to do the same. This was nominally a contraband (weapons, food, narcotics, et cetera) screening measure, but it also served to embarrass and further terrorize young recruits. I, possessing nothing in the way of contraband, avoided major embarrassment; though the terrorizing aspect was not lost on me.

Once this exercise in recruit conditioning was complete, we were lined up and marched into a dining facility (DFAC) for what was essentially a "Sorry for fucking with you. Here's a helping of Army slop" post-midnight dinner. Having choked down the raw sewage passed off as food that morning, we were then told to follow a young, relatively mild-mannered buck sergeant (E-5) to our bay, or shared sleeping area. Recruits who had arrived days or, in some cases, weeks earlier to "Reception" were sound asleep, so the buck

20

sergeant guided the fifteen of us in his charge to various bunks via his dim flashlight.

"Okay, guys, park your shit in these foot lockers," he said to each pair while kicking the wooden locker at the base of a given bunkbed. "First call is going to come at 0600hrs. That'll give you about four hours of rack. Latrine's down the hall to the right. Be ready for a long day. Now, seriously, get some rack."

And he was gone. Much like my MEPS compatriots (with whom I had parted ways hours earlier), I never again saw that particular buck sergeant. Not that there was any shortage of sergeants moseying about 30th AG. Every one of which lived to drop recruits into the front leaning rest position. Speaking of which…

…after laying down on a bunk which I thought, in that hazy moment, I would be occupying each night for the next few months' time, I adjusted my watch to Eastern Time and fell into a deeper slumber than I should have allowed myself.

I cannot reliably recall what words or images populated my weary mind prior to drifting off, but I know that thoughts of my socially vibrant senior year came and went throughout the months ahead. I think of those days even now.

But to the front leaning rest we go.

After what seemed like thirty minutes of rack, every light in that crowded sleeping bay was blazing down upon us squinty-eyed recruits. The effect had indeed been rather arresting in nature, but I did take a moment to check my watch prior to doing anything rash … like hopping out of the rack, for instance.

It was only 0400hrs. We were told to expect a 0600hrs wakeup call.

Had I parted ways with good sense? Could jetlag have compromised my otherwise well-functioning mind? I think not. Instead, I was certain the buck sergeant had been true to his word.

As I was allowing this certainty to guide me into a state of continued slumber, the sense of being watched dawned upon me. Even through tightly closed lids, it was clear that a shadow was looming over my bunk.

"What the fuck is this shit?" asked the voice belonging to that menacing shadow.

As I opened my eyes, I realized that a diminutive drill sergeant (probably about 5'6") was standing at the foot of a bunk with which I had spent a mere two hours' time getting acquainted. Realizing then that the 0600hrs wakeup call was unlikely to be honored, I jumped to my feet and looked straight ahead. Whatever punishment awaited me was by this point unavoidable.

"You think yo' ass is gonna stay asleep while all these men," the drill sergeant pointed all around the bay, "are standin' here at attention?"

"Sir, I wa—"

"*Sir*? I look a motherfuckin' officer to yo' ass?"

"No, s—. I mean, no, sergeant."

By this point, the irked NCO (non-commissioned officer) had lost patience with what he must have perceived as a grunge-haired, sarcastic, pre–Emo Washingtonian. "Motherfucker, beat yo' face."

I was lost. Completely lost. So, I did the best I could. I asked for clarification.

"I'm sorry, sir … I mean sergeant. You want me to beat my face? As in, actually be—"

"Do pushups, private!"

It all made sense in that instant, the very instant I spent dropping down into a pushup position. The act of conducting pushups itself could be said to resemble a person beating his or her face into the ground below. I understood, and do to this day.

I arrived at Fort Benning in good physical condition. What I had started during my junior year, I had continued throughout my senior. The dividends in terms of attention and ego-nourishing were too great to ignore. At around 170 pounds, I was bench-pressing well over my bodyweight, squatting a pound or two more, running the stadium stairs routinely, and conducting my fair share of curls. I was in excellent gym shape and had the physique to show for it; but nothing prepares a young man's body for minutes on end of holding the so-called front leaning rest. Note the word "rest" in that term; there is nothing restful about the pushup position, regardless of its nomenclature.

Within three minutes of metaphorically beating my face, I was nearing muscle failure. On the higher end, a bench press set lasts around $\frac{1}{6}$ of that time; most are far shorter. In other words, I wasn't conditioned for sustained pushups. That realization came early in my time at 30th AG. Within hours of arriving, in fact.

"Get off yo' knees, motherfucker."

"Yes, sergeant," I replied, my body obeying the command.

"Ten more, then get yo' pussy ass up."

I had not felt like a pussy the day prior, the week prior, the year prior. I had felt like a demigod for much of that time. That's what basic training succeeds in destroying—the illusion of power which most young men harbor within their self-perceptions. So much of my own positive self-image had materialized the previous fall, right up until the drill sergeant tacitly informed me of at least one weakness: long-term pushups.

After recovering to my feet, the drill sergeant told me to "toe the line" and to "lock the fuck up" while he strolled throughout the bay.

"Clean up yo' areas, get dressed, and fall in downstairs for chow. Now move!"

And we did. Move, that is. We straightened up our respective bunks, took a few moments in dressing and grooming ourselves, and raced downstairs for our first Army breakfast. Well, the first for about one-third of us. Many in that bay had arrived days earlier. We treated those guys like D–Day veterans for some reason.

Seniority is always relative.

* * *

The smell was so peculiar. This was all I could think of while standing in that massive breakfast chow formation. Even now, years later, similar scents will transport me to that reception station and to the enormous open areas where our bodies were tightly jammed one against the next as blocks of twenty to twenty-five men were ordered into the DFAC. Accurately describing the combination of scents has eluded me for the better part of two decades.

Imagine the aroma of unwashed athletic clothing wafting heavily throughout a high-ceilinged tunnel. Tracking? Okay, now enrich that odor with the specific smell of your least favorite food, but don't stop there. Humid air, oppressive heat, a thick assault on the olfactory—this rogue's gallery of relentless assailants was in and of itself sufficient to render the ordeal categorically miserable.

There were also the drill sergeants, the regular sergeants, the weirdly aggressive medical staff, the lines, the waiting, the pushups, the rumors, the uncertainty, and the god-awful cuisine. Despite the sense of being overwhelmed, or at least at the mercy of circumstances over which one had no control, we did have allies. Not overly powerful (or *at all* powerful) allies, but allies nonetheless.

While many of us awaited chow in that densely packed tunnel, there were a select few amongst our number whose time-at-AG (TAG) spanned days, weeks, and, in a couple of cases, even months. Yes, *months* in reception. The limbo analogy was well-worn with that group, and rightly so. Some of the senior TAG cadre had endured long enough to have seen a few of their fellow MEPS brethren make it all the way through the subsequent fourteen-week basic training/AIT (OSUT) program.

"Why were they held over?" you might be wondering.

It was almost always a medical delay, and more specifically dental in the few cases I sought to investigate during my seven-day 30th AG career. Regardless of *why* they were there, they *were* there. And in the same way we "fresh meat" recruits wrung-out intel from the Split-Ops folk while at MEPS, we also turned to the elder TAG souls for far more information than they could have provided. After all, these were not basic training graduates. They were recruits, same as us. Most of these gentlemen wore the actively cultivated persona of a sage, wise in the ways of avoiding drill sergeant fury, skilled in acquiring contraband most of us had written off for good, and knowledgeable about those policies which nominally serve to aid soldiers in need.

In other words, they were barracks lawyers.

The barracks lawyers took seriously their tacit role as guide and ally to their newcomer colleagues. And many did right by us in that respect. One of these fellows, Hamilton (a two-month holdover), would occasionally meet with the staff duty drill sergeants in order that they might communicate to us through him. We imagined these as important summits, closed door meetings the likes of which no soldier with fewer than forty-eight hours on active duty could ever hope to attend. And when Hamilton returned to the bay, all were raptly attentive to his every utterance.

"All right, guys," he began, "make sure your laundry is done, and keep your foot lockers secured. If the drill sergeants find one unlocked, they'll dump it out and make us all do pushups while the owner puts his shit back in."

Nothing of any greater importance than this ever made it back to us. Laundry, appearance, and various threats were the routine topics he touched upon with the drill sergeants during those mysterious embassies, which always came after dinner chow. During the daylight hours, there was nothing a senior TAG could do for us. We were marched around from one prescribed in-processing station to the next; uniform issue, paperwork, haircuts, paperwork, chow, formation of one sort or another, more paperwork, shots, then at last back to the bay.

It's curious how quickly a flimsy bunk, a thin mattress, and a footlocker can collectively assume a "home" feeling within one's mind. By the end of Day Two, I was relieved to recline on my bed and stare at the ceiling tiles above. My arm was sore from one of the five shots I had received that morning, but I had eaten a passable meal of casserole and white bread in the DFAC and was beginning to embrace my self-imposed fate.

The next days were not unlike the first two, though my head was now shaved, I was in my ill-fitting uniform, and I had performed something like three hundred pushups. Every now and again, I would look for Summers and the Seattle MEPS group, but the search was always fruitless. It was also pointless. I would soon be marched to my basic training battalion for one hundred days of boot camp and infantry training. Furthest from my mind were the recruits with whom I had spent one day in Seattle and one in airports/in flight. Still, I hoped they were doing well.

There comes a moment when those recruits making their way through reception (a truly severe misnomer) learned whether or not they were to be held over for some reason or another. Though I have good teeth and no medical problems, I was appropriately paranoid about becoming an elder TAG. We all appreciated what those guys did for their "cherry" brethren, but not one among us wished to join them in 30th AG purgatory.

Thus, when I learned I would be marching "down range" with two hundred fellow recruits almost exactly one week after my arrival, I was relieved. Whatever awaited me down range would be preferable to the stasis of enduring an endless reception. Such a pleasant word—reception.

On our final day at the Adjutant General, those of us preparing to march down range were assembled alphabetically into one massive formation. In just seven days' time, the non-commissioned officers charged with making our lives hell had also done good work in making us resemble real soldiers. Heads closely shaven, camouflage attire (BDUs) on our backs, and a collective sense of grimness for whatever awaited.

"Group, *attention!*" came the drill sergeant's practiced bellow of an order. For a group of recruits barely a full week into Army life, our snapping to attention was reasonably crisp and nearly in unison.

"Riiiight *face!*"

This was somewhat less crisp, less in unison … but we managed.

"Forwaaaard *march!*"

And march we did.

The battalion awaiting our arrival was 2/54, the company was Charlie. We would eventually learn to work aggressive grunts of "C-Two-Five-Four" into various cadences and affirmative responses to rhetorical inquiries. Morale is cultivated by many means.

Though there was a feeling of setting out on a long journey, the march to 2/54 took scant few moments. The building itself is somewhat visible from 30th AG, if memory serves, though I've not been to Fort Benning in the better part of two decades' time.

In any event, we were marching into the Charlie Company "quad" perhaps five minutes after hearing the "forward march" order, and within heartbeats of arriving, a familiar melody was playing for our listening pleasure:

Fall in, motherfuckers, fall in! Put yo' shit down, you limp dick pussy! Don't fuckin' eyeball my ass, motherfucker, I fuckin' whoop yo' ass! I fuckin' *whoop* yo' ass! Pick up that motherfuckin' A-bag, motherfucker, pick it up over yo' head. Now fuckin' stand yo' pussy ass right there 'til I come get yo' pussy ass. Hey, you—motherfucker—fall the motherfuck in, fall the *motherfuck* in, motherfucker!

Now, it's important to understand that the verbal chaos articulated above was wildly at odds with the largely organized manner in which the twelve drill sergeants who jointly managed Charlie Company 2/54 disassembled our group and reassembled it into four more or less equally sized platoons. This they accomplished with competence and practiced precision. As the platoon assignments were entirely alphabetical, I found myself assigned to Third Platoon, along with fifty others in the M-S range.

All frenzied insanity quickly diminished and the drill sergeants began checking names off of a roster. The recruits stood at an uneasy attention in our four blocks of alphabetized platoons, all sufficiently dazed by the onslaught of high-volume profanity as to ensure our complete stillness. Eventually, our senior drill sergeants inspected the human flesh they were charged with weaponizing over the next one hundred days.

While the inspection was underway, I kept my eyes locked firmly ahead of me. To an observer, my gaze would have appeared focused and intense. In reality, I was looking entirely inward and questioning whether or not I had one-hundred days of "suck" in me. I wasn't certain.

"Lower your damn head, private." The senior drill sergeant was standing close enough that our boots were touching.

Not realizing I had cocked my head back (a senior year habit), I sharply did as I was instructed and found myself looking upon the drill sergeant's nametape, which read "Spencer" in deep-green lettering.

You have got to be kidding me. Summers, you son of a bastard. You were so certain of the odds being impossible. So damn certain.

And so it was that of all of the drill sergeants in all of the platoons in all of the companies in all of Fort Benning's Infantry Training Battalions, I ended up in Drill Sergeant Spencer's charge. Whatever understanding of the term "coincidence" I have carried with me *since* that day, has always been informed to a high degree *by* that day.

The remainder of that afternoon was tense and rushed and weird. We were ordered to run upstairs (Third Platoon slept on the second floor), park our A-bags on a bunk, then run back down for a linen draw that somehow spanned two hours' time. Once our racks were covered in dingy sheets and scratchy green blankets, we were ordered to go to dinner chow.

Unlike 30th AG, in whose chow hall we had been allowed to speak and mingle with fellow recruits, nobody dared say a word in the 2/54 DFAC. Not one word. We ate, stood up, carried our trays to the wash station, then jogged (you mustn't be seen walking, not ever) back to the Charlie Company quad, where our drill sergeants awaited.

Falling-in to formation in precisely the order as we had found ourselves placed hours earlier, we stood perfectly still in anticipation for orders or insults. Drill Sergeant Spencer told us to make our way upstairs, to stand by our racks, and to not say a "motherfucking word" while doing so.

It was all a bit eerie.

Once upstairs, the fifty of us lined that bay in zombie-like fashion for what seemed like an hour. It was no more than a few moments. Spencer eventually made his way up and eyed his platoon with shrewdness. He paced back and forth, walking from one end of the bay to the other, all the while speaking matter-of-factly about what he expected of us, what we should expect of ourselves, and what it meant to be a Warlord. Third Platoon was known as the "Warlords" in Charlie Company, 2/54.

Spencer was an ardent believer in supra-curricular activities, an aspect of our training which he imagined would interest other platoons. If they were interested, they never communicated as much to us. We contented ourselves with the knowledge that our boot camp and AIT experience would be more active than what the official training schedule offered. Unfortunately, I was soon ordered to do the following:

Now, I want all of you to climb your asses into those racks and sleep at the position of attention. No rollin' 'round on your sides, no stomach sleepers, no feet hangin' off the end. Lie flat on your backs, keep your arms at your sides, lay still, and shut the fuck up. First call comes' early tomorrow. And then this shit is on. Move!

I have been a side and stomach sleeper since birth. According to my mother, when placed flat on my back in a crib during infancy, I would immediately roll over onto my stomach. She took it as my first act of rebellion. Regardless of my motives in rejecting the back-sleeper modus, that babyhood chapter made of me a lifelong side and stomach sleeper, which was very much at odds with Drill Sergeant Spencer's guidance.

I managed to remain at the slumbering position of attention throughout the evening and early-morning hours. It felt unnatural and made for sleep of questionable restfulness, but the mattress was narrow and I had been assigned a top bunk; I did not want to risk falling off the side. As I remember, when my eyes opened a few hours past midnight the following morning, they were looking straight up at the ceiling which was practically within arm's reach of me. Of course, I did not closely consider such things then, as we are now back to where this tome began ... with a violent wakeup call.

"Yeah, just lay in bed, motherfucker."

The trashcan had been thrown down the center of the bay and jarred all of us into a waking state. But my awakening had been met with a strong mental reaction. It materialized as an inner-monologue which might have read: *How the fuck did I end up here? Fuck.*

Spencer had taken note of my reluctance to rise from the rack. His paraphrased words thereafter, twice printed in this work, had an effect which he would (perhaps unwittingly) incite within me throughout the next fourteen weeks' time—they made me angry. I love to think and hate being interrupted when doing so. And as if it wasn't bad enough that I was questioning a major life decision, my reflection on as much had been cut short by a drill sergeant who could not care less.

So I hopped down, toed the line aggressively, and committed myself to showing them what I was made o—

"Front leaning rest position, *move!*"

And we dropped. Both sides of the bay, each looking at the other with rivalrous eyes, were in the pushup position awaiting a count.

"Fifteen, wide-arm, on your own." Spencer was seated in the bay's only chair while issuing these instructions. It was pleather, had high wooden arms, and was deep. Most of us would find occasion to occupy its comfortable frame a few times throughout the cycle, but in that moment, we executed our pushups.

A few things kept this (what would become a morning ritual) set of pushups from unfolding, for me, without incident. First, one of the larger recruits struggled to achieve fifteen repetitions and drew the ire of Spencer for that reason. Second, one of the men opposite me, Sandow, had seen fit to rise from the front leaning rest position once he was finished with his fifteen pushups. Fortunately for the struggling private, this presumptive act on part of Sandow drew Spencer's attention.

"You'd better get that ass back down, right fuckin' now," Spencer said with practiced menace. Sandow dropped with notable speed and joined the rest of us.

"Regular arms, fifteen," Spencer continued, keeping his eyes on Sandow.

I was acquitting myself nicely at this point. As I knew it would not always be so, I allowed myself a small helping of hubris. The first fifteen had barely left a mark, while the second set I completed in league with the first five or six men to also do so.

"Diamonds, fifteen."

This required me to bring my fingers together to create a diamond or triangular shape. This pushup style is more difficult, but I held it together. It seemed that a year-and-a-half of high school weightlifting, an active childhood, and my own pride were equal to the task of, well, forty-five pushups of varying style.

Blood-reddened faces now lined either side of the bay as we all struggled to conceal our heavy breathing.

"Get your PTs on and be downstairs for formation in ten mikes."

I had incidentally packed PTs on the very top of my lighter A-bag. Changing into those took mere seconds, after which I headed down with others who were similarly well-prepared.

I did notice one difference after standing in the quad for two minutes. The reflective belt! It is a mandatory component of all Army-issued PT wear, and I had foolishly forgotten it. Suddenly, what seemed like a morning off to a good start was falling apart. In those moments, most of Third Platoon had assembled in the quad and only a few poorly prepared stragglers were walking downstairs while I sprinted up them. The search took precious minutes, but I eventually retrieved that blasted belt and bolted downstairs.

Spencer watched me with hawkish, judging eyes as I fell in at the end of the third rank. As I was technically within the ten-mike timeframe, he was not as displeased as he might otherwise have been. However, he suspected I was guilty of improper preparation and communicated as much with an unfriendly glance.

"Platoon, attention! Riiiight *face*! Forwaaard *march*!"

A few lefts and rights later and Third Platoon found itself standing at attention on the physical training (PT) field which we would come to know very well throughout the months ahead. Spencer had brought us to a sharp halt, ordered a "left face" movement, then paused as if thinking closely on the matter of Army-approved calisthenics.

"Open ranks, *march*!"

We had learned this bit at 30th AG, but it was nevertheless a bit stuttered and clumsy in its execution. It required that the first rank take two steps forward, the third one step back, and the second remain in place.

We got there.

"Extend to the left, *move*!"

This was easy enough—we extended our arms outward and ran to the left until a full body length separated each man from the next. We then dropped our arms to our sides. A few more steps to place distance between each man...

...and the fun ... well, the fun did begin.

Following a comprehensive round of stretching, Drill Sergeant Spencer ran us through a wide range of pushups, side-straddle hops (jumping jacks), and overhand arm-claps that spanned the full-hour allotted for it on the training schedule.

I was forced to acknowledge my first Army PT session for the tiring episode that it was. Over the next month or so, the gym muscle I had spent nearly two years accumulating would diminish somewhat, while my physique morphed into something a bit narrower. Nearly five months later, I went to a weight room, and I was pleased to note that my overall lifting strength had not waned to any significant degree. I was simply shaped a bit differently.

Back to the quad, a quick note from Spencer regarding chow protocol, and...

"...And you all better shave 'fore comin' back down."

My mind was racing. Ten minutes is not a lot of time to unpack, change, re-pack, shave, and make one's way to formation. *Fuck!*

Once Spencer was gone from sight, I dumped my A-bag and scoured its contents for a shaving kit I should have packed on top. At that moment, I thought I should have packed *everything* on top.

Eventually, the shaving kit revealed itself. I grabbed it, raced to what was our bay's large latrine, and shaved off the mostly non-existent facial hair. There was nothing to shave, but I wasn't taking any chances ... not with Spencer.

Once again racing downstairs two or three steps at a time, I made my way into the quad and fell in at the very moment Spencer was calling the platoon to attention. As frenzied as the morning had been, and as nervous as I was about being on Spencer's shit-list, and as irritated as I was with myself (the reflective belt; the shaving kit), I was actually looking forward to breakfast chow.

For all the crappiness of the 30th AG experience—and it is crappy—the breakfast chow had not been all that bad. It wasn't the Four Seasons. It wasn't even the Two Seasons (Real place. Look it up.) But there was cereal, juice, toast, and waffles, and during lunch there was only slightly subpar soft-serve ice cream. And because we were not governed by a tight training schedule, chow was rarely rushed. We certainly didn't take our sweet time, but the dining duration was not all that dissimilar to time spent in a McDonald's while on the road.

All of that was mere prologue at the moment. While 30th AG's chow hall had been a fairly large space, its 2/54 counterpart was no larger than a medium-sized IHOP. Nowhere near spacious enough to accommodate Charlie Company's two hundred soldiers. Which, for those of us among that two hundred, meant,

Hurry yo' motherfuckin' asses up in that motherfuckin' DFAC. You think I'm playing wit' yo' ass, just try me, motherfucker. Just fuckin try my ass, motherfucker. You sit yo' dumb asses down, you eat yo' pussy ass breakfast, you bus yo' fuckin' tray, and you get yo' motherfuckin' asses back to Charlie's quad. Tracking?

[At full volume] Yes, drill sergeant!

Our DFAC instructions had been voiced not by Spencer, but by a drill sergeant on loan from another platoon. Fourth, if I recall.

Talking had been permitted in 30th AG chow hall, if not necessarily encouraged. If not for the shaved heads and ill-fitting uniforms, one might have mistaken the dining facility for a high school cafeteria. Needless to say, talking was *not* permitted in the 2/54 DFAC. It was in fact actively discouraged. And by discouraged, I mean forbidden.

And the food was worse. Again, not dramatically, but enough to be dispiriting. Coupled with the thick silence and the marauding drill sergeants—they hovered above us like birds of prey—I immediately realized that chow was not something I'd be looking forward to.

Oh, except for the fact that I preferred not to starve. And DFAC cuisine, for all its faults, does tend to stave off outright starvation. Even so, many of the larger recruits were invariably hungry. Anyone two hundred pounds or heavier tended to go to sleep feeling a bit empty in the midsection. My heart went out to those guys.

That first round of breakfast chow made fools of many of us. Our introduction to the DFAC had taken place the evening prior, with an equally rushed and silent eating experience. But the performance art exhibited by all drill sergeants had been somehow dampened in that instance. It's as though they were allowing us to develop a false sense of security.

"You done, private."

"No, drill sergeant, I..."

"That wasn't a question, dumbass. You done."

You can certainly understand my certainty that the drill sergeant had inquired as to whether or not my breakfast experience was complete. It had a sort of interrogative lift to that final syllable. Though I may have imagined it.

"You deaf, private?"

This was certainly a question.

"No, drill sergeant."

"Then bus that tray and get out my DFAC."

When bussing my tray, I inadvertently made eye contact with one of the civilian food workers whose relationship with recruits was always a bit curious. We treated them with supreme respect, knowing full well that anything less would be reported. For their part, the food workers seemed to enjoy their position of pseudo-prestige, casting unsympathetic glances towards hapless privates and occasionally issuing commands, which we treated with silent disdain.

I was soon running back to the quad with a slop-laden abdomen and wondering whether or not my lungs would fully adapt to Georgia's oppressively humid air. Seriously, the very act of drawing breath was around twenty-percent more difficult in that thick climate than had it been in my beloved Washington.

And just like that, I was homesick.

This would be a recurring theme throughout the early weeks of my 2/54 experience. A thought of childhood, a school memory, clouds formed in the right shape, and I was yearning for a land I had only subconsciously cherished for nearly two decades' time.

I was perhaps the tenth Third Platoon recruit to return to the quad following chow. With no drill sergeants in sight, we stood in an awkward formation until more joined us. First one, then three, then ten, and then all ... followed by Spencer. The other Charlie Company platoons were largely intact as well, their drill sergeants leading them God knows where. As for us, we were ordered upstairs, where some interesting paperwork awaited. And it was interesting...

Fast-forward about a month or so. The whole of July had seen our platoon transform into something fairly respectable from a soldiering standpoint. We had run endlessly, road-marched, learned to shoot, taken a few

Army Physical Fitness Tests (my run improved slightly from the first to the second; considerably from the second to the third) and I was within spitting distance of earning a maximum score of three hundred. I needed a victory of that sort, as I had screwed up in a number of ways early on, including drifting off during a class on, um, one topic or another.

The latter of these had made for a long morning. I had performed more push-ups than the human organism should be capable of performing. Mind always wandering, I found myself silently questioning if I would ever have put myself through physical/psychological torment of this sort had I remained in Marysville. As a budding gym rat, I thought largely in reps and sets. The idea of doing push-ups for an hour's time would have been comical and dismissed out of hand.

Yet there I was flutter-kicking for two hours. I also thought briefly of Ariel, and what she might be doing that very moment.

There were friendships, too. Third Platoon was mostly men whose names started with M–S. Everyone to my right was an M, most to my left were N. Across from us were O–S. To my immediate left was a man named Joseph Naylor.

I have known many a fine soldier. Naylor was among the very best. His uniforms fit well, he was disciplined, he took seriously the work of protecting these United States, and he was honest. Always honest.

There was Douglas Rohde. As fine a physical specimen as the Warlords would know that summer. He was athletic and clever. He was also a target of humorous drill sergeant ire on occasion. We bonded quickly.

There was Matt Mann. If ever 2/54 has graduated a more comically gifted soul, I would very much like to hear his stand-up. Mann regaled us with tales of his high school years, offered spot-on impressions of our drill sergeants, and brawled absurdly with his bunkmate while those of us who remained (the platoon had shrunk by this point) watched in raucous amusement.

There was William Roum, a fine soldier and sarcastic kid, with a devil may care quality we all came to appreciate by cycle's end.

I could go on about the good and selfless Warlords with whom I endured the suck of basic training. But this is a book about the 3rd U.S. Infantry. Speaking of which, Matt Mann and William Roum would be joining me there.

Here's how it all came to be.

Sometime in late July or early August, the Warlords were busy firing away at a machine gun range. We were learning the finer points of operating the formidable M240B, a lethal weapon system with which I would become closely acquainted.

"Roum! Mann! Mongoose!"

"[All] Yes, drill sergeant!"

"On me. Move!"

And we moved.

We moved to where Spencer stood with an unusually relaxed staff sergeant of some height and a powerful build.

"These men are too short, Spencer. You tryin' to make me look like a dumbass?"

"Nah, man. They're good. Maybe a height waiver for one or two, but they all good on PT and GT."

What Spencer meant was that those of us who had joined him and the heretofore unknown staff sergeant had all scored well on our recent physical training tests (the APFT) and had sufficiently high General Technical scores (one section of the ASVAB) to be considered for…

"…the Old Guard. Private, are you listening to me? Do you want to go to the Old Guard?"

I had become lost in my thoughts momentarily. I did that often. I do still.

"Yes, drill sergeant."

"You see a round-ass hat on my head, private?"

"No, dr—no sergeant."

"Then why you callin' me a drill sergeant?"

"I guess I just…"

"Never mind. You wanna go to the Old Guard up in D.C.? Or do you wanna play in the mud for the next four years?"

"I hadn't really…"

Turning to Spencer, he said, "You sure about this one, Spencer? He having trouble catching on."

At this I bristled. Who the hell was this guy? And why was he putting me on the spot?

"Yes, sergeant. That sounds perfectly fine, whatever it is."

"See what I mean, Eagleton?" Spencer chimed in. "Mongoose'll run his mouth on you. Fit right in up at the Guard."

So that was his name. Eagleton.

"All right, listen up, men." Eagleton alternatingly looked us each in the eye. "Your old contracts are gonna be canceled and I'm gonna write new ones for you. Wherever you were going, forget about it. I'm taking you men up to the Old Guard. Understood?"

"Yes, sergeant!"

We had started the day as young grunts heading to the M240B firing range and were ending it as The Old Guard's newest recruits.

What the hell is The Old Guard? Variations on that question populated our minds.

As it happened, our very own drill sergeant had served in The Old

Guard, and would be returning to it at some point in the near future. We learned from the man a bit here and there, but knew not to press him.

"You'll learn for yourself when you get there, private. Ain't nothing I can say that will prepare you for what's to come."

Spencer was largely correct in this regard. In any event, we still had quite a bit of basic training ahead of us—the hard stuff. We had largely escaped from the so-called "Total Control" phase and were being treated with increasing degrees of respect with every passing day. A smoke session was still just a hair-trigger away, as we learned when Mendoza came down to formation unshaven (in Week Eight, mind you) and Spencer opened up on us with unbridled fury.

The sheer quantity of push-ups, flutter kicks, up-downs, and mountain-climbers collectively performed by the Warlords on that particularly hot, sticky August morning would likely require NASA's assistance to correctly calculate.

"Get up! Get down! Get up! Get down! Beat yo' faces! Turn-over, flutter kicks! Turn-over, mountain climbers! Get up! Get down!"

This went on for about an hour's time. We struggled stubbornly to keep up. We mostly failed. At some point, I lost any reliable sense of what was happening around me.

Here is what I do remember:

Naylor was working like a man possessed to stay exactly even with the drill sergeant's every command. He maintained impressive composure for a time, but even the sturdiest of bodies have their limits.

Rohde was in remarkable physical condition, but he was not overly flexible. The constant changing of position, the conflicting commands, the sheer rapidity of what was happening eventually overwhelmed him.

And then there was Roum's contribution to the chaos. Being fully aware of Mendoza's infraction and now experiencing brutal punishment because of it, Roum exclaimed with uncharacteristic intensity, "Motherfucker!" around the half-hour point of our mercilessly long punishment.

So relentless was the smoke session that even Roum, our most carefree soldier by a wide margin, parted ways with his cool in order to voice his rage. For my part, I had believed we were past such insanity by that late date in the training cycle.

For the most part, we spent our days on firing ranges, performed live-fire drills, learned land navigation, practiced hand-to-hand combat, and acquainted ourselves to some degree with first aid. All very useful stuff.

Our cycle was split-up at the Week Nine mark by a so-called "Family Day" which spanned thirty-six hours' time and saw us reuniting with those friends and family who were able to make the trip to Fort Benning. While my immediate family planned on attending the graduation ceremony some six weeks later, they were absent for this pass. Surprisingly, my future brother-in-law, Travis, and three of our good high school friends had made the drive to Georgia and were more than willing to accommodate my every meal request.

I ate pizza, ice cream, and fried chicken. I ate more pizza. I drank soda. I ate crappy cinnamon rolls, and more pizza.

And then it was time to return. The drive to Sand Hill from our final restaurant stop was but a mere ten minutes. We believed ourselves to be on schedule. I had no watch and no cellular phone. Travis and our friends had not thought to adjust their watches to Eastern Time. We were not on schedule. I was around five minutes from being late. And the drive spanned...

"Ten minutes? Holy shit! Are you sure?" I was rightly panicked.

"Yeah, ten minutes. Come on, get in." Travis knew where we were going and risked a Georgia traffic violation to have me returned in an on-time arrival.

After speeding through side streets and cutting off a number of irritated Southerners, I was dropped off in the 2/54 parking lot a few moments after the official report time. With no time for a proper farewell, I hollered "Thanks, guys!" over my shoulder and gunned it back to the quad. While doing so, I found myself wondering which of the cars in that parking lot belonged to Spencer.

"Platoon, atteeeen-shun!" I heard just prior to turning the corner. "Dismissed!"

Oh, fuck. I thought to myself. "What now?"

When I rallied enough courage to turn the corner, I found an utterly empty quad. Entering the area as though negotiating a minefield, I cautiously made my way upstairs where my platoon brothers (we had bonded closely those past two months) were readying for our "lights out" ritual. Somewhat pensively, I approached my bunk as though expecting Spencer to leap out from my wall locker and place a knife to my throat.

Spencer was nowhere to be found, my wall locker was devoid of any human lifeforms, and my throat went unthreatened. After changing into PTs, I visited with Mann and Rohde. We swapped food ingestion tales and spoke about the six weeks ahead of us. I then returned to my bunk and wished Naylor a good night before climbing under my scratchy blanket.

The evening's closing thoughts were of Travis and my high school friends, all of whom had sacrificed several days of their post-high school summer to ensure I would not be alone during the mid-cycle pass.

I was honored then.

I am honored now.

* * *

The final five weeks of 2/54's Basic Training/AIT program were notably different than the first nine. For one, we had lost a couple of guys for medical reasons. Two or three had gone AWOL. And one or two (I truly cannot recall) were split-ops.

They had completed the nine-week basic training and were returning home for their senior year of high school. I remember wondering if, that following summer, they would be looked to for guidance and wisdom by incoming recruits, in the same way I had looked to Summers for any insights.

We had also picked up a few returnees, all of whom had completed their first nine weeks the previous summer.

The Warlords were a changed group.

Prior to Family Day, we were told to have our rucksacks packed for a road march upon our return. True to his word, Spencer (who had said nothing of my being tardy the night prior) awoke us at 0600hrs that following morning, and our five weeks of Infantry School were underway.

It's uncanny, the feeling of being equal to a hard task. The feeling of belonging in a way of life which only weeks earlier seemed alien, and overwhelming, and incompatible with my character. But there I was, road-marching on a morning of notably mild temperature, and feeling perfectly capable of keeping pace and performing as a soldier should. Perhaps it was the restorative effect of crappy food, or the eleven hours of uninterrupted sleep I had enjoyed while on pass; whatever the explanation, I was in fine form for that ten-mile road march.

I recall making eye contact with Roum and being proud for having trained alongside him. Rohde and I exchanged a knowing smile at one point, as we had cultivated a conversational garden rife with countless in-jokes. Naylor was focused and intensity incarnate. I wanted very much to prove myself his equal as both soldier and warrior.

What a high bar.

Things got harder in some ways throughout the weeks ahead; less difficult in others. We were no longer scum in the eyes of our drill sergeants, though we had yet to fully prove ourselves. A careful and unspoken balance was struck between trainer and trainee: we didn't screw-up, they treated us like men; we screwed up, it was back to the fundamentals. I liked it this way.

The road marches grew longer, the live-fire drills more intensive, the days a bit more slogging. One day in particular stands out as having been a point of no return. The day I knew I would graduate. The day I knew I was capable of good soldiering. The day I learned what it meant to suffer. Whatever pain we Warlords had collectively endured while being smoked into oblivion would prove rather negligible in relation to what awaited us on a wet Georgia evening, perhaps a week or so into AIT.

We had enjoyed an uneventful round of cattle-car transportation to a firing range. Ordered to bring our rucksacks along, we did precisely that. What followed was around nine hours of incessant shooting on the M16 range. We shot, and shot, and shot. And when we imagined ourselves done shooting, we shot some more. Any civilian gun enthusiast who imagines himself a seasoned triggerman has likely never endured so many hours of constant range firing. So many rounds down range, so much brass to retrieve. So. Much. Shooting.

And then more shooting. Whatever excitement had once accompanied the thought of firing an assault rifle down range had abated. I never again wanted to see the damned thing.

When our time on the range was done, it became clear that the very cattle cars we'd used to transport us to the range of infinite shooting would not be treating us to a return journey. Our packs were with us because we would be road-marching back to 2/54. It was twelve miles, and we would be moving at a good clip, even though we were exhausted from a day on the range.

Drill Sergeant Spencer, in his infinite wisdom, decided Rohde and I would make good road guards.

Being a road guard sucks. It is a very taxing duty.

Rohde and I would each lead one column of men on either side of the road. When nearing an intersection, our job was to run ahead and block flanking traffic (which was negligible to the point of being non-existent) while the columns of men we led made their way through. Once the last man had passed us by, we ran (packs, weapons, and all) to reclaim our place at the head of the line.

Coming off of that brilliant ten-miler a week or so prior, I began this road march with a feeling of invincibility, of sublime confidence. The fact that this march was coming at the end of a day-long shooting extravaganza, that the distance was greater, that rain was upon us, and that I was tasked with being a road guard—none of that found purchase within my naïve mind. I would whip the shit out of this march, and Spencer would respect me.

Plus, Rohde, a dear comrade by this point, was also a road guard. I would not let him down.

Around three miles in, after having sprinted the length of the marching column perhaps a dozen times, only to keep up the four-mph pace once there, I was beginning to tire. The rain continued to fall, and Rohde was wearing the familiar look of fatigue upon his usually smiling face.

This one's gonna take a toll. I recall having acknowledged to myself around that point. *I'll not give Spencer the satisfaction of seeing me struggle.*

But I probably did. If Rohde was visibly exhausted, so was I.

On it went.

Stubborn step upon stubborn step, cruel mile upon cruel mile. Somewhere around the halfway mark, Spencer called two others to replace myself and Rohde. I can't recall who because I didn't know then; I was relieved and hoped the latter half of this rain-drenched gauntlet would be less miserable.

The damage was done. I had blown through my energy reserves with those repeated sprints, had consciously held my head high and my back straight for Spencer's sake, and was now running on fumes. The next six miles were completed via force of will; my feet had long since abandoned the effort.

When at last 2/54 entered the Warlords' shared field of vision, the relief was palpable. Even Naylor, stony knight that he was, was pleased for the sight of home. Yes, home. If Roum (the poker face) was happy, he concealed as much masterfully. He almost invariably, more than any of us, refused to show his hand.

After a brief quad formation during which most of us struggled to stand, we were ordered to bed. It was an order that went entirely without saying. Had I pulled back the abrasive green blanket to see a king cobra, three black widows, or a particularly hostile Brazilian yellow scorpion had taken up residence in my bed earlier that day, I would nevertheless have gladly made myself at home in the warmth of their venomous company. My state of exhaustion was sublime in its purity.

Prior to falling asleep, I afforded myself the luxury of a clarifying realization: I would complete Infantry School and join the soldiers of The Old Guard.

With three weeks remaining, the days seemed to pass quickly. Morning PT was rather perfunctory, the chow hall experiences less depressing, the rapport between recruits more brotherly, the relationship between trainee and drill sergeant less tense. As "They of the Round Hat" readied the Warlords for the coming Bayonet, I realized that graduation was within reach. What stood between us and it was the following:

1. A fifteen-mile road march.
2. Six days of field living and tactical operations training.
3. The final road march, spanning twenty-five miles, with missions awaiting each platoon at various junctures along the way.

All of this would come to pass within a week.

The night prior to our embarking on the fifteen-miler was unusual (favorably so) for a few reasons. First, the drill sergeants left us largely to ourselves. We had been briefed prior to dinner chow as to what the coming week would entail, then told to make our way upstairs for an evening of packing and preparation. The packing list was written out on a white board and was simple enough to follow. Most of us were finished within thirty minutes' time, after which we spent several hours in conversation, reading, with our thoughts, or writing letters.

We reminisced about the veritable shit-shows that had unfolded early in our cycle, about the various afterhours brawls which had allowed for the venting of considerable pent-up tension, about the platoon-sized wrestling match which saw one soldier (herein unnamed) execute a flying wipe of his genitalia across the face of a pinned man, of chocolate milk politics (that's a book unto itself), of the whip Naylor had fashioned mid-cycle, of the morning in which a junior drill sergeant had subjected us to an hour's worth of overhand arm-claps, and of Spencer's decision to park his Warlords at the position of parade rest one afternoon, only to consume the contents of a two-liter bottle of Pepsi while we looked on in wonder. That was simply bizarre.

We talked of writing one another letters, of what to expect at our respective duty stations, of the fairer sex, of Airborne School (which awaited perhaps 10 percent of the Warlords), and of the foods we longed to ingest once Infantry School was behind us.

And we talked of home. Most of us, though not all, had developed a greater appreciation for the towns and states we came from. Many would be returning in support of the Hometown Recruiter Assistance Program, or HRAP. All of us who would be returning for HRAP looked forward to it greatly. HRAP ran for twenty days' time, and was fairly casual in its concept.

When the lights came on that following morning, there were no trash cans being tossed about, no sets of push-ups being knocked out, no cursing or frenzied activity. We rose as professionals, calmly shaved, dressed ourselves, moved our equipment downstairs, placed it in formation, and awaited our orders.

We donned our rucksacks and moved to the hardball road. Once there, the Warlords looked to one another, to Spencer, and to the miles ahead. We were a family of sorts, and would see one another through this trial. There's not a thing I would not have done for Mann, that clever soul; for Naylor, that born warrior; for Rohde, that endlessly lighthearted recruit; or for Roum, the rakish and aloof soldier whose heart was (and is) far more golden than ever he let on.

We would see one another through this final week, and do right by Spencer; his guidance, his tough love, all of it.

We marched professionally, in a steady, quiet, and determined rhythm.

And fifteen miles later, we reached the firebase in and around which the week's training operations would unfold, and where our field proficiency would be assessed.

The following six days were tiring. We ran operations from sunrise to sunset, maintained perimeter security at all hours, and moved inexorably closer to the Bayonet—those twenty-five miles of road marching which stood as a monolith between the Warlords and graduation.

When the Bayonet was at last upon us, things unfolded similarly to how they had taken shape a week earlier. We packed our rucksacks, took in a few hours of rest, and rose early the following day.

A couple of blisters which had taken up rent-free residence on my feet during the fifteen-miler were far from healed by the day of the twenty-fiver. I did what any sensible recruit would do under such circumstances and wrapped each foot in a couple layers of duct tape. It ultimately wouldn't matter. Somewhere around the Bayonet's ten-mile mark, I knew the tape had either worn through or slipped enough to expose the open wounds. So I welcomed the pain as a traveling companion and continued the march.

Every four to five miles we would be ordered to stop and take up defensive position on either side of the road. From there, our next mission was given. Of these, the ammo-carry stands out in my mind as having been the most memorable, and difficult. We were tasked with carrying empty ammunition cans around a kilometer (or klick) from the hardball road, only to return with full cans. As a standalone activity, this would have been a bit tiring. As but one task of many we would undertake while covering twenty-five miles in the space of a day? It was brutal.

On we went. One step after another, one mission to the next, until at last we set out on the home stretch; a stretch of perhaps three to four miles.

Morale is a very physical force within the human organism. Realizing we were an hour's walk away of the battalion was positively restorative for the Warlords. We rallied loudly and marched energetically. And when 2/54 was within clear sight, Roum, always so detached from it all, seized the platoon's guidon and ran up and down the length of our marching column. He was among the best of us. I knew that then, in that moment, as the otherwise devil-may-care recruit expended the last of his strength to see his brothers through to a proud finale.

As we closed in on what was a finish line of sorts, recruits, battalion support personnel, and even a few drill sergeants cheered us on from either side of the road. It was, in all its fatigue-induced haziness, a profoundly uplifting scene.

After crossing the finish line, we were guided some distance from the battalion itself towards a small clearing wherein we were instructed to drop our rucksacks. In a long list of things that went without saying, that particular order sits comfortably on top.

The Warlords stood in a loose and open formation. We were taking part in a ritual which had been spoken of only as rumor throughout the preceding months. Our drill sergeants went from one man to the next, looked him in the eye, bestowed upon him the Infantryman's blue cord, and firmly shook his hand. I had made things hard for myself time and again throughout the one-hundred days leading up to this point. But in that moment, I was overcome by a sensation of true pride which felt worthy, lasting, good.

That night, like the evening of the twelve-miler, I slept like the dead. We could expect a solid eight hours of uninterrupted rest before arising for the Warrior's Breakfast come morning. If I dreamt at all, I do not remember. But I remember saying good night to Naylor, and thanking him for something. It might have been for that handful of chocolate chips he'd stolen from the DFAC while on kitchen duty, only to gift me with them upon returning to the barracks. This had happened around mid-cycle; my gratitude had apparently been undiminished by the passage of time.

The Warrior's Breakfast was a simple affair. It was unexpectedly casual, and, by extension, enjoyable. Absent were many of the restraints on behavior which had rendered meals an exercise in strict and practical food ingestion. On the morning of the Warrior's Breakfast, there was conversation, laughter, coffee cake by the sheet, and there were drill sergeant impressions.

That afternoon, we turned in equipment, cleaned the barracks, messed about, placed phone calls to family members, and discussed the weeks and months ahead. A few of us were bound for Airborne, others for their duty stations, and a smaller percentage were reservists readying for a return to civilian life.

My parents and sister made it to Graduation Day. They had been shocked by my decision to join the Army. That shock was now replaced by a feeling of pride which was, perhaps, a bit exaggerated. I sincerely appreciated them making the trip, particularly my mother, who is somewhat averse to air travel.

What was to follow was a bit more training, a homeward jaunt, and history itself.

(Omitted from this chapter are innumerable humorous anecdotes, dozens of personality profiles, more smoke sessions, and a number of screw-ups [my own, in many cases]. The story of Naylor crafting a whip from 550 cord, for instance, is worthy of alluding to.)

IV

Airborne School and a Temporary Homecoming

Following a seventy-two-hour reprieve from duty, I bade farewell to my family and joined a half-dozen of my fellow Warlords in the 2/58 battalion some distance from 2/54. It was our holdover residence as we waited for Airborne School slots to materialize. This was, in many respects, akin to our 30th AG experience. Though now we had earned our blue cords, had developed toughened feet, had run ourselves into the ground, and were proficient with a number of weapon systems.

If we thought that counted for anything, we were fools. The drill sergeants tasked with keeping order at 2/58 were a sarcastic bunch. They loved to harass recent OSUT graduates with the sole purpose of reminding us that we were still very much in the Army, and had a good deal to prove before our infantry credentials would be regarded as legitimate in the eyes of our brothers "down range." By this, they meant those men who were immersed in the 11B way of life by living it ... on the line.

Early on during the holdover period, we took an APFT. It was mandatory to pass that one for admission to Airborne School. While I was a very good runner by this point and had, by virtue of my frequently employed sarcasm, developed remarkable push-up stamina, sit-ups were a vulnerability.

On that day, I failed the sit-ups. If memory serves, I missed the passing score by one repetition. Nobody's fault but my own. We had not, as a platoon, conducted sit-ups since prior to the Bayonet, and I had not performed them independently. This was devastating, to say the least. Failure meant not joining the Warlords at Airborne School.

But there was hope.

The Non-Commissioned Officer in Charge (NCOIC) correctly presumed that this APFT was, for me, an aberration. He afforded me an opportunity to re-take it in two days' time. I humbly accepted his offer.

Two days later, I reported to the PT field with a handful of soldiers who were, for one reason or another, in need of taking the APFT. Some were battalion functionaries needing to keep their scores current. Others were readying for a promotion board. And me. I hoped to accompany the remaining Warlords to Airborne.

The push-ups went over swimmingly. If I didn't achieve a maximum score, I came within one or two of doing so. Next were the sit-ups. There's something about being flat-waisted that works against otherwise physically fit soldiers in the performing of this exercise.

Sit-ups are the only partner-dependent APFT event, in that another soldier is required to hold the performing soldier's feet while sit-ups are cranked out. Counting is left to the grader, almost invariably a non-commissioned officer.

"One, two, three…"

The NCO counted steadily, I sat up repetitively, the other soldier kept his palms pressed firmly on my feet.

"…thirty-seven, thirty-eight, thirty-nine…"

There's that feeling again. It was the feeling of achy, crippling fatigue in my abdomen. *What is it about skinny guys and sit-up weakness?* I was not alone here. A number of the Warlords had struggled with this exercise, while the thick-in-the-middle gentlemen could be counted upon to achieve scores in the ninety-percent range.

"…forty-five … forty-six…"

I slowed, and time was running out.

The event runs for exactly two minutes. A maximum score required seventy-eight repetitions, a score I had achieved during one of my AIT tests. Passing required that I perform at least fifty-three sit-ups. And at around 1:40, those last seven were far from a certainty.

"Don't you fucking quit on me!"

I knew that voice, but processing as much took about a second. A valuable second.

It was Roum. The unpredictable bastard had followed me out to the PT field and was observing me.

"Don't you *fucking quit!*"

There was no question of it now. Failing myself was an awful notion; failing a fellow Warlord was unthinkable.

"…fifty-three, fifty-four, fifty-five."

When the counting stopped, two things became clear. (1) I had passed the sit-ups and would undoubtedly be joining the Warlords to Airborne School, and (2) I would never again struggle through the sit-ups. Whatever degree of training was necessary, I would ensure a passing score within the first minute, and enough repetitions in the second to put me near, or over the maximum.

As I stood and readied myself for the two-mile run, Roum vanished. Because of his Native American ancestry, Roum would often joke about being "fleet and silent of foot." He had a way of being self-deprecating without forfeiting his self-respect.

The run was easy. I crossed the finish line with a solid time, thanked the NCOIC for trusting his hunch, and went to find my brothers.

In much the same way my 30th AG experience had lasted one week, so too was the 2/58 holdover. By Friday, Roum, Rohde, Naylor, and I had all received our Airborne orders. We would report that Sunday. I recall seeking the right moment to thank Roum for showing up on the PT field as he did, but it never materialized. The regrets had begun to pile up.

* * *

Fort Benning is big. It is, at over 180,000 acres in size, *quite* big. Being both sizable and home to a number of distinctive units, Benning is organized into four primary cantonment areas, or districts. There is Sand Hill, wherein Infantry recruits are trained. Kelley Hill, which is home to the 3rd Infantry Division (not to be confused with the 3rd U.S. Infantry Regiment). There is Harmony Church, which is, among other things, home to the 316th Cavalry Brigade Armor School. And the Main Post, which is exactly that: the base's main post.

It was to the Main Post we were headed, and to Airborne School. On a warm Sunday afternoon, we joined Alpha Company of the 507th Parachute Infantry Regiment. After quickly (very quickly, by military standards) in-processing with HHC, we made our way to A Co. and drew linen for a three-week's stay. We were assigned rooms by a buck sergeant, and then ordered outside to the formation area.

"This is a gentlemen's course, gentlemen!" spoke a detached, world-weary soldier.

I confess to being rather unsettled by these words. They had been spoken by a senior non-commissioned officer who was overseeing the reception of Airborne School reports.

"We don't have any intention of fucking with you for the sake of it. Fuck with us, we'll fuck you back. Otherwise, just behave like a professional and we'll be good. Roger?"

"Roger," Naylor responded for the group.

There were around fifteen of us, mostly from Charlie Company, 2/54. As we were all new basic training/AIT graduates, the senior NCO could speak to us in this frank manner. That would not always be the case, as Airborne School welcomes trainees of all ranks, military occupational specialties (MOSs), and branches.

Because the school welcomed such a broad cross-section of the military into its temporary keeping, there was no way to run the place like a medium-intensity boot camp. And high-intensity was, naturally, out of the question. So, it was a gentlemen's course.

There was a martial atmosphere to the place, and rightly so, but it was as casual a professional situation as any of the Warlords had experienced since reaching Benning. And the food was good.

Making sense of the situation was simpler once the higher-ranking trainees began to arrive. The instructors (known as Sergeants Airborne) could not treat such trainees with anything other than firm respect. It essentially homogenized the whole school; mess with all or mess with none. Unless, that is, the lower-enlisted guys screwed up ... which many did ... including myself. These were then singled out and messed with (read: punished) accordingly.

After being acquainted with the school's policies and given a brief overview of the following week's schedule, we were released to the barracks prior to evening chow. We took an APFT the following morning. It would be my third in seven days' time.

I'll be well-prepared for The Old Guard at this rate. I thought to myself, remembering something Eagleton had said about the unit performing PT twice daily in order to keep its men fit, trim, and capable of slipping effortlessly into a pair of dress blues. This was, I later learned, a partial fiction.

First-call came early on Monday morning. Autumn was well upon us, and the darkness was persisting well into first formation. Rohde and I stood shoulder to shoulder somewhere in the second rank. We would march out to the PT field for the APFT. (This was actually a weeding-out measure, as tickets to the Airborne School extravaganza had apparently been overbooked.) Failing scores would see students dropped from the program. And unlike 2/58, Sergeants Airborne were disinclined to offer second chances.

I owed that 2/58 NCO a good deal of gratitude. There was virtually no chance of my failing the sit-ups this time 'round, while push-ups and the run were, of course, a given.

I'll not elaborate on the specifics of that particular APFT, other than to say that all of the Warlords passed, and it was an unexpectedly cold morning. I scored something in the 280/300 range, I believe, with the sit-ups eating heavily into my score.

The cold made for a noticeable difference. Literally every such test we 2/54 men had taken had been conducted in middle to high temperatures. Running in the cold was an experience with which I would soon become intimately acquainted.

The next three weeks were broken down as follows:

1. Ground Week
2. Tower Week
3. Jump Week

We ran most mornings, executed pull-ups by the hundreds (it's sort of the staple Airborne exercise), practiced falling, practiced falling, practiced falling, and then practiced knitting.

Joke.

We practiced falling more.

It's known as the parachute landing fall (PLF), and mastering it during ground week is beneficial for those who plan on jumping from an aircraft. We also learned a good deal about parachutes and their proper post-fall packing (this made their return to the pick-up point more manageable). In all, it was a useful and rewarding school, and a fine capstone for what amounted to around five months in Fort Benning.

During Jump Week, based on the day, we jumped from either a C-130 or C-17 aircraft. We boarded at Lawson Army Airfield, then flew a negligible distance to Fryar Field—named for Medal of Honor recipient and World War II paratrooper Elmer E. Fryar—over which our jumps were conducted at an altitude of twelve-hundred feet. We jumped day and night, landed as we had been instructed, ran back to the gathering point, and began again. We graduated twenty days after having reported.

At one point, I nearly found myself kicked out of Airborne School.

I intentionally tripped a fellow Warlord while marching in formation. We had grown a little comfortable during those casual 2/58 days, had remained so during the gentlemen's course, and had taken to messing with one another. I got caught. To this day, I can't say why I took leave of my senses; but that is precisely what I did.

That error in judgment took place in Week Two. By Week Three, the incident was mercifully forgotten. I jumped, I graduated, and my Benning experience was within a day or so of being complete.

I was sad to a degree that would have been impossible, *simply impossible* to fathom during those depressing 30th AG days, or during the first few weeks of my 2/54 experience.

There were not many of us from Third Platoon, 2/54 in the Airborne graduating ranks. It was Naylor, Roum, Rohde, myself, and perhaps three or four others.

I believe we moved to some sort of transition room for a day or so, as the PIR barracks needed to be cleared after graduation.

From there, I worked with an administrative specialist in securing my homeward air travel documents. The airfare had been purchased some weeks earlier. I was heading home for HRAP, a twenty-day stretch of time. Naylor and Rohde were destined for a Ranger Battalion, and to adventures all their own.

The end had materialized before any of us realized what had happened. We blinked and had awoken under Spencer's austere training. We had blinked and the Bayonet was upon us. We had blinked again and were falling from the sky. And then it was time for a very painful farewell. Naylor and I hugged.

A mere five months earlier we were complete strangers. On that cold autumn day, we would have taken bullets for one another without a moment's hesitation. I loved those guys.

Having said goodbye to the others, Roum and I were on our own. Heading to a PX somewhere on the Main Post, I convinced a civilian cab driver to drive us one-hundred-fifteen miles to Hartsfield-Jackson Atlanta International Airport. He reluctantly agreed, though only after insisting that he would lose money on the deal. I was not convinced.

Roum and I had not been close during those early weeks at 2/54; bunked, as we were, on opposite sides of the bay. We bonded somewhere around mid-cycle. I came to respect him and was grateful for our sharing that cab ride to Atlanta. Not much was said; I was lost in thought and Roum speaks rather sparingly.

Upon reaching the airport, we paid the driver (tipping generously) and made our way to the terminal. There was an unexpected feeling of sensory overload. Having spent so much time on a comparatively isolated and quaint military post, Hartsfield-Jackson may as well have been Times Square. After securing our boarding passes, Roum and I shook hands.

"You wanna give me a call when you land, don't sweat it," Roum said.

"Okay. If not, I'll see you at Myer."

And that was it. I had said farewell to a fellow Warlord under circumstances which would've seemed odd a half-year earlier. Making my way to the terminal, a trace amount of that high school confidence began to resurface. This would be a very different homecoming than the one when I had danced with Ariel.

Though I had a fairly late departure time, the three hours "gained" (I had spent the previous five months trying to reclaim those) in flying east to west had me arriving around mid-evening. Awaiting me at the airport were my sister Megan, her boyfriend, my childhood classmate Travis, and a new friend by the name of Kyle, the latter of whom took it upon himself to carry my massively over-packed green duffel bag to the parking garage.

On the long drive to Marysville, the questions came one after another.

"What was the worst part?"

"Did you get in trouble?"

"How was the food?"

"Have you heard of Linkin Park?"

This last question was asked by my future brother-in-law Travis, who apparently possesses no understanding of my taste in music.

By the time I had answered every inquiry, we were nearing the first of Marysville's exits. It was past sundown by that point, so I had not laid eyes upon my beloved hometown to the extent that I would have liked. Doing so the following day and throughout the coming weeks, however, was nothing short of sentimental. Not much has changed.

I spent around an hour in conversation with my parents before heading upstairs to my bedroom which was so familiar ... and so foreign. Everything was precisely as I had left it, with the exception of my window, which was closed. I typically kept it cracked year-round. I opened it a palm's width before laying down for a night's rest. The following day, I was to report to the very recruiting station in which I had been, well, recruited at the previous spring.

Waking up in my own bed had a strange time-distorting effect upon on me that first morning. For a heartbeat, it felt as though I had never left at all. As if I had never endured the humbling experience of remaining in the front-leaning rest position for hours on end; had never been violently divorced from a resting state by way of a clanging trash can careening down the center of a bay's long linoleum floor; had never been forced to stare my limitations in the eye and acknowledge their rightful place upon the terrain of my identity.

It was as though the dream of adolescence had not yet collided with a training regimen designed to wrench such illusions from those who harbor them.

I took inventory of my countenance, of my eyes, and of my high-and-tight haircut. On that cool November morning, the unfortunate "style" reminded me of two things: (1) I was Army property, and (2) I was expected at the local recruiting station by 0900 hours.

"Morning, Mom," I said while eating a bowl of cereal.

"Hello, offspring," she replied with a smile, "what time do you have to go?"

"In a few minutes. Where's the Prelude?" I had gifted Megan with my 1985 Honda Prelude the day I departed for MEPS. I'd imagined she'd allow me to make use of it while home.

"Your sister took it to school."

I was wrong. "Bollocks. Suppose I could use the Camry?"

"That's *my* car. What if I need it?"

"I'll be near. For all I know, they won't have me work a full day."

"Ugh. Okay, but let me know when you're heading home."

"Roger."

And I was off. What struck me as odd was how reflexively the commute unfolded. The Camry drove itself as I took in as much of Marysville as I would cover in the ten-minute drive; which is to say, most of it. I couldn't seem to suppress that persistent question: what if I had never left?

Parking in the small shopping/dining plaza where the Army recruiting station was located, I reported for duty and experienced an entirely different flavor of military service. My own recruiter, a former Special Forces NCO who had returned to the line, had moved on, though the corporal working under his leadership was still around. The senior figure had been replaced by a staff sergeant with a civilian approach to his work.

"Hey there!" SSG Lager bellowed through the practiced smile of a motivated car salesman.

"Hello, Sergeant!" I was standing at firm parade rest as I had been instructed to do when speaking with any non-commissioned officer.

"Relax, relax—this ain't Benning, son." Lager approached me, patted my shoulder, and pointed to a chair.

"So, glad to be back?" the casual staff sergeant asked as I took a seat opposite him.

"It is, Sergeant, yes." I was a bit uneasy, as though waiting for Lager to switch gears and unload on me with a smoke session.

"Good, good. Well, listen, you got any buddies who might wanna enlist?" I was taken aback by the man's urgency.

"Uh, well, Sergeant, I hadn't really given it much thought." This was entirely true. "But I might have one or two who…"

"Great! Great! When can we get them in?"

"Oh well… I don't know." I was beginning to relax, as the man's commitment to his sales role was now apparent. Whatever "down range" intensity I had been preparing to confront would have to wait until I reported to Fort Myer in twenty days' time. "I was going to visit some friends this evening. Maybe I could talk to those guys."

"Yeah, get them down here. Peters (a corporal assigned to the station) is gonna have you sign some paperwork and then you can get outta here. Be back tomorrow at 0900 or whenever you can. And bring those dudes in, okay?"

I don't know what I had expected of HRAP, in truth. Whenever the subject came up during OSUT and Airborne, we tended to focus only on the "H" portion of the "H-R-A-P" acronym. The thought of being home for three weeks' time was enough to see us through many a trying ordeal.

That said, we certainly did not expect that our time in the recruiting station would be so informal in nature. I had anticipated something very regimented. Perhaps even a PT session? Wouldn't that have been something? Executing push-ups in a parking lot which I had walked, bicycled, or driven past thousands of times in Marysville.

PT was not a priority for these guys.

Before leaving, I turned to Corporal Peters, whose acquaintanceship I had made the previous spring, and who operated in a mostly administrative capacity. Making certain the station's senior NCO was not within earshot, I asked, "Is Sergeant Lager a bit more aggressive in his approach than your former boss?"

At this, Peters laughed. "Jesus, man, I'll probably hear the guy trying to convince some chicks that the Army has a cheerleading MOS. He's always going on about the Army having more aircraft than the Air Force, trying to pull those guys away from our next-door neighbors."

Indeed, contained within that modestly sized strip mall were three recruiting stations—Army, Marine Corps, and Air Force.

"Well, I'll try to bring in a couple of good guys. No idea if they'll have any interest in joining, but I'd bet one of them has nothing else going on."

As I left the station, I breathed in the crisp, cool, November air. Aside from my brief drive over to the station, this was my first daylight glimpse of Marysville, Washington in nearly half a year's time. It struck me deeply in that moment. Leaving would be difficult when twenty days had come and gone.

But as of then, I was home, and I meant to make good use of my time.

I should think the most unsettling feeling is the clear knowledge that all continued on as it had prior to my departure. It's a bit awkward. Nobody knew quite what to do with me, not at first.

The feeling that people were re-arranging their schedules on my behalf was unavoidable. Routines and obligations were messily moved about in order for a coffeehouse trip or visit to the local pizzeria (Alfy's, in this case).

At first, I was uncomfortable in seeing and re-connecting with friends and family. But eventually that passed, and a sort of makeshift pattern took shape.

I hung out with my sister and Travis during the evenings, and saw a couple of my college-attending friends during a non-class day. I even stopped in to visit my high school teachers. This last I did in full-on Class A uniform. I might have been showing off, but it wasn't clear either way. Nominally, I was there to generate recruitment interest. If it worked, I never knew one way or the other.

When I brought a couple of high school friends down to the recruiting station, the effort proved unfruitful. Neither were overly interested. One friend cast a look of "fuck this" my way and hinted that he was ready to leave.

Interestingly enough, my joining up had contributed to the decision of three others to do exactly that. One was a close friend, while the other two were loose acquaintances. In hindsight, I should have asked Lager to credit those towards my HRAP record. Not that my doing so would have been met with success. The guy had a quota to meet.

I don't recall if those twenty days of HRAP passed quickly. Time at home plays tricks on the mind of a soldier. There were certainly blocks of leave where I found myself genuinely taken aback with how fast Monday transformed itself into Thursday, Thursday into the following Tuesday, and that Tuesday into Saturday ... my usual departure day.

But HRAP was different. Time's passage might have been slow, steady. So much so, that I was eager to board my flight and report to The Old Guard. I managed to get a good deal done. I saw my grandparents over dinner, spent time with my parents, God bless them. I spent time with my sister, Travis, and the family into which Megan would one day marry. I knew it then— Megan would be an Ahre.

I took in my beloved Washington. God, how I love Washington. So much so that returning permanently (I write these words from my current Arizona home) seems out of the question. I dare not risk tarnishing my Pollyanna vision of that remarkable state. Let the beauty persist in my mind's eye, even if it may not withstand the scrutiny born of full-time residence.

As it happened, I would leave my family, and our pets, and my friends, and my home state, and everything I had come to cherish since boyhood on Thanksgiving Day of 2000 Anno Domini. Whereas my mother had dropped me off at the recruiting station in rather errand-like fashion some six months earlier, she was a complete mess the morning of my departure for The Old Guard.

I hugged her farewell, shook my stepfather's hand, spent a moment in "goodbye" with our two dogs (Patches and Cinnamon), and left the house to breathe in a puff of thick, cold, Washington air. That was enough to summon tear-jerking sentiment to the surface.

I would experience homesickness again, of that much I was certain.

My sister and a high school friend of mine, (one of those who had made the drive to Benning months earlier), would shuttle me to Seattle-Tacoma International Airport. It was a cloudy day, not unusual for a Puget Sound Thanksgiving.

Rather than a mere curbside drop-off, Megan and our friend insisted on accompanying me to the gate. This was nearly a year prior to September 11th, 2001, and airport security was a rather relaxed affair. While we waited, my sister began to weep. Fortunately, I knew what was necessary to mitigate her sadness—a partial rendering of a *South Park* song performed in the voice of one Eric Cartman. This was a largely successful effort.

And then I boarded my flight. I was off to Fort Myer and to a wealth of ceremonies, stories, screw-ups, SNAFUs, successes, sorrows, and service with some of the finest human beings I would ever know, let alone have the privilege of serving alongside.

V

The Old Guard
Welcomes Its Newest

The Seattle to Washington, D.C., flight is a bit lengthy. It's around six hours in favorable flying conditions.

A beautiful blonde flight attendant took notice of the fact that I was flying in my Class A uniform.

"Are you in the service?"

At this I looked down at my attire, then back at her. I couldn't quite make out whether the question was serious in nature.

"Uh, yes I am."

"That is so incredible. I could never do it. Good luck, wherever you're going."

"Yes, ma'am."

It was a nice gesture and one for which I was, on that cold and lonely day, quite appreciative. Such sentiments often have me feeling uncomfortable. For instance, I'm always a bit uneasy when someone says "Thank you for your service" or voices other such sentiments on Veterans Day, Memorial Day, and Independence Day. I immediately think of all those souls who sacrificed their very lives, of those whose time overseas dwarfs my own, of those who made careers of the military. Somehow, that gratitude seems better spent on them.

But in this case, I found myself sincerely moved. The words were earnest, not a trace of self-interest to be found. I was grateful.

And then we landed.

I was familiar with Dulles International Airport for the following reason: *Die Hard 2* was a TBS fixture for the better part of five years prior to my joining the military. This occurred to me only very briefly as I made my way to baggage claim, then out to the cold night to locate a taxi.

"Are you familiar with Fort Myer?" I asked, uncertain.

Smiling knowingly, the cab driver responded, "Of course. Throw your bags in the trunk."

Illustration depicting the Military District of Washington (with obvious emphasis on Arlington National Cemetery) (3d U.S. Infantry Regiment, "The Old Guard").

Fort Myer (now known as Joint Base Myer-Henderson Hall; just rolls off the tongue, doesn't it?), was originally named for Civil War hero Amiel Weeks Whipple (1818–1863), a brigadier general who would tragically meet his end during the Battle of Chancellorsville.

Despite the gallantry and worthiness of its namesake, Fort Whipple would operate under that name only until 1881, when it was renamed for Albert J. Myer, also a brigadier general and brilliant signal officer who had served in that capacity during the Civil War. For that reason, Fort Myer was home to a Signal Corps for more than half a century prior to the 3rd U.S. INF (The Old Guard, as Gen. Winfield Scott nicknamed it) laying down its roots.

Prior to the 1940s, the 3rd had enjoyed a long, storied, and impressive history, beginning on 03JUN1784. Known then as the First American Regiment, the unit was composed of companies from four states: New York, Pennsylvania, New Jersey, and Connecticut. And from that point forth, the First American Regiment would go on to see action in every major (and minor) war.

The regiment would experience innumerable re-designations, consolidations, reorganizations, deactivations, and reactivations. So many, in fact, that it might have taken a team of elite archivists (if such a thing can be said to exist) to accurately trace the Regiment's origins back to its 1784 founding.

But there it was, on 06APR1948, more than a century and a half removed from its founding, being activated at Fort Myer, VA. Mind you, this reactivation did not set things up precisely as they presently sit. The 2nd Battalion was activated across the river at Fort McNair, and Regimental reorganization would take place twice between 1948 and 1986. But by and large, the 3rd U.S. INF was essentially assuming the form for which it would become militarily famous throughout the latter half of the 20th century.

Arlington National Cemetery, a sacred ground which, in addition to being recognized and cherished throughout the nation, also serves as the emotional and psychological bedrock of both Fort Myer and The Old Guard. As perhaps the most enduring, visited, and significant hallmark to have sprung forth from the national trauma that was the American Civil War, Arlington National Cemetery is emblematic of something so fundamental to a proper understanding of our republic's profound story.

Established on 13MAY1864, the date of its first military burial (that of William Henry Christman), Arlington National Cemetery is as intertwined with American history as is any piece of land in the country. At the outset of

Arlington National Cemetery shortly after dawn (3d U.S. Infantry Regiment, "The Old Guard").

the Civil War, Arlington belonged to George Washington Parke Custis, a grandson of Martha Washington, whose daughter, Mary Anna Randolph Custis, would marry Confederate general and renowned military genius Robert E. Lee. For his part, Custis passed away a few years prior to the South's secession from the Union. Mary Anna inherited the land, which was both a plantation and home to the now famous Arlington House.

By virtue of its proximity to Washington, D.C., the estate was confiscated in its entirety by the United States government early in the war, just under three years prior to the burial of Christman. Mary Anna had taken it upon herself to safeguard (by way of burying) a number of family treasures, many of which were tied in one way or another directly to the Washingtons.

The Battle of the Wilderness, which was fought in the early days of May 1864, resulted in a tragic number of deaths on both sides, with over two thousand dead in the Union Army alone. As cemeteries in the area that pre-dated the Civil War were no longer viable, having reached their respective capacities for obvious reasons, new land would need to be appropriated for purposes of honorably burying the fallen.

Arlington was recommended, and formal burial authorization was, in June of 1864, officially granted. Some two decades later, in 1883, following a curious situation in which the land had been returned to the Lee family by Supreme Court verdict, the land was deemed a military reservation. From that point forth, Arlington National Cemetery's six-hundred-twenty-four acres would stand as our healing republic's most sacred of lands.

It should go without saying that very little of this was on my mind some one-hundred-seventeen years later, as my forty-five minute Dulles-to-Myer cab ride was nearing its end. We entered through what I later came to know as the Iwo Jima Gate. This is not its official name, but names are a fluid concept within the military ranks.

To his credit, the cab driver did a good job of reasoning just where I should be dropped off. To my discredit, I hadn't the faintest notion.

Turning left on Sheridan Avenue, which would later be known to me as "Barracks Row," the driver slowed to a crawl and scanned the buildings to our right for signage. When he stopped, I saw that we were in front of an older looking structure, more like a good-sized house than a regimental headquarters. Not long after my arrival, a new headquarters building would be built, leaving this one to serve as a post museum.

"Thank you, sir," I said, while handing the driver cash and insisting that he keep the change.

"You bet, buddy. Good luck to you."

And he was off, leaving me standing at the base of a short staircase that led to the building's large double-doors. I exhaled, made certain my overcoat appeared presentable, secured my A-bag, and made my way up the stairs.

As I sit writing these pages, I cannot recall with any certainty what specifically I expected upon reporting for duty on that cold Thanksgiving evening in the late autumn of 2000. Though it was nearly midnight, and a holiday, I was nevertheless braced for a smoke session of some sort. This had also been the case upon my reporting to Airborne holdover, to Airborne itself, and to HRAP. Basic Training leaves an indelible mark on those who experience it.

What I had not expected is what actually happened.

Entering the rundown building, I heard the familiar sounds of a video game being played. This may as well have been Geoff's house some eleven years earlier, though the game was not *Kid Icarus*. Taking a few steps inside, I slowly turned the corner to see a couple of shaved-head soldiers engaged in a game of Risk™ ... via electronic interface—that of a Nintendo.

Upon noticing me, those two must have thought my face was a veritable case study in curiosity. As for my own thoughts, they went something like this: *I can't imagine Risk™ is improved from a gameplay standpoint when experienced in this format.*

"What's up, man?" This was asked by Staff Sergeant Saxon, and in far more casual a tone than I had anticipated. Where were the obligatory push-ups?

Shouldn't I be in the front-leaning rest position this very moment? I inquired of myself.

"Where you coming from, man?" Saxon was still casual and keeping one eye on the video game.

"From Fort Benning, Sergeant."

"No shit, man. You're an infantry guy reporting to The Old Guard. I mean where *from*?"

"Oh. From Washington, Sergeant." I felt a bit sheepish.

"Cool. Welcome to the show."

"Thank you, Sergeant."

"Have a seat. We'll get you squared away in a min ... hey, fucker, don't make a move without me looking."

This last he had directed to his runner, Specialist Paxton.

"Well take your turn, man, come on."

What the hell was going on? An E-4 was speaking to an E-6 in the tone of an equal. I wanted some damn answers. And I wanted them right n...

"Do you want a doughnut?" Saxon pointed to a box of Dunkin Donuts.

What was I to do? The last thing I wanted at this late hour was a doughnut. But when was the last time a staff sergeant had offered me anything in so kind a tone?

"Okay, Sergeant."

I made my way over to the box and selected the least-stale doughnut. After one bite, I thought to indulge my inherently curious mind with a question.

"Which company will I be going to?"

Saxon pointed to a white board. "Says right there."

And there it was, in blue marker and crappy handwriting: "next 5 to alpha"

Oh shit. I didn't know all there was to know about The Old Guard, but I did know about Alpha Company. I also knew I had no interest in being a part of it.

"What company are you from, Sergeant?" I asked, though for what reason is anyone's guess.

It was Specialist Paxton who responded. "We're from Bravo." This, he said, while pointing across the way, indicating the Bravo barracks were very near.

What was not nearby was Alpha Company. Alpha was based out of Fort McNair, in Washington, D.C., proper. The company's specific location had absolutely nothing to do with my disinclination towards joining its ranks. It was that wig. I simply had no interest in donning a powdered wig.

The 3rd U.S. INF is somewhat labyrinthine in its organization. And in the interest of confusing former TOG soldiers, that organization has undergone two restructurings since the summer of 2004.

Suffice it to say that the core line companies, those being Bravo, Charlie, and Delta, belong to the unit's 1st Battalion, along with a battalion HQ com-

The 3d U.S. Infantry Regiment at the 58th Presidential Inauguration on January 20, 2017 (U.S. Army Photos by Staff Sgt. Kelvin Ringold/Sgt. George Huley/Pvt. Gabriel Saliva).

pany and the guys over at Hotel. While we could certainly and irretrievably lose ourselves in this maze, just know that (a) the lion's share of funerals (full honors and otherwise) are carried about by the 1st, 2nd, and 3rd platoons of Bravo, Charlie, and Delta companies, and (b) that these three companies all sit at Fort Myer, Virginia.

Also on Fort Myer is Honor Guard (or Echo) Company which is comprised of the unit's most vertically gifted soldiers and houses the excellent Continental Color Guard along with the Tomb of the Unknown Soldier platoon. There are also the Specialty Platoons, some of which belong to Hotel Company. These included the United States Army Drill Team, the United States Army Caisson Platoon, and the Presidential Salute Battery (the Guns).

I've not said a word about the Fife and Drum Corps, nor about "Pershing's Own," also known as The United States Army Band (TUSAB), which provide, respectively, 18th and early-20th century music during certain parades, shows, retirements, et cetera. And I have yet to make mention of the S-Shops, two of which I would come to know from within during my second full year with the regiment. With luck, I will get to most of this.

As noted, things have changed since my time with the regiment. Organizationally, companies falling under a given command structure might have moved or been reassigned to the now reactivated (as of 2008) 4th Battalion,

Above and opposite: A 21-gun salute carried out as the Presidential motorcade makes its way through ANC. Veterans Day, 2016 (U.S. Army Photos by Spc. Brandon Dyer).

but, to my understanding, Bravo, Charlie, and Delta remain the grunt companies where performing daily burial ceremonies is concerned.

What also remains is the inexorable fact that Alpha Company, or the Commander-in-Chief's Guard, sits not at Fort Myer, Virginia, but at Fort McNair in Washington, D.C.

"I thought I might be going to Bravo Company," I said aloud. "One of my Sergeants Airborne came from Bravo."

This was true. One of the NCOs under whose training I learned to fall from an aircraft had, like Spencer, come from the 3rd U.S. INF, and had been a part of Bravo Company. Prior to Jump Week, he had said something offhand about hoping I ended up there myself.

"Ain't up to us, is it? Next five are Alpha's." Saxon was intently engaged with his video game. There were certainly staff sergeants throughout the unit who would have been far less patient with my imprudent inquiries.

"Relax for now. We don't have trans to get you over there tonight." Saxon looked to Paxton. "Who's got the desk over at Bravo tonight?"

"It's Rickson."

"Give him a call, ask if he's got room for another report."

Paxton picked up the phone. "We got another dude here. Wanna come get him?"

After hanging up and resuming engagement with his video game, Paxton assured Saxon that there was indeed room for "one more" over at Bravo.

A few moments later, Sergeant Rickson entered the building, asked if I needed help with my A-bag (I didn't), and led me across the street to the Bravo Company barracks in Building 402. I later learned that 402 was virtually condemned and that all occupants would soon be relocating to a new barracks. But none of that mattered to me on that cold Thanksgiving night.

I recall Rickson filling out paperwork, though it was not a time-consuming process. A moment or so later, he placed a bundle of linen in my arms and led me into a room near the Charge of Quarters desk. (There are a few CQ (and one Staff Duty) stories to relate throughout the chapters ahead.)

Upon opening the room's door and turning on the lights, I saw two beds, one to the left, one to the right. The bed to the right was empty and devoid of linen, the other was occupied and linen-clad. Its occupant was familiar to me. It was Roum.

While I might have anticipated Roum's arrival aligning almost perfectly with my own, what I could not have counted on was our ending up in the same room shortly after reaching Fort Myer.

"Roum! What's going on, buddy? When did you g—"

"Shut the fuck up and go to sleep."

"Come on, man, are you kidding? What are the odds of our ending up in the same company?"

"I think we're going to Alpha." Roum was now sitting up, though his eyes were half-closed.

"That's what they said. You think we'll go tomorrow?"

"I don't know, bro. Just hit the lights and go to sleep."

"All right, man. It's good seeing you here."

"Yeah, whatever." Roum was characteristically (though not convincingly) terse.

Turning off the lights was easy enough; falling asleep less so. Leaving my home state earlier that day had made for a deeply painful experience, one made all the more so by a lonely flight towards the unknown. But the sight of a fellow Warlord—and Roum, no less—was enough to mitigate much of the pain. What's often most important is that which exists on the margins of experience.

Eventually, I fell asleep. And quite unexpectedly, I awoke with the sunrise, not to the sound of a trash can crashing to the floor, nor to the sound of heavy knocking upon the door, nor to the sound of a singing Moor. That's likely the final rhyming passage you will read herein.

It was the day after Thanksgiving and the unit was effectively closed for business. Roum was already awake and dressed in civilian clothes.

"You're not going to wear your BDUs?" I asked, sitting up.

"Nah, man. I've already been out. Nobody's here, except Mann."

At this I lit up. "Mann's here?"

"Down the hall. I saw him yesterday."

"So what do we do today?"

"You ever been to D.C.?" he asked.

"No."

"Let's go get chow and hit the city."

This was all a bit odd. It was our first day in our assigned duty station. We were supposed to be subjected to … *something, anything.* Stress was a natural ingredient in the welcoming of new soldiers to a given unit. What we were experiencing was something far too indeterminate for my liking.

"All right. Should we try to find an NCO?"

"Don't worry, man. I got this. The CQ guy doesn't give a shit what we do, as long as we don't fuck up."

"Aren't we supposed to be heading to Alpha?" I asked.

"Do you *wanna* go to Alpha?"

"Not particularly, no."

"Then shut the fuck up."

At that moment, I wanted nothing more than for an angry staff sergeant to burst in with a vengeance. Push-ups and flutter kicks would have been preferable to uncertainty. In the Army, if you're not following some set of orders from someone for some reason, you're doing something wrong. And spending that Friday milling about in the Washington, D.C., area felt … incorrect.

"All right. Where's the latrine?"

After a brief shower, I joined Roum at the nearby DFAC. Mann was already there.

"What's up, man?" Mann was all smiles.

"Matt-Mann, how the hell have you been?" I, too, was all smiles.

"Not bad, man. Been here for a couple of weeks. Everyone's on pass or whatever. We're on our own. How was Airborne?"

"It was good, man, thanks. Are you assigned to Bravo?"

"Yeah. And you?" Mann asked.

I looked to Roum, then back to Mann. "Apparently, we're going to Alpha."

"Ahh fuck, dudes. Fuck that." Mann was sincere in his sympathy.

"Hurry up, guys, let's hit D.C." Roum had eaten lightly and was ready for a day of exploration.

And explore we did.

Not one among us owned a car, at least not one we had with us at Fort Myer. In truth, I didn't expect I would need a vehicle while in the infantry. My vision of Army service had been one of life largely limited to the base.

So, on that cold November day of 2000, we Warlords walked … and walked far. I wagered by nightfall that we had covered something approaching ten miles throughout the preceding hours. We exited the very gate through which I had been driven the evening prior; this is technically called the Wright Gate, though we knew it almost exclusively as the Iwo Jima gate.

Washington, D.C., is the nation's most landmark-rich city by a wide margin, even in comparison to Marysville, Washington. This made navigation a fairly simple task for The Old Guard's newest reports. We eyed a major monument and walked towards it. Having passed the Iwo Jima Memorial upon exiting Wright Gate, we had agreed to take in as many such sacred and historically consequential structures, sculptures, and landmarks as we could during the daylight hours.

Led by our collective sense of direction, we found ourselves crossing Arlington Memorial Bridge, which extends across the Potomac River thereby connecting Arlington with D.C.

I confess to having been consumed with a sense of patriotism and feelings of humility as the Lincoln Memorial came into full view. As much as I may have doubted my decision (not that there had been much of a choice) to forego service in a standard infantry unit, the sight of so much history, so much Americana encapsulated within the paramount architecture by which we were surrounded was breathtaking. I knew then that I was blessed to be, in some small way, a part of The Old Guard.

It was apparent I was not entirely alone in this respect. Though a lifelong student of history, that sense of the sacrosanct by which I was overcome had been visited upon Mann and Roum alike. Neither was as attuned to the sense of historical narrative with which my own psyche was (is) intertwined, but they seemed awed by the grandeur. Namely, the statue of a seated Lincoln flanked on either side by larger than life inscriptions of his two most well-known speeches: his Second Inaugural and the Gettysburg Address.

From there, we moved about the nation's capital in something not unlike road marching fashion. Speed and purpose had been relentlessly drilled into us, and neither would soon abate. Laying eyes upon Iwo Jima and Lincoln had made for rather moving experiences, but our lungs were still adjusting to the cold fall air. By 1000hrs that morning, we moved with what must have appeared to those around us as unnecessary haste.

Mann and I had not dressed well for the weather, having been deceived by the beauty of a sun-rich, cloudless sky. Along the way, I purchased a black hooded sweatshirt with the letters "FBI" emblazoned upon the front. There were no plain options available. This particular garment would become the source of considerable ridicule from a number of platoon mates.

For the time being, it kept me warm—and that was enough to warrant the purchase.

On we moved.

The National Mall, the Washington Monument, the Reflecting Pool, the

Capitol—we saw more or less all there was to see on a grand scale. A couple of exceptions worth noting: (1) we did not visit the Jefferson Memorial, and (2) we spent no time in Arlington National Cemetery. I would visit Jefferson at some point the following year. As for Arlington, that sacred land would become well known to each of us, as it does for most all infantry soldiers assigned to The Old Guard.

Shortly after sundown, we had dinner in the city. Having experienced the Fort Myer DFAC some eight hours earlier, we agreed that a civilian restaurant was indeed preferable. Besides, DFAC cuisine would be a hallmark of our time with the regiment. No need to overly indulge in its culinary splendor at the moment.

The Hard Rock Café was perfectly willing to accept our Army-issued greenbacks. Then we walked to Fort Myer. It dawned on me as we neared the gate that had anyone in the company (or in the unit) inquired as to our whereabouts, or requested our presence for in-processing purposes, the responses would have been decidedly unsatisfactory. We had checked-in with nobody, and had mentioned to not a soul just where it was we were headed … or for how long we would be gone.

But upon returning to the Bravo Company barracks, I came to understand that the Thanksgiving four-day weekend was honored within the military as it is in the civilian sector. Truly, not an Old Guard soul had any interest in our activities on that sunny, crisply cool day.

"Suppose they'll take us to McNair tomorrow?" I asked Roum after we had returned to our makeshift room. Mann had taken a phone call and was out of sight the remainder of that evening.

"Who knows? Prolly not. If they didn't take us today, why would they on a Saturday?"

This made sense, but I couldn't shake my disappointment at having been so unlucky. I kept seeing that marker-scrawled sentence (as in "sentencing") in my mind's eye.

If I was unlucky at all, evidence of as much would not be made known to me for some time. It had nothing to do with the company assignment. On that matter, I had dodged a proverbial bullet.

The following two days were low-key, given the circumstances. The barracks were almost empty, save for a handful of soldiers. Mann and I had spent Saturday exploring Fort Myer and reminiscing about Benning. We ate all three meals in the DFAC. The following day, Sunday, Mann introduced me to the company barber, Specialist Niles, a redheaded gentleman who had cut hundreds of heads scores of times by the time I entered his lair.

He did a good job with the fade and told me to have fun with Alpha. Mann and I spoke about keeping in touch after I went to McNair. This seemed unlikely, but I was willing to maintain the possibility for a day. I called home, told my mom to pet the dogs on my behalf, asked my sister to take care of the Honda, and hung up happy to have spoken with them.

That night, Roum and I packed in preparation for what we imagined would be an earlier departure from Fort Myer.

Even so, we rightly presumed that the 0600–0900hrs uniform would be PTs (Winter or summer? That much we didn't know.) and so I laid those out for the following morning. Roum spoke with unusual openness and sentiment that evening. He was, like the rest of us, uncertain as to what the future held, and his voice betrayed as much. We fell asleep having set an alarm for 0545hrs.

Then came the knock. Roum and I were already awake, shaved, and in our PTs. It was a training room clerk I would later know as SPC Nelson. At the moment, he was a PT-clad soldier several years my senior, and was ordering us to get downstairs for formation.

We guessed correctly as to the uniform. Roum and I had donned our winter tops and our knit caps. These we had barely seen and never worn during basic training and AIT, though each had seen a bit of use at 2/58 and throughout Airborne School. The temperature was perhaps another ten degrees cooler than anything we had experienced in Benning, but we had begun to adapt to it.

Somewhere along the way, Roum and I were split-up. I think he ended up falling in with First Platoon (Mann's platoon) for the time being. While walking out to the formation area, I mentioned to Nelson something to the effect of…

"I was told I'd be going to Alpha Company. Were you aware of that?"

Not knowing the man's rank, I chose to omit from my speech any guesses. This carried with it its own risk, but I hated the idea of referring to an NCO by a lesser rank. And I *really* hated the idea of referring to a lower-enlisted soldier by "Sir" or "Sergeant."

"What?" Nelson was incredulous. "Who told you that?"

Shit. I had forgotten the name of that staff duty NCO. It was Saxon, and I would remember it later that morning.

"It was um, he was on the…" I was mumbling at this point, "…the desk over in the…"

Nelson mercifully spared me another moment of half-formed speech.

"No, *fuck* that. We housed you over the weekend, you're staying with Bravo."

Relief is the only way to describe my reaction. It was palpable, sincere, heartfelt relief.

"You're going to fall-in with Headquarters Platoon for PT. We'll figure out where you're going later on."

Bravo Company numbered well over a hundred souls, from what I could make out in observing the morning formation. Perhaps thirty-six per platoon and another dozen or so in the Headquarters group. I fell in alongside Nelson thirty seconds prior to the First Sergeant appearing before us. We were called to attention, listened to a brief statement about being ready for a few backup missions (whatever that meant), and were instructed to perform some hard PT.

The Headquarters Platoon was very small in number. And of those who had been present for first formation, only around half had any intention of performing PT after the 1SG released the company to its individual platoons. Nelson excused himself for legitimate training room business, while a couple of others voiced (less legitimate) explanations along the lines of finishing an inventory process.

This was an aspect of both Bravo's Headquarters Platoon and of the Regiment's Headquarters Company which I'd come to know closely. A good number of those who serve in support/administrative roles become highly adept "shammers" upon reaching their respective units. Shamming is the act of avoiding duties which are less than appealing. This includes, but is not limited to, (a) physical training of any sort, (b) anything remotely resembling a ceremony, (c) field time, and (d) walking more than seven steps in any one stretch.

That said, every (and I do mean *every*) Headquarters group, whether at the company, battalion, or division level, has a couple of PT studs populating its ranks. It usually breaks down like this: (a) a gazelle-like runner, (b) a former high school powerlifter, (c) a 5'7" fireplug, (d) a male cheerleader who is too enthusiastic about, well, everything. The latter of these is typically insufferable. We all know one.

On that chilly morning, I experienced my first run in the Washington, D.C., area, and labored to keep pace with a fellow 11B—SPC Mike McGuinness, who had been temporarily assigned to the Headquarters group. I had left Benning in very good running condition, better than most of the Warlords. But we had run in warmer climes. The bite of that late-autumn East Coast air was deep. And the guys I was running with from The Old Guard on that first Monday were pretty damn fast.

None more so than McGuinness himself. Fitting, given his belonging to the combat arms, like myself. By the latter half of that five-mile jaunt, he and I had left the others behind. By the final mile, I knew I, too, would be left behind unless I found that gear generally reserved for shorter, faster two-mile APFT runs. This was a pace with which I'd soon become supremely comfortable.

Soon was not yet upon us that day. I was only just appealing to the higher gear for sustained usage over a longer distance, and the negotiation would take some time.

Inhaling deeply and expanding my stride by a foot or so, I resolved to beat this unusually fast SPC across whatever it was that constituted a makeshift finish line. Passing through the Iwo Jima Gate, I was only a stride or two behind McGuinness.

The end was near. We were back on base and, Myer being rather modest in its dimensions, could not have had much more than a half-mile remaining. If Spencer had done anything, he had conditioned his men to make short work of half-mile sprints.

I was ready to do exactly that. I would outsprint McGuinness in this final stretch, and earn the respect of an established TOG soldier in the process.

And then I remembered something which I had no business forgetting in the first place.

The hill.

It was the very hill Roum, Mann, and I had walked when returning from our tourist outing. The hill is steep, curves slightly to the left, and seems endless at times.

And it is not to be taken lightly.

In the years ahead, I would learn to make short work of that hill. So much so, that I would often allow my platoon mates a generous head start, only to overtake them one by one when finishing a long run.

Those days were months away, and would've seemed out of reach as I watched McGuinness bolt with impressive speed up that lengthy incline. I remember wondering if Roum (having been the Warlords' swiftest runner) could have overtaken the man. It's possible. But McGuinness was fleet of foot and well-conditioned for that particular stretch of paved gradient.

And so too will I be. I like to think that words to that effect ran through my mind as I forced myself to finish the climb within at least twenty seconds of McGuinness. We had experienced some tiring runs with Spencer, but this might have been my toughest to date. Throughout my TOG tenure, I would go on to routinely achieve APFT scores north of the three-hundred maximum. My being compelled to perform at that level was in no small part attributable to the standard set by Specialist Mike McGuinness.

I had been instructed by Nelson to eat breakfast after PT and to report to him "down the hall" at 0900 hours. There was a bit of paperwork.

Walking to the barracks utterly exhausted, I wasn't convinced of being spared a wigged fate. The guillotine of an Alpha sentence loomed over my vulnerable neck, and until something was formalized, I would harbor a sensible quotient of skepticism.

After dressing in BDUs, not yet pressed, I headed over to the DFAC with Mann around 0815hrs.

"Apparently, I'm not going to Alpha after all," I said as we walked.

"No shit?" Mann enthusiastically replied.

"That Nelson guy said something about housing us over the weekend. Sort of a finders keepers rule, I suppose."

"I hope he wasn't fucking with you." Mann tended to fret, and over the strangest of things. When introducing me to the barber Niles on Sunday morning, he had explained the situation as though imparting State secrets.

"He gets one day off each week in exchange for cutting heads on Sunday, okay?" The graveness of Matt's tone was as amusing as it was confusing.

"Yes, Matt, I understand."

That was Sunday, and this was Monday. To my knowledge, I would not be visiting Fort McNair. At least not yet. There would be a trip over that way for unrelated reasons down the road.

After breakfast chow, I asked Mann if he'd show me to the training room ... and if he'd tell me what it was.

"It's where a couple of turds sit all day. They do the company's paperwork and schedule ranges and shit."

Mann was being a bit unfair. Of the two training room soldiers I met that morning, one of the two would go on to become a good friend and Operations colleague a year later. His name is Jason Telgren, and his mind is well-suited for bureaucracy and administrative matters. Telgren, still fairly new, was the junior of the two TR administrators, with Nelson being a few years into his Army enlistment.

"You thought you were going to Alpha, huh?" Telgren posed this rhetorical question while manipulating a generously sized wad of chewing tobacco from one patch of oral real estate to another.

"Yes," I replied.

"That shit ain't happening," Nelson assured me. The "sham shields" were visible on his uniform. He wasn't a sergeant, after all. Glad I spoke indefinitely earlier that morning.

I should say here that the rank of E-4/Specialist carries with it a distinctive rank insignia. It is somewhat shield-shaped and places its wearer in a sort of grey area, rank-wise, which tends to result in a good deal of shamming on part of said wearer. Hence, the term "sham shield."

"We went to the trouble of bedding you over a holiday weekend. You're in Bravo, kid."

This was a mere reiteration of what Nelson had said earlier that day. Nevertheless, it was good to hear, even if Nelson had spoken the words in an oddly punitive tone. I later realized it was his way of sticking it to the powers that be. He's a good man, and fearless.

"Telgren is in-processing you. Once that's done, the 1SG is gonna wanna sit down with you. Guy your size, you're probably going to the firing party."

Nelson was right. I probably should've been assigned to Third Platoon, which provided Bravo with three firing parties. Instead, I was assigned to

Second Platoon, which provided Bravo's three casket teams. It all came about strangely.

After the training room, I was directed down the hall to meet with the company 1SG. Without question, First Sergeant Triton was the most impressive, intimidating, serious, and credible soldier I had yet encountered in the U.S. Army.

Every soldier leaves basic training convinced that their drill sergeants were the toughest, deadliest warriors walking the planet. That misconception is quickly dispelled upon reaching one's unit, where one can train alongside former Special Operations soldiers, seasoned warriors of wide-ranging backgrounds, and talented field operators whose craft has been forged in the fires of real-world missions.

Triton was just such a soldier.

It was me, Roum, and a taller kid, Private Welling, sitting in 1SG Triton's narrow office. Triton aimed to take our measure, and I was humbled by the prospect.

"Where do you see yourself in a few years?" Triton directed this to Roum.

"I've thought about S.F. or maybe Delta, but I don't know yet," Roum replied.

This was a revelation to me. Roum had never spoken a single word on the topic of Special Forces. I scarcely had a moment to register my surprise, as Triton's response was equally unexpected.

"I'll tell you right now, son, that I can outrun, outjump, outswim, and outfight every man in this company, and I'd have a hard time keeping up with Delta Force. You want that, you'd better start training the moment you leave this office."

A couple of points on this: (1) It is difficult to express how credible Triton seemed in delivering what might otherwise have amounted to mere boastfulness. The man was not boasting; he was articulating an irrefutable fact. (2) If any among the Warlords would have been ideal for S.F. training, it would've been Roum. Observing the Triton/Roum exchange made for engaging theatre.

"All right, stand up, you three." Triton was himself standing and was readying to issue platoon assignments.

Welling was by far the tallest of us and assigned to First Platoon, the marching platoon, which typically recruited all soldiers over 6'0, with a few exceptions.

Roum and I stand about the same height, which meant the remaining platoon assignments might have been decided by a coin-flip. Triton's determination was made by assessing muscle tone. After a squeeze of my upper arm, it was decided.

"You seem sturdy. Hope you can carry a casket."

He had not, to my recollection, done the same to Roum, who was by default assigned to the firing party platoon. I would learn the art of ceremonial flag-folding; Roum the art of the twenty-one gun salute.

The next six months would see my Bravo Company experience intertwine with Triton's in ways that were humbling, edifying, stressful, and necessary.

For the time being, however, I would report to Second Platoon.

VI

Second Platoon and a Cold Inauguration

Old Guard platoons are highly archetypal in their make-up, more so than other U.S. Army infantry platoons. The taller, leaner, and often ganglier soldiers are almost invariably assigned to First Platoon, the marching platoon. These gentlemen are trained to march flawlessly in tight formation for the primary purpose of rendering full honors funerals particularly prestigious. Which is to say, First Platoon accompanies the casketed remains of deceased senior military figures who, when being laid to rest, are ceremonially conveyed through Arlington National Cemetery, that hallowed garden of stone, via horse-pulled caisson. This level of elaborate funeral ceremony is reserved, in most cases, for field-grade officers and above. Exceptions, however, are often made; specifically, for others deserving of high honors.

For its part, Third Platoon, the firing party, is home to soldiers both too short for marching service and inadequately built for casket-bearing. Firing Party soldiers tend to fall in the 5'10–5'11 range, and are generally lean in build. Again, there are exceptions, but Third Platoon generally welcomes guys of average height and build into their ranks.

To say I didn't fit the Second Platoon mold would be to invite upon myself legitimate accusations of understatement. These guys were big. Imagine your high school football team's defensive line. Now add around twenty pounds (ten of those around the middle, two around the jaw, eight on the forearms), grizzle the face a bit, apply an unfortunate high-and-tight haircut, toss in a dose of cynicism, and boom—I give you Bravo Company's casket platoon circa late-2000.

There were exceptions. Just as every football team has its wide receivers and kickers, Second Platoon had a handful of mesomorphs in its ranks. I was such a mesomorph, though even then I was the smallest platoon member by at least ten pounds. Height-wise I was on the shorter end, though there were two or three I could look straight in the eye, and at least one who was, to my surprise, visibly shorter. This gentleman was nevertheless considerably heavier and made an excellent casket bearer.

Sergeant First Class Wilde seemed to register all of this within seconds of my reporting to his office.

"Shouldn't your ass be in Third? What am I gonna do with you?" Wilde was half-smiling while asking me a question for which I had, quite literally, no response.

"I was sent here by 1SG Triton, Sergeant." What a truly pointless thing to have said.

"Yeah, I know. Think I'm gonna put your small ass in Second Squad. See what Dussard can do with you."

I would soon learn the platoon politics, but, for now, a squad was a squad.

"Roger, Sergeant."

"We got a lot going on right now. The building you're standing in is falling apart. We gotta move our shit 'cross the street before Christmas."

"Roger, Sergeant."

"All right. Just keep that shit in mind for now. I don't know what Dussard's gonna have for you, but things are about to get real busy here, man. So do what you can stand."

That was the first time I heard Wilde employ what I later came to recognize as his favorite slogan. *Do what you can stand.* It was intended to be both encouraging and cynical, I suppose, but Wilde never elaborated.

SSG Michael Dussard resembled actor Daniel Day-Lewis to an uncanny degree. The similarity was suitably strong to have me commenting on it within days of meeting the man. Dussard was also unusual. He was tactically minded in the extreme, had a pronounced distaste for "corporal punishment" (unless it proved necessary), was mostly impatient with ceremony, and treated his men well.

To a newly arrived lower-enlisted soldier, Dussard was the best squad leader one could reasonably hope for. The man held the same rank/paygrade as did Drill Sergeant Spencer, but behaved in a rather civilian-like manner. For some, years of military service do nothing to dampen the inherent kindness within. And Dussard was, above all else, kind.

He liked me immediately, either despite or because of my wit; we would ultimately develop a friendship, of sorts. But between the lower-enlisted soldiers and their squad leaders stand the middle-men: team leaders. My first experience with this dynamic was less than pleasant. Much of the heat brought down upon my person by Sergeant Rickson (the very same man who had walked me over to Bravo Company on Thanksgiving night) was owed entirely to a sarcasm I was too often unwilling to harness.

"Welcome to the squad." Dussard spoke while exhaling in what could've been mistaken for exasperation. It was not. The man exhales in that manner every fifth or sixth breath. This was not indicative of any respiratory disorder; Dussard was a steel-lunged soldier with a gift for endurance running. I could best him by thirty to forty seconds on the APFT two-miler, but found myself fighting to keep up with Mr. Day-Lewis on our seven-mile trots through D.C.

"Thank you, Sergeant," I replied, still basking in relief for the Bravo Company assignment.

"What did the platoon sergeant say to you?" Dussard asked, as though looking for guidance himself. It was a rather odd tone, as I think about it some sixteen years later.

"Sergeant Wilde said we'll be moving soon. Also, something about ROP and EIB."

"Yeah. The move." Dussard was *actually* exasperated at this point.

"When is that happening, Sergeant?"

"Next couple of weeks or so. It'll probably continue past Christmas. Most of us will be on leave for the second half of December. Do you have any leave saved?"

"Yes, Sergeant, but I've just spent twenty days at home. I'd prefer to accumulate a bit of leave and take a longer stretch this summer."

"That's good. You may as well get yourself into the Old Guard mindset. Summer will be here soon enough."

"Roger, Sergeant."

"Let's get you assigned to a team. There's a lot going on, and we could use extra hands."

After this entirely relaxed and informative meeting, I was re-introduced to Sergeant Rickson, who would be my team leader for two months' time.

Building 402 was inadequate for the tri-purpose of housing on-post soldiers, providing off-post soldiers with locker areas, and functioning as an administration center for officers and senior non-commissioned officers. It was ideal for the first of these, as every room in the building was designed for two beds and a few pieces of basic furniture. Offices and off-post locker areas were nothing more than re-purposed bedrooms.

Such was the case for the Second Squad off-post locker area, wherein a number of those guys who lived in the D.C.-Metropolitan Area civilian housing kept their dress blues and other equipment/uniforms. This tended to be where team and squad leaders spent their downtime, as offices were limited to platoon sergeants, the first sergeant, and the officers.

Entering the locker area rendered me a bit tense. If hazing or verbal abuse of any sort was going to be directed my way, it would be in such an environment. Platoon sergeants and squad leaders are largely too restricted by the bureaucratic hamstringing of rank and responsibility to openly visit disparaging language upon their soldiers, however tempted they must be on occasion. Buck sergeants, "sham shield" E-4s, and senior privates—those guys were far less concerned with decorum and maintaining professional appearances, at least when left to their own devices.

Here, in the locker area, they were left to their own devices. And, in the locker area, stood Second Platoon's freshest meat.

"What's up, man?" asked a slightly older (23?) E-4.

"I'm looking for Sergeant Rickson. I've been assigned to his team."

"Next room over. Second Platoon has three of these off-post areas."

"Thank you, Spe—"

"It's Hoffman."

"Thank you, Specialist Hoff—"

"Just Hoffman. Don't worry about the rank."

Hoffman will feature rather regularly throughout the pages to come. As mentor, friend, leader, and as a colleague. But in that moment, having pointed me in the right direction, he went back to polishing his uniform brass. I observed that intricate process for another second or so and left.

Entering the next room over, I recognized Rickson immediately. Though much of that Thanksgiving evening amounted to a blur (the late hour, the darkness, the uncertainty), Rickson had spent a good deal of time issuing me linens, filing preliminary paperwork, and showing me to the room I had shared with Roum. At the time, I had no reason to expect that the man would be responsible for me in any direct leadership capacity.

After all, "next 5 to alpha" had been clearly scrawled on the Staff Duty office's white board.

It was, in fact, next two to Bravo. In my case, from Bravo to Second Platoon, from Second Platoon to Second Squad, and from Second Squad to Rickson's fire-team.

"What's going on, man?" Rickson was sitting comfortably in one of the room's two chairs. He had a tobacco dip lodged in one corner of his mouth; nearby sat a two-liter spitting bottle.

"Hello, Sergeant."

"You ready to get started?"

"Roger, Sergeant."

The two weeks that followed were at no point dull. Within a day of being assigned to Second Platoon, I was sent to the firing range. Dussard had decided I would make a fine SAW gunner, meaning the soldier assigned to carry an M249 Squad Automatic Weapon. Though I had qualified with the weapon system during AIT, re-qualification was mandatory once I was officially assigned to wield it as part of a fire-team.

The range was enjoyable and a welcome reminder that I was, indeed, an infantryman. I was very much at home on the firing line. Nothing about the SAW's functionality had perished from memory, nor had my marksmanship diminished in any significant way.

Bravo Company soldiers reveling in the joys of maintaining their marksmanship at a French Foreign Legion firing range (3d U.S. Infantry Regiment, "The Old Guard").

Returning that evening, I ate alone in the DFAC and, after calling home from a payphone, returned to the room I continued to share with Roum. He had played basketball with some of his fellow Third Platoon soldiers and seemed content with how things were shaping up.

The following days were entirely labor-oriented and allowed me to better acquaint myself with Second Platoon. In Second Squad, there was SSG Dussard and Specialist Hoffman, fine soldiers and good men each; there was SGT Rickson with whom I was fated to clash; First Squad was led by SSG Rivera, a fit, disciplined, and serious NCO I would come to know and respect greatly; SPC Codd, the platoon's strongest runner and a brilliant soldier whose example I labored to equal; SPC Brady, a powerfully built and well-read former carpenter with whom I'd develop a close friendship; PFC Travis Smith, a talented and skilled soldier; there was SPC Bob Williams, a college-educated man who had joined up in his early twenties; SPC Bill Palmer, another college-educated "Degree-Four" with a rapier wit; and there was Sergeant Christopher Bradley, a man who would ultimately demand that I demand from myself nothing short of greatness.

I did not meet these soldiers in any such concentrated capacity. The introductions were spread out over the course of a week or so, during which time we did, indeed, move the contents of condemned Building 402 to the sparkling new Building 248.

Moving sucks. I would rather have been doing anything else. The CS (*o-chlorobenzylidene malononitrile*) gas chamber? Sure, bring that on. Two hours of flutter kicks? Count me in. Another twelve-mile road march with six miles of road-guard duty? Uh … maybe not. A diagnostic APFT? Well, that was already in the cards.

"Mongilutz!" Specialist Nelson called out my name during close-of-business formation on a cold December evening.

"Yes, Specialist?"

"You got a APFT tomorrow morning. It's gonna be at McNair. Trans will be leaving from Echo Company at 0600hrs. Roger?"

"Roger, Specialist."

I was curious to see what sort of score I was capable of achieving coming off of a few days of moving heavy furniture. Sit-ups and crunches had been a part of my daily routine since that close-call at 2/58.

As Bravo readied itself for another day of conveying furniture to another building, I walked alone towards Echo Company. Boarding the large van, I sat in silence with five or six soldiers who, for varying reasons, found themselves joining Alpha Company for a morning APFT.

While exiting the Iwo Jima gate, it occurred to me. *Guess I'll be seeing Fort McNair, after all.*

This was my first APFT in seven weeks. My push-up and running strength were more than equal to the task, and I acquitted myself rather nicely on the sit-ups. The score was around 285/300. I had scored higher during AIT … and would score *much* higher in years to come. At that time, I was happy to have done well on short notice.

Back on Myer, I hauled lockers over to 248. Things continued thusly for the next week. We moved, we claimed rooms, we went to the DFAC, we moved a bit more, and then the holidays were upon us. The vast majority of Bravo Company soldiers would sign-out on leave somewhere around the nineteenth or twentieth. A small number stuck around.

This reminds me of something the United States Army does very well—taking care of its lower-enlisted soldiers, an often-vulnerable bunch.

Our platoon leader, Lieutenant Gary Stucker, made certain to ask each man in the platoon about their Christmas plans. Most were heading home, a few of the married guys were spending the day with their immediate families. I was doing neither, nor was Brady. We were both invited, along with one other soldier, to Gary's home for Christmas dinner.

The three of us made the drive together and reached Gary's beautiful home around mid-afternoon. We enjoyed a good meal, played a game of

Trivial Pursuit, and departed well after nightfall. I called home upon reaching the barracks (the new building) and read throughout the evening. The days that followed were an extended version of the Thanksgiving weekend which followed my arrival the previous month.

I acquainted myself with the Fort Myer gym and visited Washington, D.C., once or twice. I read and called home. I spent time with Mann and Roum, though we were increasingly invested in our new platoons. I was now rooming with a fellow Second Platoon soldier, Matt Diller, and would see less and less of the Warlords in the months ahead.

When Bravo Company began to reassemble after the New Year, things picked up a bit. The Presidential election had been decided, George W. Bush was President-elect, and the Regiment was focused on the impending Inauguration ... and nothing else.

None of the new guys had gone through ROP, the Regimental Orientation Program. This meant our role in the Inaugural Parade would be less than prestigious. Most of Bravo Company would be marching; a few of us would dot Pennsylvania Avenue in the manner of living, breathing mannequins.

In calendar year 2001, the twentieth of January fell on a Saturday. For

A scene from the 2017 Presidential Inauguration. Old Guard soldiers reliably shine when displaying their marching prowess for the onlookers, for the President, for the country (U.S. Army Photos, by Staff Sgt. Kelvin Ringold/Sgt. George Huley/Pvt. Gabriel Silva).

those of us in The Old Guard, it was a very, *very* early morning. Regardless of one's role in the day's ceremony, first call came at 0300hrs. The marchers boarded one set of buses, the rest of us another. And the day was long.

I saw neither Roum nor Mann that day. Instead, I shared a bus seat with a new First Platoon soldier by the name of Daniel "Jake" VanMeter. In conversation, we learned that our basic training experiences had overlapped almost week-for-week, with my having reported to 30th AG earlier.

What ensued for myself and VanMeter was a day of cabin fever symptoms played out on the bus which we occupied for hours on end prior to filing off one by one to perform our statue-like duties on Pennsylvania Avenue. Despite the invisibility, which characterizes cordon duty of that sort, I did internally acknowledge the significance of the ceremony which the 3rd U.S. INF was playing a big part in realizing.

The Regiment acquitted itself marvelously that day. Watching from the sidelines, I counted Old Guard platoons as they marched by one after the other. I was acquainted with enough Bravo Company souls to recognize most of its members as they marched past. Charlie and Delta were interchangeable. And anyway, the day belonged to Echo Company, officially the Presidential Escort Platoon. These guys are typically in the 6'3"- 6'6" range and march with something bordering on superhuman precision. They represented the Regiment brilliantly.

President George W. Bush was sworn in as the forty-third President at 12:01 postmeridian on 20 January 2001 with over a quarter-million people in attendance to witness the Inauguration. For Mr. Bush, it was likely a relief, given the legal battle which had preceded. For the Regiment, it was a relief for an entirely different reason—we were bloody exhausted.

VanMeter and I had fully succumbed to cabin fever. We found everything hilarious and kept one another awake via easily induced laughter throughout the afternoon bus ride back to Myer. When we returned to the barracks, I realized that the marchers had arrived ahead of us. Entering the room I shared with Diller, I was surprised (and a bit amused) to see about seven Second Platoon soldiers lying motionless on the floor. They were essentially comatose, as I would be momentarily. What struck me was the temperature—it was hot, a sharp contrast from the icily frigid temperatures we cordon soldiers had endured for hours in stillness while observing the Inaugural procession.

None of this was sufficiently interesting to keep me from collapsing on the inviting bed I had abandoned in a weary state twelve hours earlier. It didn't occur to me in the moment before a deep slumber welcomed me into its seductive embrace, but I had just taken part in my first Old Guard ceremony...

VII

Regimental Orientation
and the Expert
Infantry Brigade

Nothing in the way of a *literally* lost weapon would plague this period of my TOG experience. But something along those lines did befall me a couple of months after the Inauguration.

With the Inauguration as prologue, R.O.P was now the foremost priority for all of us who, under normal circumstances, would have undergone that training within days of reporting to the Regiment.

R.O.P., or the Regimental Orientation Program, is three weeks in duration and amounts to a very effective conditioning process. At its core, R.O.P is a marching, standing manual, and uniform maintenance program, with ample composure training tossed in for good measure.

The Old Guard is essentially a stage production. Appearance counts for everything. Height, physical fitness, uniform care, synchronization of movement—these are the ingredients of a mission-capable Old Guard platoon. Even if height is often negotiable (here's looking at you, Third Platoon), the other elements are not. You must be in good shape. Your uniform must be flawless. And your movements must be sharp, crisp, consistent, and, when called for, synchronized with those of your platoon mates, period.

R.O.P. instructors, of which there are usually three to four summoned from throughout the Regiment at any given moment, do very good work in producing competent marchers capable of maintaining their dress blues to a high standard. Physical training is also central to the unit's mission, and there's plenty of running, push-ups, flutter kicks, and pull-ups to go around during R.O.P. Though, in truth, Second Platoon's brand of PT was indeed far more worthy of my physiological investment. Much of it would provide the framework for the PT I would conduct when permitted to train independently.

Diller was my R.O.P. sponsor, which is to say that he ensured I departed from Bravo Company each morning with a well-pressed uniform and all of my necessary materials. Sponsors do not accompany the sponsored to R.O.P., but they do right by the uninitiated in readying them for those days of intensive scrutiny.

* * *

One aspect of Old Guard service deserving of its own book is that of uniform preparation and maintenance. It is simply central to one's duty in so prestigious and visible a ceremonial unit. And though thousands of words could be employed in illustrating the tediousness inherent in readying one's dress blues for the unit's sacred work, I will keep this overview brief.

There is the blues blouse, the single most labor-intensive piece of apparel one is issued. It is a woolen coat of a deep-blue color that falls comfortably below one's waistline. Though the overcoat (also woolen and deep-blue) and raincoat (sort of a purplish blue) are larger garments, neither is worn with medals, badges.

And that makes all the difference.

If ever you have seen a soldier in formal attire whose chest is bedazzled with various ribbons and colorful accoutrements, you have an idea as to what is required to be worn upon a blues blouse. Anything ever awarded to a given soldier is due its sliver of real estate upon that coat. For an Old Guard professional, there are also a few standard items.

1. The blue cord, which denotes one as an infantryman. This fourragère (a cord artfully braided) is worn on the right shoulder.
2. The buff strap, which represents the Regimental colors of black and, yes, buff. This thin strap (which is worn on the left shoulder) is actually *two* straps of leather, the slight buff interwoven with the larger black. An attractive uniform component, in truth.
3. The distinctive unit insignia, which is worn on both epaulettes as well as on the blouse's right side.
4. The brass crossed rifles. Worn on the lapel, this emblem denotes service in an infantry unit. Keeping any such brass piece polished and properly aligned is the source of many a headache for young TOG soldiers.

Now, before this explanation ventures too far into esoteric detail, allow me to arrest its momentum here, as there is the matter of uniform pressing to cover.

Uniforms. Require. Steam. Pressing.

And a good deal of it.

When first issued, the blouse and overcoat are rather ... poofy. They are

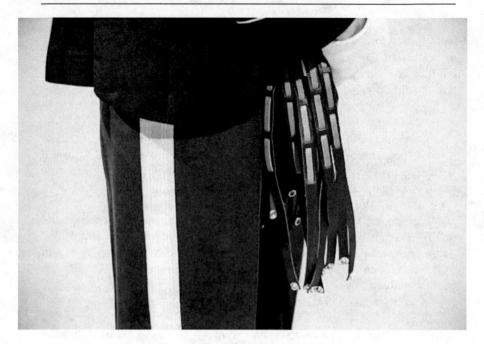

Bundle of "Buff Straps" soon to be awarded.

simply too thick and unbecoming to allow for their being seen by civilian eyes. Correcting this requires a time-intensive process of long-term steam-pressing, a bit of light burning (hairspray, lighter, skill, luck) and a bit more steaming. To properly ready a blouse and overcoat for ceremonial wear is necessarily a three-hour process, if not far longer. Each company barracks is equipped with at least two expensive (thousands of dollars) steam presses. These are effectively in a state of constant use; holidays and deployments notwithstanding.

From that point on, subsequent steaming and proper storage will continually shape and form the apparel into something almost (*almost*) comfortable and progressively more appealing to the eye.

By comparison, the placement of those aforementioned standard items, along with any other badges and medals, takes only a little while. With a skilled mentor guiding one's hand, this bit should run perhaps forty-five minutes to an hour. Although, there is the matter of preparing a so-called "rack."

The "rack" (which should not be mistaken for the blessed bosom of a well-endowed woman) is one's array of gleaming medals. Proper creation of a good rack requires the use of a well-traced and precisely cut tin frame upon which stretches of ribbon are delicately but firmly emplaced and fixed via hot glue. From there, a thin hook contraption is suspended to allow for the dangling of the medal itself. Based on the size and scope of a given rack, this process can persist for hours on end … as I would myself learn when preparing a series of racks for a Command Sergeant Major and for his successor.

So, there it is. Steam, fire, and patience are the ingredients one must possess in varying quantities when transforming a poofy blues blouse into the lean, flat, crisp, measured garment it is fated to become. Time, glue, tin, and a sharp blade will suffice for the creation a rack.

I should also note that once a blues blouse has reached the apex of its career, a mere forty minutes of maintenance each week will typically suffice where keeping it in good fighting shape is concerned. Turds will get by with about half that time, sterling soldiers insist on doubling it, and the Tomb Sentinels (who truly do set the standard) invest far more of themselves in the process.

* * *

"All right, buddy, just don't move around too much. Your uniform looks good." Diller had inspected my Class B attire with a trained eye and found it acceptable.

"Thanks, Diller. Anything else I should know?"

"Yeah, don't smart-off too much. It's not Benning, but the R.O.P. guys can make your life hard."

By this point, my reputation for sarcasm was well established within the platoon, and within the company. Unless I heeded Diller's sound advice, it would be established across the Regiment.

"Tracking," I glumly replied.

"You'll be all right," Diller said with a wry smile. He hoped I'd ignore his advice, and return with stories of being smoked while in dress uniform.

But I took R.O.P. seriously. More so than I had Airborne School. I wanted very much to be a useful Bravo Company soldier, both tactically and ceremonially. I shut my mouth (uncharacteristically), heeded the advice of my sponsor, listened to the instructors, and readied myself to join Battlehard (Bravo's moniker) as a qualified marcher, ready to learn the arts of casket-bearing and ceremonial flag-folding. Those skills were taught in-house, just as firing party soldiers learned their craft at the squad level.

VanMeter and I were attending the same R.O.P. class, which was welcome news to my ears. We had cultivated a friendship predicated upon fatigue-induced laughter. The furthering of that friendship was a foregone conclusion, given the nature of what it was we had ahead of us.

"All right, guys—fall in." One of the R.O.P. instructors spoke to our group in a disarmingly mild tone.

We came to attention and awaited the follow-up order.

"All right, at ease."

There it was.

We stood at ease and listened to the man's clearly spoken words. He told us what to expect for the day, for the week, for the program. When he had finished speaking, there was no question as to how our time under his guidance would be spent. It all unfolded as follows:

There were daily uniform inspections. These were tense, as the instructors were looking for "gigs," uniform errors which resulted in either (a) a quick correction, or (b) a round of ridicule followed by a correction.

There was ample marching. We practiced the precision steps and the right shoulder to left shoulder rifle transitions in the Echo Company quad. After an hour or so of perfecting the process in a confined space, we took our show to the road. By which I mean, we marched around the entirety of Fort Myer. Though not at all large in relation to Fort Hood, Myer covers more than enough ground to make for long stretches of uninterrupted marching practice. I distinctly recall a Week Two afternoon when our group marched after lunch chow (around 1300hrs) until just prior to being released (around 1600hrs).

Even those of us fated to carry caskets or perform twenty-one gun salutes were expected (*required*) to be proficient marchers. And the general discipline instilled during those long hours spent taking one precision step after another overlapped considerably with the baseline composure necessary to perform all ceremonial missions in support of the Regiment's unique charter.

So, we marched for miles on end.

To this day, I often hear that mine is a distinctive gait, that my posture is notably erect, that my movements are unusually precise. You can take the soldier out of The Old Guard...

There was standing manual, or the prescribed manner by which one is to ceremonially manipulate one's weapon, fix bayonets, perform "eyes right" head movements, and so on. This comprised perhaps fifteen-percent of our R.O.P. training.

And there was standing.

Standing perfectly still for very long periods of time.

The training is necessary. I knew why at the time; I would come to know even more so that August.

This portion of the training, which accounted for perhaps twenty percent of our time, was also rife with humor. None that we trainees were permitted to enjoy as it unfolded, but plenty about which we could laugh in years to come. The suppressed laughs resulted from our instructors' incessant efforts to have their trainees break composure. Methods varied from one instructor to the next, but they tended towards the inventive.

These efforts reached an apex during the final "Test Out," an hour-long stretch of time of standing positions in complete stillness. A single parting of ways with one's composure would result in immediate failure and a recycling through the program.

R.O.P. was hardly Infantry School, but none had any interest in spending more time in its ranks than was absolutely necessary.

Not that the instructors cared a smidgeon for any such disinclination. They worked hard to undermine our composure in hopes of breaking at least one among us. Mind you, this didn't extend to acts of violence or outright sabotage; they merely agitated, each to varying degrees.

Surprisingly, what came nearest to breaking me of my stillness was an irritation measure upon a soldier standing a few feet to my fore and right. The R.O.P. NCOIC, a particularly cunning staff sergeant, had taken to pacing in and around those three ranks of his pupils who stood like statues. Eyeballing each of us in turn, the coy SSG would thrust his face directly into that of a hapless soldier, in hopes of yielding a flinching response. He had in hand a thin metal ruler that measured precisely six inches in length. These are emblematic of the Regiment and, upon being revealed, denote its soldiers immediately. They are suitable for the work of placing various uniform accoutrements (medals, ribbons, insignias) in their correct places. They are also neat in their appearance. Surgeons have their scalpels, ceremonial soldiers their rulers.

In this SSG's devilish fingers, the ruler was a lethal weapon.

When the close-range facial thrust failed to break its target, the SSG would scan the face, neck, and ears of said target in search of adequately dense peach fuzz. This he would then lightly caress with the small ruler's ultra-thin edge … while emulating the sound of a buzzing mosquito. "*Bzzz.*"

That last was very nearly more than I could bear. I was largely unfazed and preferred that tactic to some of the others being employed by instructors and NCOIC alike. However, when observing the measure in action, I very nearly succumbed to a fit of laughter. The SSG was *so intensely focused* on the work of targeting a single piece of fuzz, and with every assault came a hilariously rendered "*Bzzz.*"

However, the looming threat of repeated R.O.P. training was enough to subdue my otherwise insistent impulse. I distracted myself from the SSG's cruel project for the remaining ten minutes or so by training my eyes on a patch of blank wall measuring two inches squared. When we were placed at ease, I breathed a sigh of relief and afforded myself the luxury of a smile; not the violent laughter which would have overtaken me had I responded to the peach fuzz assault in real time, but the sacrifice was perfectly acceptable.

And then it was over.

I recall Spencer telling us what to expect of R.O.P. This he had shared with me, Roum, and Mann at some point after we completed the Bayonet. At the time, is had seemed daunting. This may have been attributable to Spencer's spoken word delivery.

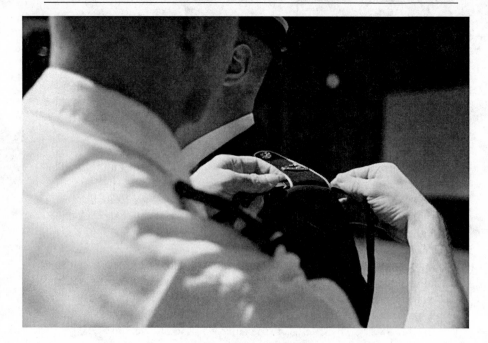

Buff Strap being awarded.

In reality, R.O.P. was perfunctory in nature. There had been a few moments of stressful uniform inspection, the marching days were wearying, and that final test nearly got the better of me, though not for reasons of physical/mental prowess. That "*Bzzz*" had been the very essence of funny.

Returning to Bravo Company with VanMeter that afternoon, we learned that most of the soldiers had been released for the weekend. There were the standard two men (one sergeant, one lower-enlisted) on the CQ desk and a couple men performing extra duty for punitive reasons. Otherwise, it was an empty barracks.

The friendship had taken firm root during R.O.P., as VanMeter and I came to recognize in the other a kindred spirit. Our common ground stemmed from a shared commitment to achieving a high level of tactical/ physical competency. Coming off three straight weeks of training, VanMeter and I found ourselves missing the feel of rucksack straps digging into our respective shoulders. We craved the climbing of a rope, the burning lungs brought on by long-distance running, and the general sensation of training-induced pain.

That Saturday, our first following graduation from R.O.P., we packed our rucksacks with forty-fifty pounds of gear and headed out for a six-mile march through Arlington, nearby Georgetown, and Fort Myer itself.

It felt damn good, marching about the area with weight upon our backs. We had known nothing but ceremony for the better part of a month. Rucking under such circumstances was not unlike saying hello to an old friend. We cherished the familiar burden, commented on the salt accumulating on one another's cheeks, and reveled in the sense of improving our combat viability. In The Old Guard, prior to the terrorist attacks on September 11th, 2001, we felt it necessary to keep ourselves braced for the hardship of warfare. Our drill sergeants had instilled a lasting sense of purpose in that regard.

To some degree that purpose is with me still.

Though VanMeter and I would continue this extracurricular training regimen for another few weeks, we eventually fell in closely with our respective platoons. I had seen less of Roum and Mann, and would interact with VanMeter very little throughout the coming spring and summer. He belonged to First Platoon, the marchers, while there were caskets whose physical burdens needed muscular bearing—which is how I'd spend much of February and a week or so of March.

It was during that time that two of my more enduring friendships would be forged, but I had no way of knowing as they were taking shape. Instead, I focused upon the work of becoming a good casket bearer.

In many respects, my formal casket training with Second Squad, Second Platoon was more intensive than what I had experienced in R.O.P. There was no uniform inspection of which to speak, as we practiced both flag folding and casket carries in either PTs or BDUs. So, in that regard, the casket training was preferable to R.O.P. But what was absent in the way of uniform inspection, the platoon's senior members made up for with impossible levels of repetition.

We folded flags...

...again...

...and again...

...and when we had folded the flag for the hundredth time...

...we folded it another hundred still.

The art was so thoroughly ingrained in me that I often dreamt of its individual steps.

We practiced casket carries. This generally meant weighing down our platoon's empty coffin with several 45 pound plates and moving about the company quad while maintaining composure and synchronized steps. In truth, synchronicity of stepping was often compromised within Arlington National Cemetery, as uneven terrain and the like tend to disrupt that aspect of even the best casket team's excellent precision.

After around six days of intensive practice, I was deemed ready for a "live-fire" within those "gardens of stone" (as Nicholas Proffitt termed them) adjacent to Myer.

I entered with Second Squad and, as part of a six-man casket team, did lay to rest a deceased veteran. For the other five members of that team, this was business as usual. I believe the team consisted of five ANC veterans and me, the "cherry" of the group. That meant that even the most junior among them would have performed dozens of ceremonial funerals prior to my joining them in the art.

I was not nervous.

I was, on that grey morning, solemn in my bearing and demeanor. I aimed to perform this duty with utter gravity, particularly given that it was my first. I had correctly deduced from the start that, eventually—no, inevitably—these would become all too routine.

In this moment, for this funeral, at this point in my fledgling Old Guard career, I'd treat the mission as though it were a matter of life and death … rather than strictly a matter of death.

All went well. The six of us stood motionless on the cemetery's winding road. The hearse arrived. We came to life. We marched forward, turned sharply to the left, approached the hearse, and stopped. The "drag" man (insert cross-dressing joke HERE) broke ranks to pull or *drag* the casket from the vehicle. As it was extracted, each of us assumed its weight within our white-gloved hands, until the casket rested wholly within the cradle of our collective strength.

In practiced fashion, we ferried the casket, which between vessel and occupant weighed between four hundred and five hundred pounds, to the mockup situated directly over the grave which provided our deceased passenger with his final resting place.

Once firmly atop the mockup, we turned inward, knelt slightly, secured the draping American flag by its edges and corner, stood slowly, and, on command, took a very small step back. This allowed for our taut holding of the flag, a position we would maintain throughout the chaplain's speaking of those holy words which meant very much to the gathered friends and family, but which we effectively drowned out for professional purposes. Becoming overly engrossed in verbally articulated sentiment might compromise one's composure, or, at very least, his ceremonial timing.

With the chaplain's speaking concluded, we reanimated, and the flag-folding was underway. The process is as mechanical as it is fluid. First, the flag is narrowed lengthwise in half, then in half once more. From there, the Stars and Stripes are ceremonially folded together one triangle at a time. Once there, the senior casket team member, the fold man, tucks the remaining material, or tail, into the now tri-cornered flag. The finished product is sent to the "present" man, who both (1) presents the flag to the team's NCOIC, and (2) salutes that same man before falling back into place.

During this process, the firing party, with whom we casket bearers share a bus ride into the cemetery, perform their twenty-one gun salute.

The tri-cornered flag now firmly in the family's possession, the casket team turns, makes a right or left face (based upon which side of the mockup one stands upon) and marches off into the distance. These ceremonies are of enormous and memorable significance to those bidding farewells to their loved ones. We labored to keep ourselves cognizant of that truth.

As my casket-bearing/flag-folding qualification was completed only weeks prior to the Regiment's annual EIB training and testing period, I performed perhaps as few as ten such ceremonies before finding myself swept up in a struggle largely of my own manufacture. Again, Regimental records might tell a different story in terms of precise count, but it wasn't a great many funerals before I was off to A.P. Hill for an extended stay.

* * *

The Expert Infantryman Badge was established in November of 1943 and is limited to those Army soldiers who belong to either the "11 Series" of Military Occupational Specialties (the Infantry) or to the "18 Series" (the Special Forces). Earning the badge amounts to an enormous rite of passage; the tasks required are numerous, complex, conducted beneath the architecture of actively cultivated stress, and often come down to mere luck.

EIB was upon us a bit too soon after R.O.P. for my liking. I was developing proficiency as a casket bearer and had hoped for a few weeks of ANC duty during which to perfect that craft. And besides, EIB is the very sort of training process for which my young mind was terribly ill-suited. Less so nowadays, perhaps, but I often managed in my youth to compound otherwise manageable stress quotients into something wholly unmanageable.

There was an element of self-consciousness that so often accompanied my emergence from the books which had, throughout childhood, been to me such close and indispensable companions. When entering the present moment, and interacting with fellow humans, I was invariably aware of myself being seen. The phenomenon tended to place my mind at a disadvantage in making sense of new concepts, as though in seeing myself being seen, I delayed the intake of practical knowledge.

Though I had managed to synchronize these two selves during adolescence, their autonomy often became apparent when the practical aspects of training were married to the superfluous aspects of stress. And EIB was nothing if not a sublime union of training and stress.

I was an infantryman and was expected to earn my Expert Infantryman Badge. More importantly, SSG Dussard, my squad leader and a good man, believed me capable of doing it my first time 'round. Would that I had proved equal to the task of affirming Dussard's misplaced faith.

EIB took me to Fort A.P. Hill, VA for the second time since my having reported to the 3rd U.S. INF three months earlier. As Fort Myer is rather small, and as the surrounding area is densely populated, much of the unit's tactical and firearms training takes place some seventy miles south, in the very remote Fort A.P. Hill.

Though we didn't always allow ourselves to register as much, the land is somewhat beautiful; in the absence of ballistic weapons fire, it might be thought of as serene.

The Old Guard was not visiting A.P. Hill, Virginia for purposes of enjoying its natural beauty. We were there to train in the myriad tasks whose flawless completion was requisite for the earning of one's EIB. Many of these tasks were familiar to me, as they were covered to varying degrees during basic training. Others were alien. Before we got to any of that, there were tents to be setup and fixtures to be emplaced. There were also supplies to be loaded or unloaded, ammunition crates to be transported to the firing ranges, and barracks to be readied for the arrival of what must have been more than half of the regiment. There was a lot of work to be done, and both tester and soon-to-be-tested were seeing to its being carried out.

I rather appreciated this aspect of EIB. I was coming to know fellow lower-enlisted soldiers and a select few NCOs from Battlehard. I was slowly blurring the lines of rank with a few of the latter, a process I would inadvertently replicate throughout my time in the Army. Which is to say, the bonds of friendship were often sufficient to render rank a secondary factor in my interactions. If the blurring had begun during my casket training, it had rendered itself fully in effect during EIB setup.

The Regiment had, within the space of a few days' time, setup over thirty testing stations across three lanes. Within two or three days, we EIB hopefuls would be, to quote SPC Dennis Brady, "…eating, breathing, and shitting those damn lanes." Brady said it as well and as truthfully as it could have been said. We would spend hours upon hours visiting those various stations.

There were preliminary tasks to be completed. Candidates must first overcome a handful of hurdles before advancing. These include: (1) Day/Night Land Navigation, (2) M16 Expert Qualification, and (3) earning an APFT score of eighty-percent or higher.

At Fort A.P. Hill in the spring of 2001, the Land Navigation Phase, M16 Qualification, and APFT were conducted immediately prior to the Lane Testing Phase, while the Twelve-Mile Forced March was scheduled at the end.

We visited the firing range as a platoon. An expert score requires thirty-six of forty targets knocked down at distances of fifty to three-hundred yards using only iron sights, or the fixed aperture/sliver of steel whose visual alignment allows for accurate targeting. I fired thirty-eight out of forty (missed one three-hundred and one two-fifty) and took one step closer to the earning of my EIB.

Land Navigation would follow.

Map reading and a bit of compass work had been covered during AIT, but the Warlords had not engaged in any intensive land navigation training. I suppose those infinite flutter kicks needed doing and were, in effect, the priority. Fortunately, The Old Guard erred on the side of caution and tasked a Ranger Battalion veteran with educating the EIB hopefuls in the art of navigating long stretches of woodland via map, compass, and terrain association. Within a couple of hours' time, most of us were largely competent in the plotting of our respective points.

Even still, I forgot to adjust my azimuth to account for Fort A.P. Hill's true north deviation. This meant that when negotiating the daytime land navigation course for what was, mercifully, a mere practice run, I missed my first point by a hundred yards or so. The cruel reality of land navigation is that failing to reach one's first point will almost certainly undermine the second.

It was 1SG Triton, with his expert fieldcraft, who drilled the correction into my stubborn cranium. Because of the man's excellent instruction, I made short work of the Day Land Navigation Phase when the time came...

...with one exception.

Since reporting to Fort Myer a few months prior to EIB, I had been improving as a runner with every passing day. PT was typically conducted at the squad level, and our squad leader SSG Dussard was as committed to running as a way of life as was any soldier. We ran early, often, far, and fast. And if that wasn't enough (hint: it wasn't), I had taken to running through Georgetown on the weekends. Coupled with the road marching regimen with which VanMeter and I had enthusiastically burdened ourselves, I was morphing into a human/gazelle hybrid.

A necessary transformation, as I had some excellent competition in Second Platoon. Dussard was, among us, arguably the strongest over extended distances, but Specialist Codd and PFC Travis Smith were demigods in the middle-range. Anything between three to seven miles, and those two were bipedal missiles. I reveled in the challenge of rendering myself their equal in that respect.

In that spirit, I had committed myself to a swift Day Land Navigation completion time. This sub-project of mine was coming together as planned, and I reached my final point well ahead of schedule. After marking my card with the necessary information, I raced to the finish point wherein my navigation card would be checked and an inventory of my assigned equipment would be taken.

The soldier who approached me at the finish point was, I believe, a

Charlie Company chap, and a nice enough professional. He was doing the job which was his charge when, after verifying the correctness of my navigation card, he looked quizzically upon my equipment and asked, "Where's your weapon?"

To my understanding, the fastest recorded human footspeed has been clocked at just under twenty-eight miles per hour, a speed achieved over a very short running distance. Even so, I would not be surprised in the least to learn that the footspeed I achieved when racing from the finish point to the land navigation point at which I *knew* I had stupidly left my assigned weapon was something north of thirty miles per hour ... through woodland terrain.

I was the human embodiment of panic, a state of being that manifested very palpably in my heart, lungs, feet, and eyes. I ran with animalistic fervor, and had taken with me neither map or compass. I needed neither. I was drawn to my abandoned weapon with a magnetic force born of a very legitimate fear—that of another soldier reaching it before I could.

It was worse than that. Just as the navigation checkpoint (and my lonely M16) came into clear view, so did an approaching figure.

Was it a fellow private who might keep mum on the matter? It was not.

An NCO who might fuck with me on the spot but ultimately squelch the matter immediately thereafter? No.

Was it a commissioned officer who would feel compelled to make known exactly what it was he had observed in the deep, dense woods of A.P. Hill? It was.

It was a young lieutenant, and he was shaking his helmeted head in a "Tut-Tut" sort of manner. I would've found it maddening in the extreme, had I not been seething with self-loathing.

"Hello, sir," I said through labored breathing. We both knew the score.

"Hello, Private." His eyes were as judgmental as ever a pair of eyes has been.

I sheepishly secured my weapon, saluted, and prepared for another swift run through the woods. Literally half-a-heartbeat before my first step struck the soil below, a taunting voice interrupted me.

"You do know I'm going to tell your platoon leader, right?"

My back was turned to the officer. I briefly suspended my departure, looked sharply over my shoulder through eyes which must have seemed either plaintive or resentful, and responded in the only sensible manner. "Fuck you, sir."

Okay, I didn't *actually* say that. I wanted nothing more than to say that.

"Yes, sir," I *actually* said.

And I was off. Knowing that my fate was sealed, I didn't move with quite as much swiftness as I had moments earlier. I ran, as I still hoped for a respectable completion time, but the fuel of legitimate panic was now absent in my stride.

Upon returning, the sympathetic Charlie Company soldier marked me complete, nodded politely, and suggested I board the truck which would return us to the barracks.

* * *

I went through EIB with Battlehard soldiers from throughout the company. Only PFC Smith (the excellent runner) joined me in representing Caskets within our Bravo cross-section of a group. We were led by a First Platoon buck sergeant who was an EIB candidate. He was a respected colors marcher and took seriously his task of seeing this hodgepodge bunch through the training.

Things had been going well, for the most part, though this NCO didn't respond well to my sense of humor. He also didn't respond well to learning that one of his temporary charges had been caught emptyhanded in the woods. Hands empty, that is, of his assigned weapon. Had I reported back to, say SSG Dussard, the repercussions might have been brutal, but they wouldn't have been tinged with the salt of mild disdain.

And so, this respected First Platoon buck sergeant smoked the shit out of me.

I had it coming.

I left my weapon at a goddamned land navigation checkpoint. That I could stand at all following that well-deserved smoke session is a testament only to the resilience of youth. Teenaged bodies are quick to recover from physical strain.

It is with some regret that I recall matters never being anything less than tense between myself and that First Platoon colors marcher. The remaining days of EIB amounted to a rather dispiriting affair. This might not have been the case had I been moving through the lanes with a strictly Second Platoon group. But platoon cohesion is untenable during EIB.

* * *

Night Land Navigation requires the same basic principles necessary for completion as its daylight counterpart, but the process is more linear. In the pitch-black woods on a cold moonless night, one determines the correct azimuth (true north adjustment included), after plotting points with flashlight in hand, walking in as straight a line as the terrain allows. With a bit of luck, a reliable pace-count, and strict attention to the compass, success is attainable. If the question crossed your mind, allow me to address it here and now: I clutched my M16 with sufficient strength to nearly compromise the weapon system's structural integrity.

I don't recall how the numbers looked by this point, but to my knowledge a good majority of candidates passed the Land Navigation Phase. Between that and the preceding M16 Qualification, I can't imagine more than ten soldiers across the Regiment were eliminated from EIB candidacy.

The attrition rate begins its most significant upward climb on Day Two of the Lane Phase. Plenty dropped on Day One, and a few terribly unfortunate souls fail on Day Three. But Day Two seems to detonate many EIB candidacies.

There are typically around ten-twelve stations per lane. This varies from unit to unit, and from year to year, but the total number of stations is around thirty-five. We come to know these well.

To SPC Brady's earlier mentioned point, candidates eat, breathe, and shit those stations. A full three days are set aside for the numerous groups to move through each of the lane's stations in their entirety. The stations, which are home to specific fieldcraft tasks, welcome each group into their tented woodland retreats for an hour, during which the tasks are demonstrated by EIB holders and then performed by the candidates themselves. By sundown, candidates have been inundated with copious quantities of information.

Following dinner chow, candidates are "encouraged" (read: required) to visit miniaturized versions of the stations as they exist within the barracks themselves. The badge-holders construct tiny clinics near their respective bedsides and "invite" EIB hopefuls to drop-in for continuations of the practice. This regimen continues well into evening hours until, it all comes to a short-lived halt as both tester and tested retire to their bunks.

These are long days, and demanding. For most, EIB training amounts to something of a strenuous experience. For some (perhaps ten-percent), the tasks come easily. For others (perhaps eighty-percent), their correct and timely completion requires very close attention. And for a final ten-percent, EIB is of little interest. I knew a fair number of infantrymen who had either not earned their EIBs on account of never having pursued the badge at all, or, having failed once or twice, simply decided to be done with it. Priorities—they do indeed differ greatly from man to man.

I observed something consistent about the ten-percent who moved easily through EIB. Those possessing a mind for the mechanical, those who had a mind for, say, engineering, those who had perhaps grown up working on vehicle engines, or those who had been woodworkers or builders of some sort—picked up the thirty-five tasks quite readily.

Opposite that way of thinking was the bookish sort, such as myself, who tended to complicate EIB tasks, at least enough of them to jeopardize the candidacies we struggled so hard to keep afloat. I belonged to neither ten-percent; not to those for whom EIB was a largely perfunctory process, not to those who could care less about the badge. I did very much care, but the process would not be perfunctory.

Tasks, I will note here, were wide-ranging. There were precision tasks such as range estimation, calling for indirect fire, and GPS usage. There was the proper applying of camouflage to one's face, the correct usage of field communication equipment, and the rapid donning of one's gas mask. There was the loading, unloading, and correct functions checking of numerous weapons systems. There was also the anti-tank mine and its effective emplacement. Among others, these comprise EIB's thirty-five testable tasks.

By the end of the third training day, I was optimistic. I knew from listening to countless anecdotes that certain luck-hinging stations had claimed the candidacies of very competent soldiers in years past. Chief among these was the grenade throw, a station for which considerable practice could improve one's odds, but which ultimately existed under the specter of chance to a far greater degree than did any other task.

Even correcting for such factors, my outlook was positive. Every soldier had been afforded ample training time and I had practiced each task no fewer than ten times when I fell into a light slumber of the third training day.

And then it was time.

First call was 0500hrs on Day One of the Lanes Testing Phase. Days Two and Three would start a bit later, for the simple reason that neither of those days would begin with an APFT.

We candidates knew full well that prior to testing on a single task, we would need to pass an APFT with a score of at least eighty-percent in each exercise.

Just prior to the test, the respected First Platoon marcher inquired of me, "Are you gonna pass this, Mongilutz?"

He was asking out of a sustained sense of anger regarding the lost weapon incident. If he had also hoped to piss me off, he had succeeded.

When the dust had settled and all candidates had completed the push-ups, sit-ups, and two-mile run, mine was among the higher scores of all tested. I had made certain to look that respected First Platoon Colors marcher dead in the eye upon crossing the finish line among the fastest runners.

We ate breakfast chow quickly and formed up en masse at a sort of staging point near the lanes' respective trailheads. Following some ostensibly motivational words from Regimental Command Sergeant Major Aubrey Butts, the formation broke up into thirds; about ten-twelve groups comprising each third.

Each would move through one lane that day, its surviving candidates would rotate to the second lane the following day, and those to have survived two days of testing would rotate to their final lane on the third day.

A "No Go" is to be avoided at all costs. Candidates must achieve a "Go" at *every* testing station. Period. If a soldier is so unfortunate as to fail a given task, a "No Go" is marked on their task checklist. That soldier may re-test once—and only once—as a second "No Go" on any one station results in the elimination of that poor soul's EIB candidacy. Likewise, a candidate may carry no more than two "No Go" marks upon their checklist, as a third results in the elimination of their EIB candidacy, regardless of the "No Go" marks having been received across three stations.

Soldiers moving through the lanes with two "No Go" marks on their checklist are said to be Blade Running. I always appreciated the term linguistically, if not for its rather stress-inducing implications. Myths abound on the topic of Blade Running candidates falling asleep on the evening of Day Two only to wake up with a head full of grey hair the following morning. Eliminations on Day Three of Lanes Phase? It is a cruel fate.

Those who earn their EIB without so much as a single "No Go" are described as "True Blue." There is not, to my understanding, a name for those who complete the Lanes having been hit with only one "No Go," but I can't say there should be. If you're going to claim that badge, either do so via close call or without so much as a single misstep.

My sense of self-assuredness held fast initially. I completed perhaps five to six stations without so much as a shred of uncertainty. But things took a downward turn quickly.

To my surprise, when outlining this work, I was forced to confront a void in my memory. The receiving of a "No Go" score is something which plagues the dreams of many soldiers. They remember the precise task as well as the circumstances of their failure. And while my recollection is not wholly incomplete on this topic, it is indeed partially so.

I do not recall which station I received my first "No Go" on that dreary March day in the woodlands of Fort A.P. Hill. If forced to wager it, I'd say it was either the gas mask station or the grenades. Whichever it was, I re-tested and attained a "Go" before advancing to the next station.

In any event, at some point, our entirely intact group made its way to the Anti-Tank Mine station. This was a task which many (myself included) found needlessly meticulous. Not in the activating of the mine, but in the absurdly precise concealment measures required. But this was the task and it was not my place to question, only to perform.

"You are a No Go, at this time."

"Sergeant?" I was distressed. I was now a Blade Runner. One more "No Go" at *any* station would doom me to a badge-less existence for at least a year's time.

"You failed to *blah-blah-blah-blah*."

I wasn't listening. I should have listened, but I didn't. I wanted to motherfucking re-test, and I wanted to motherfucking re-test immediately. I wasn't

going down to this anti-tank mine. Let a *tank* go down to an anti-tank mine—
I would do no such th—

"Did you fuck-up in there?"

The respected First Platoon Colors marcher made of me this inquiry
the *very moment* I exited the testing tent. He and the others were sitting in
the uncovered holding area, with only a grey sky and a well-worn concealment
net over their helmeted heads.

"Yes, Sergeant," I replied, struggling with a temper which yearned for a
target. The anti-tank mine would have been impervious to the impact of my
thrown punch. A human face, on the other hand…

"You wanna take a minute to get your shit together?"

This was unexpected. The respected First Platoon Colors marcher had
assumed an understanding, even *kind* tone. My anger abated, my anxiety did
not.

"No, Sergeant. I'd like to re-test right now." I was insanely foolish in my
teenage years. Just so very foolish.

"All right. Get it done, Private."

He didn't know it, or maybe he did, but the respected First Platoon Colors marcher had eased my tension with his change of tone, and considerably
so. Would that it had been enough to yield a favorable outcome.

"You are a No Go, at this time," the EIB grader spoke in a matter of fact
tone. It was not personal.

"Sergeant?"

"You failed to *blah-blah*…"

I was gone. I exited the tent in a fury, blew past my (former) group, and
continued towards the lane's primary trail.

"Mongilutz. Mongilutz. Private!"

The respected First Platoon Colors marcher bellowed out after me. And
because I apparently harbored a death wish, I completely ignored the non-
commissioned officer under whose charge I presently fell.

What was he going to say to me? What did it matter? I had rushed
through one of the lane's easier (if needlessly meticulous) tasks not once, but
twice, and had sunk my EIB candidacy. Nothing needed saying.

"*Private!*"

"No, let him go."

The voice was English-accented and belonged to SSG Yates. He was the
Anti-Tank Mine station's NCOIC, an Alpha Company Squad Leader. He sympathized with my plight, seemingly agreed with the pointlessness of anything
more being said on my failure, and outranked the respected First Platoon
Colors marcher by one pay-grade. Yates had overruled my group leader,
thereby allowing me to escape the patch of land on which I had, through
haste and pride, sabotaged my EIB candidacy.

The sentiment was buried deep beneath several layers of self-contempt and blinding anger, but I was profoundly grateful for Yate's siding with me. Me, the hotheaded private who, had I not reported on a holiday weekend, might very well have reported to Yate's company three months earlier.

I joined the scores of Old Guard soldiers who had also accumulated one "No Go" too many and awaited the conclusion of this demoralizing episode. What had been a largely successful transition into the Regiment's mission and way of life throughout the preceding winter was now diminished by a disappointment of which I would be routinely reminded for a year's time.

Those among us who earned their badges would wear them proudly. And while I often scraped together sufficient character to be happy for those men, I occasionally felt regret upon seeing that beautiful blue badge, long musket framed within, and yearned for the opportunity to do right by those who had invested in my success.

VIII

A Running Summer
and a Long Day
on Summerall

The return bus ride had been curiously cathartic. For the past few weeks, I had forgotten there was an external world. Expert Infantryman Badge training and testing had been all-consuming in its execution. While I had failed to return with the badge, I soon afforded myself the luxury of realizing that I could nevertheless be a good and worthy and useful Old Guard soldier.

I reflected closely on that. What would I do to make myself a good and worthy and useful Old Guard soldier? What would I do to ensure EIB was but a formality come next year? What would I do to ensure I earned (truly *earned*) the two-week block of leave I had scheduled for that coming June?

For one, I would continue my extracurricular running and road-marching regimen. No matter my having not earned the coveted EIB—and I did covet it—I would run myself into the ground, rise, and run more. I would perform nightly sit-ups, would conclude my every run with a few sets of dips, and would render myself equal to Battlehard's strongest PT performers.

I would conduct myself well ceremonially. This went without saying, of course, but on that long bus ride home, I chose to think it all the same. There are traditions unique to Old Guard service, just as there are with service in any military unit. Among those to which I hoped I would never fall victim was that of Summerall Field comedy.

There are aspects of just how it is the sausage of The Old Guard is made which you should find rather surprising. As stony and perfectly still as any Regimental marching platoon might seem to the untrained eye, there's a bit more movement and (mostly unspoken) communication underway than you might realize.

In at least one instance, I recall the singing of a semi-familiar song in response to an unsightly image. The song in question was Eric Carmen's "Hungry

Eyes," a popular single linked with the 1987 film, *Dirty Dancing* (which many critics have convincingly described as unwatchable).

Ceremonial blues pants have the potential to ride upwards, particularly in the case of bulkier soldiers (read: casket bearers). During a Summerall Field retirement ceremony, one such soldier found himself both (a) suffering from that very sort of upward ride, and (b) standing a rank or two ahead of two clever Bravo Company soldiers.

One of the two, an endlessly inventive creature, began to quietly sing a slightly modified version of "Hungry Eyes," with "Butt" cleverly substituted for "Eyes."

I was nowhere near when this scene played out, as I had fallen in with a separate marching element. Even so, I have it on credible authority that the non-singing party, an otherwise unflappable professional, very nearly gave in to a spell of debilitating laughter as his colleague carried forth with a *complete* rendering of that appropriately reimagined song.

> With this hungry butt
> One look at you and I can't disguise
> I've got hungry butt

And on it went, from first re-purposed verse to last, nearly claiming a soldier's composure in its unfolding.

Such coping measures are often employed in the spirit of seeing one another through difficult ceremonial circumstances. Not so much irreverent as necessary where enduring sustained engagement with a mentally taxing profession is concerned.

As for that return bus ride—

I would return to Myer with a sense of invigorating purpose. I would awake the following morning (a Saturday, if I recall) and run for miles. How far? Until my lungs gave out. What I had started in working to match Roum's basic training pace I would continue to match Dussard's. I would keep to myself for a time. I would eat chow alone. I would work to do right by my platoon. And I would read, of course.

To paraphrase Woody Allen, "If you want to make the gods laugh, make a plan."

Summerall Field, full parade (3d U.S. Infantry Regiment, "The Old Guard").

Much of the regimen I outlined for myself would take shape as I had envisioned it. I did run in my spare time. I interacted less and less with my platoon brothers on the weekends. And I read nightly.

But the Army often has plans for its soldiers. And by "often" I mean to say invariably.

Second Squad, I learned after returning from EIB, had been regarded as the "problem squad" by platoon leadership. Its leader, SSG Dussard, was a field guy through and through. He never invested much of himself in shaping the casket team into an elite ceremonial machine. He made us strong runners and taught us a good deal about proper fieldcraft, but our primary mission was one of laying to rest deceased soldiers in a highly formal and polished manner.

First Squad was the platoon's premier casket team. They were the eight-man team responsible for performing full honors funerals; high profile, manpower-intensive affairs complete with marchers, a caisson, and two additional casket bearers.

Third Squad was, like Second Squad, a six-man group. But they were good. Very good. Their squad leader, unlike Dussard, was closely engaged on the ceremonial front. He had something Dussard did not—a skilled team leader under his charge. That team leader's name was (is) Tim Pennartz. He

A full honors funeral presided over and led by the Regiment's command sergeant major (photograph by SSG Jedhel Somera).

was a buck sergeant who demanded nothing short of perfection from his casket team. With a squad leader who left him to his devices, Pennartz, a trained Tae Kwon Do practitioner, molded Third Squad into a highly skilled group of professional pallbearers. To his great credit, Bob Williams played an enormous part in that process and drilled his men day after day in order that they might achieve unequaled ceremonial excellence. He was successful by any measure.

Second Squad was perfectly competent and had not made any notable mistakes in the cemetery. But we were, at that time, the platoon's weak link. The measures taken by our platoon leadership in strengthening the chain would succeed in doing exactly that.

My individual experience with the Regiment, with Bravo Company, with Second Platoon, and with Second Squad would improve at this point. What I had taken upon myself—the process of self-improvement—was augmented once I found myself under the wing of skilled leadership at the team level.

Dussard was as remarkable a squad leader as could be hoped for, but it was team leader Sergeant Christopher Bradley, an esteemed casket-bearing/flag-folding master, who invested of himself in the elevating of Second Squad's ceremonial performance.

Though I could not have known as much at the time, Bradley was among the most influential forces in my young life. And, my god, how I did so often take for granted his excellent leadership. I didn't know enough to be ashamed at the time. I know enough to be ashamed now.

"Where you from?" Bradley's was a North Carolinian accent of the sort I had encountered frequently while at Fort Benning.

"From Washington, Sergeant." I didn't know what to expect of the burly NCO standing before me. It was clear he was taking my measure.

"What part?"

"About an hour north of Seattle."

"How long you been with the unit?"

"I arrived on Thanksgiving, Sergeant."

"That long ago? Why don't I know you?"

It was a good question, and I took my time in formulating a useful response.

"Unit was largely on leave in December, Inauguration followed. I was in R.O.P. for three weeks' time and then E.I.B."

Bradley seemed satisfied.

"What's your PT score?"

"I'm usually within a few points of 300. When I don't exceed it, that is."

"Good. Means we can focus on getting you better at caskets."

That was precisely why Bradley had been transferred from First Squad. He was a well-regarded casket veteran with a strong sense of mission. He knew how to instill and maintain discipline without compromising morale; a balance which eludes many NCOs.

To his credit, Dussard handed Bradley the reins almost entirely. Apart from PT, which Dussard led every morning, we belonged to Bradley. This was for the best. We trained on caskets as often as ever we had, but under skillful instruction our precision improved.

Within a month's time, we were no longer a source of concern among the platoon's leadership. Within two, we were equal to our fellow squads, though Third Squad would never acknowledge it. Under Bradley's patient guidance, we graduated to higher planes of ceremonial performance.

The spring months of April and May were an extended proving ground, a period when we perfected our craft and labored to do right by Sergeant Bradley. He was a fine sergeant who had left the prestige and prominence of First Squad to impart his knowledge (quite selflessly) upon a junior team which was not always worthy of his sacrifice.

It is said that teachers are like candles—they consume themselves to light the way for others. Bradley covered himself in glory by embodying the essence of those words. My thanks to him then, my thanks to him now, my thanks to him for the remainder of my days.

He also beat the shit out of me from time to time.

Well, that's putting it harshly. Bradley had a penchant for hand-to-hand combative training. Carrying over 200 pounds on his 6'2" frame, the man had accumulated terrific muscle strength over three years of physical conditioning by the time my 175 pounds came into grappling contact with him.

He never did me the disservice of easing up in terms of intensity.

I was outmatched in strength and experience, but I fought hard. Bradley took note and set a high bar for me to overcome. Had he done anything less, those countless hours of training would have been cheapened.

My high school confidence with which I had parted ways while at 30th AG began to resurface. If I could face Bradley in what we jokingly termed "The Octagon" (the off-post locker room), if only for five minutes at a stretch, I was more than a match for a majority of American males my age.

That was the benefit of training to so a high standard in all things: doing so kept me within proximity to an understanding of my limits, while compelling me to surpass them. We in Second Squad came to know our worth under the combined leadership of Bradley and Dussard. It was a blessed way of life.

At last, a routine took shape. Now well-trained ceremonially and in good physical condition, Second Squad was pulling its weight within Second Platoon and reveling in our sense of purpose, of professionalism, of near-perfection.

The Old Guard funeral cycle is very straightforward. Bravo, Charlie, and Delta rotate weekly through a series of tasking levels. Being on "Primary" requires that company's platoons to absorb as many funeral missions each day as humanly manageable. The "Backup" company absorbs overload missions. The "Down" company typically spends the week training. Ranges, road marches, land navigation, and funeral practice are commonly scheduled.

During Primary week, PT was brief and medium intensity. A day of carrying caskets was PT in and of itself. We would run perhaps two-three miles, perform a few sets of pull-ups, then race to the DFAC for chow before donning our dress blues and heading out to the cemetery. We never, to my recollection, performed more than six funerals in a day. And we rarely performed fewer than four.

Backup Week was a wildcard. We might find ourselves taking on two to three funerals, just enough to rule out any downtime or additional PT. In other instances, we might have nothing in the way of ceremonial missions. This left it up to team and squad leaders to decide how we spent our time. The motivated NCOs tended to use these days for professional development. Those less concerned with such things released guys to their rooms or the off-post locker room.

Down Week often saw us heading to Fort A.P. Hill for machine-gunning, land navigation, or tactical drills. But such excursions were not always in the cards, as even The Old Guard operates on a budget. Can't have their men blowing through tens of thousands of M249 rounds every day.

Down Week was a good occasion for additional casket training. SSG Dussard, who, realizing no ANC missions awaited that day, appreciated the opportunity to take his men on long runs through Georgetown and Washington, D.C., respectively.

Dussard's runs whipped my ass. I reveled in being his fastest soldier at this point, and took too much pleasure in seeing Bradley struggle to keep pace, as he routinely tapped me out in our off-post room sparring sessions. However, speed came at a price, and those interminable Second Squad runs were bloody draining.

On and on that routine went, with Second Platoon (and Bravo Company in its entirety) acquitting itself nicely in the spring and summer of 2001. Only two marring episodes come to mind when I reflect upon those nearly perfect five months. The first demoralized Second Squad, while the second reminded the Icarus within me that I had, perhaps, flown too closely to the sun.

The first of these came to pass somewhere deep in the heart of that splendid five-month stretch of time. Dussard was elsewhere. He often was. He had priorities which extended well beyond The Old Guard. We respected these. He deserved as much. Bradley was nominally in charge of the squad in Dussard's absence, but he had competition. There was a recently promoted NCO with whom he shared team-leading duties. Normally, a casket mission would see Bradley on Fold, the position reserved for either senior team members or those most skilled in tucking the flag's tail into the triangular mass.

Dussard's job as NCOIC was easy. He observed the process, then took possession of the flag once the Present man (occasionally myself) had placed it in his care, presented arms, and fell back in. Dussard would then bestow that folded flag upon the bereaved and join his casket bearers in making a solemnly executed departure.

But Dussard was elsewhere, and Bradley was indispensable on Fold. It was decided, the recently promoted NCO would stand-in for Dussard.

Flag-folding sometimes goes wrong. Very rarely. The Fold man is good at what he does; elsewise, he'd not be the Fold man.

Occasionally a flag proves uncooperative, or the Fold man errs. Again, very rarely.

In either case, the NCOIC has at his disposal a signal by which he can silently command a ceremonial unfolding and refolding. This he does as the Present man attempts to place the flag in his care. Rather than embracing the flag, the NCOIC may choose to Tap the flag on top and bottom at once, thereby signaling the start of an elaborate unfolding of that cloth triangle.

The double-tap befell a casket team only twice during my time with Second Platoon.

Both occurred that day.

Both occurred that mission.

It was effectively a double-double-tap

This was, to my knowledge, unprecedented.

Bradley had completed the folding, the flag had been sent down, and the Present man (Billy P, in this case) had attempted to place it in the care of our stand-in NCOIC, who rejected it.

We unfolded. We refolded. We gently passed it to the NCOIC. And it was, again, rejected.

Truly.

Whatever our team knew of flags and of their folding, we *knew* that Bradley had not screwed up twice. We *suspected* he had not screwed up even once. Palmer, to his credit, held the flag in place for a heartbeat following that second double-tap, as though to say, "Are you certain you want to embarrass the squad in this way?"

The stand-in NCOIC maintained his position.

Rather humorously, the ANC liaison, a civilian who interfaces with the bereaved, approached the stand-in NCOIC as we unfolded/refolded for the second time and quietly spoke words to the effect of, "What the hell are you doing? Take the damn flag!"

And he did. When presented with the flag for a third time, the stand-in NCOIC accepted. The rest of the mission unfolded (so to speak) in ordinary fashion. The bereaved accepted their flag, Second Squad marched off into the sun, and moments later regrouped with the stand-in NCOIC...

...for whom Bradley had a few words.

"I'll speak for the whole team when I say that was complete fuckin' bullshit."

Had we not been in a cemetery, let alone Arlington National Cemetery, Bradley might have yelled. He might've thrown a few punches. But we *were* in Arlington National Cemetery, so he did neither.

"Flag wasn't to standard," was the NCOIC's succinct riposte.

"Oh it *wasn't?*" Bradley, eyes wide, was fuming. "Bullshit."

"That's your opinion. I saw a flag not to standard." This led to a standoff of no longer than five seconds' time, after which the NCOIC excused himself in advance of the next funeral.

As we awaited the hearse in silence, Bradley, astutely sensing his men had been shaken by the unprecedented circumstances, broke ranks to speak a few encouraging words.

"Listen, guys, we all know that was total horseshit. You know what you're doing and so do I. Let's perform as the elite team we are and carry the fuck on. Strength and honor."

Reflexively (and largely in unison) we replied, "Strength and honor."

I don't know whether Bradley had David Franzoni's *Gladiator* screenplay in mind when speaking those words, but they were as necessary in that moment as ever they were on a film set. More so.

Years later, when in communication with Bradley regarding the incident, he revisited the topic in a way I had not anticipated. He acknowledged the flag in that instance had been of the shorter variety (there were at least two makes in circulation during that time) and entertained the idea that our folding process suffered because of it.

As I think on it, the stand-in NCOIC did not mean any harm. He was a career soldier and had served his country for many years by that point. What had happened was regrettable, but might also have been more the result of uncertainty than any other likely factors.

Our remaining missions came and went without incident, both that day and throughout the remainder of the week. The incident was ignored outright, as the Company was too busy that summer to allow for a squad-level schism to disrupt its efficacy.

We carried on, and soon that miserable episode was a minor blight on an otherwise flawless summer career. If anything, we tightened up our performance following that dreadful incident.

The second marring was one wholly of my own making, and heaped humility upon only myself. The summer of 2001 was my running summer. I have been a relatively routine runner since leaving Drill Sergeant Spencer's platoon in the fall of 2000. But in the summer of 2001, I ran early and often. I ran with the squad, on weeknights, and on Saturdays.

I realized I had ascended to a level of running aptitude quite advanced in relation to the unit, and certainly better than anything I achieved as a civilian. During a Backup week, Dussard deigned to treat his squad to a seven-mile bridge-to-bridge run. This was a good, scenic route, but unusual for Second Squad. We tended to run through D.C. or Georgetown.

This route saw us link the former with the latter, crossing Key Bridge from the south, taking a sharp turn east, then making our way towards Arlington via Arlington Memorial Bridge, that same bridge Mann, Roum, and I had crossed into Washington, D.C., upon my reporting to the unit.

"Sergeant," I said, while maintaining a comfortable seven-minute mile.

"What's up, Mongilutz?" Dussard, too, was running comfortably, but I had more energy in reserve, and knew it.

"Mind releasing me for the remaining distance?"

This meant that, rather than staying within sight of the squad, I would be free to run at my own pace. Dussard seemed curious as to what I could do.

"Go ahead. I better not beat you back to Myer."

If I didn't accelerate to a six-minute pace, I was damn close. Just prior to entering Iwo Jima Gate, I turned to see who was nearest. It was Dussard, and he was at least a hundred yards to my rear. I would have to stop for coffee for him to gain on (let alone surpass) me.

Instead, I found another gear. I took CIF Hill—the hill on which McGuinness had put fifty yards between us in fifteen seconds' time—as fast as I could.

The hill was easy.

I saw fit to run to its midpoint and join my battle buddy Jason Barnett in his ascent of the latter half. It was easy enough that I felt immortal that morning.

It has occurred to me in recent years ... or at least since I began authoring this work ... that so very many of my problems during those years with The Old Guard might have been mitigated, maybe even averted entirely, had the sensation of hubris not found such fertile soil in my nascent psyche. It's true—arrogance found in me an all too accommodating traveling companion ... and frequently.

Arrogance is nothing if not humility's deceptive midwife.

During the height of that summer, Bravo Company was released for the weekend following a very busy, very hot week. If forced to wager it, I'd say it was a Primary week, but at times even Backup could leave the lot of us feeling drained to the core.

Weekends were spent differently across the board. Guys with families were with those families. Single guys living off-post tended to be rather reckless at times. The stories abound on that front.

Barracks rats are an Army-wide phenomenon. For the guys stationed in, say Fort Polk, holing up inside the barracks is perfectly understandable.

The barracks rats stationed in Washington, D.C., however … well, their behavior was difficult to explain. A thin majority of these rats were video gamers, and avid ones. And a strong majority of that thin majority were obsessed with *EverQuest*, an online, massive multi-player role-playing fantasy game. The game's most devoted of enthusiasts knew far more about the fantastical lands they navigated than they knew about, for instance, Arlington National Cemetery.

These same guys found it bizarre that I'd spend time doing on the weekends what we were required to do each weekday morning.

"Bro, you're goin' for a fuckin' run? Are you kidding? Dussard's gonna have us eating pavement Monday morning!"

I was not alone. A Third Platoon barracks soldier was a well-conditioned marathoner and triathlete. His off-time training was the stuff of legend. Two of my platoon brothers were big-time weekend weightlifters, as they found our weekday PT unsuitable for muscle growth. Another Second Platoon soldier was often seen performing dead-hang pullups in the company quad following five-mile runs around and near Fort Myer.

For a handful of us, physiological development was a way of life. And the barracks gamers were many. Those guys loved *EverQuest*, alongside other games.

After being released for the weekend following the hot, busy week, I decided (foolishly) to forcibly graduate to a plane of sublime fitness. Saturday, I would engage in a grueling gymnasium regimen. Dips, pullups, pushups, and, yes, a good number of sit-ups, though these had not been a problem since reaching Myer.

On Sunday, I would run seven miles midday.

I had good reason to believe I would be perfectly fine come Monday. So, on Saturday, I executed the regimen as planned and went to sleep in a particularly sore state that night. On Sunday, still a bit sore, I donned my PT uniform around 0900hrs, sans reflective belt because I did not want to wear it.

And I ran. Fast. The steps turned so quickly into miles that it was only around the midpoint when I realized the day was hot. I had left late. Typically, my running regimen had me leaving the barracks no later than 0800hrs and returning no later than 0900hrs.

Here I was, mid-run and it was nearly 1000hrs. The heat was swiftly laying claim to Georgetown, with my poorly hydrated body caught in the middle.

I had reached the midpoint and turning back was exactly what I had to do. But there was no metaphorical turning back. I had committed myself to running seven miles.

It was a slog. I had been stupid about nutrition that summer, even more so about proper hydration. Youth? Hubris? Ignorance? Pick one. Those last miles were simply a slog. However, pleased with myself I had been when completing the same distance ahead of Dussard just a week or so prior was now wholly absent from my mind. It'd been replaced with petulant relief.

The hill was slow going, but still faster than my first experience with it. Jogging to the barracks, I showered, changed, and made my way to the DFAC a short while later for lunch chow. A mild headache made itself known to me that afternoon, an introduction I could've done without.

Monday came early, and with it a reminder that Bravo Company and much of The Old Guard would be at Summerall Field, Fort Myer's parade ground, upon which large-scale retirements for senior military officers routinely take place. There are other occasions which warrant gathering the Regiment onto a single patch of earth, but sending off general officers is the most common.

The missions run long because generals love to hear generals speak. I've nothing but tremendous respect for those rare officers who do ultimately achieve the rank of general. It is no mean feat. What I might say to one or two of them, however, is that brevity in speech will win you the heartfelt respect of many a soldier.

Particularly the respect of a soldier whose state of self-induced dehydration is about to bring him down while you speak. I was assigned that morning to what is known in the Regiment as "States & Territories" duty. Which is to say, I, along with fifty-six others from throughout the Regiment, stood at the back of the field while holding a state flag (Maryland, I believe) high over my cap-clad head.

There couldn't have been a worse assignment, on a worse day, with a more loquacious general … and I'd stupidly invited a weakened state upon myself two days prior.

Arrogance. It inevitably makes a fool of its every bearer.

I held out. The ceremony was approaching an hour's length, and I'd already seen several men in the marching ranks collapse in loud fashion.

I closed my eyes briefly and attempted to convince myself that my head was not spinning wildly. This was a fool's errand. I was going down, but I wouldn't take the flag with me. Falling out in the marching platoon is one thing, that's relatively inconspicuous based upon your placement within the platoon, and only holding a M14 rifle.

The state flags are prominent, and would be visible to all in attendance. To contain the damage (and this would be rightly damaging to me personally),

I placed my left arm behind my back. While doing so, my knees buckled. Thankfully, a backup soldier reached me in time, strategically took control of the flag, and left my weakening organism in the care of two medics whose sole task was seeing to those who had succumbed to the heat and long-winded speech.

Now, if I were a complete cunt, I would've taken comfort in knowing that I wasn't alone in having fallen out during the ceremony. But I wasn't, and I was angrier with myself than ever before.

While taking in fluids, I taunted myself with the question, *How will you ever recover from this?*

There was no clear answer. I had been a fool and it had cost me greatly. The blame rested solely with me.

What pained me most was the thought of having let down Bradley, Dussard, and a few others whose faith in me would be shattered. More than fifteen years hence, the thought is often enough to cripple me where I stand. I'll carry that shame until my dying breath.

This and the flag-folding debacle were by no means characteristic of the spring and summer of 2001; not for me, not for the squad, not for the platoon. We had performed scores of successful funerals, had marched our fair share, had spent time on the range, and engaged in PT whenever possible. Our friendships had been born and strengthened throughout those five months.

Just prior to the ceremonial peak season picking up steam, a few new soldiers reported to Second Platoon. Two of these, Davidson and Drake, joined Second Squad, while the third man, Eric Ebner, would report to Tim Pennartz in Third Squad.

I liked these guys immediately. Which was good, as I was assigned to serve as their R.O.P. sponsor. This is regarded as a high honor, and I took the work seriously. All three graduated within the minimum three-week timeframe, which was a source of pride.

Davidson and Drake were rural in background, in personality, and in ruggedness. Southerners by way of geography and in spirit, they were as trustworthy as anyone I would encounter while in uniform. They were also *big* guys. Davidson probably stands 6'3" and, at the time weighed two-hundred-thirty pounds. Drake was of similar height and weight. Both were scrappers, which meant Bradley would have his hands full, which is not to say either posed a threat individually. Bradley made sure to annihilate that misconception within days of them finishing R.O.P.

In looking for a legitimate threat to his combative supremacy, Bradley invited the two boys to attack him at once. Bradley fought *very* hard; he was ultimately forced to acknowledge defeat. He had made those guys earn it, and the squad's respect for the man grew in that moment.

We assigned Drake and Davidson a joint moniker: the Bash Brothers.

They were inseparable from that moment on. Second Squad was lucky to have them in the family.

The one I had taken to regarding as the "third twin" was Eric Ebner. A bit more reserved and thoughtful a soul than most in the platoon, Ebner is an inherently cerebral creature, given to thought experiments, riddles, and abstract humor. We became close immediately.

Bill Palmer, a Second Squad soldier who had preceded me in reporting to the unit three months previous, earned his degree prior to joining the unit. Palmer could (and did) enlist as an E-4/Specialist. The term "Degree 4" was used disparagingly in referring to soldiers who were regarded as having by-passed essential lower-enlisted ranks of PV1, PV2, and PFC. Palmer was wit incarnate. I've never known a cleverer human, his sarcasm manifested aggressively and relentlessly.

Another Degree 4 was Robert Williams, a big guy who hailed from Phoenix. He was argumentative but not boorish, proud but self-deprecating. He was also given to saying things the rest of us were merely thinking. This penchant resulted in Williams' enduring humiliating punishments, but even the leadership found his frankness endearing.

I developed an unlikely rapport with both Palmer and Williams, the three of us a sort of "Three Musketeers" group, with the collective aim of publicly articulating our shared irreverence.

And there was John "Hooph" Hoffman, a soldier who had served four years with the 101st Airborne in Fort Campbell prior to his Old Guard stint. A fellow Second Squad soldier, I bonded closely with Hoffman. He was, like Ebner, a thoughtful, curious soul. He recognized in me a kindred spirit where literary interests were concerned. I had formed another trio, this one predicated upon common ground of a non-martial sort. It was like having my childhood friends Geoff and Andy with me; albeit in uniform.

Beyond Second Platoon, I spent time with a few non-casket bearers. Roum and I still spoke on occasion, but less so after E.I.B. However, I did come to know a fellow Third Platoon soldier of his. Brett Thurman had reported to the Regiment that winter (February 2001), not long after which we found ourselves sharing a bus seat as we were transported to the Capitol Building for a low-key ceremony.

Now, let us step foot into September of 2001, and to the second Tuesday of that fateful month.

IX

"I think the Pentagon got hit"

The Spirit of America. That is the name of an Army roadshow in which The Old Guard had traditionally played a big part since prior to my time with the Regiment. It was slated to once again play a big part, and since September had dawned, the companies had been contributing soldiers to that cause.

Coming off a spring and summer of virtually non-stop ceremonial activity—did I mention having returned home that June? That round of leave often escapes my memory, as it was preceded and followed by so very much.

I returned for my sister's high school graduation. It certainly didn't feel as though an entire year had passed since my own, but, to paraphrase the Bard, we are Father Time's subjects, not he ours. It was a splendid two weeks. I enjoyed every moment of every day, and made up for lost time the previous summer, having made inefficient use of my HRAP stretch in November.

In any event, the Spirit of America was essentially a singing, marching lightshow of an Army production held in Columbus (or was it St. Louis?), and it was consuming many of our waking hours. We were scheduled to be on the road early that autumn.

But here we are now in September ... of 2001.

I trust it goes without saying we were delayed. In fact, I have neither witnessed nor participated in, to this day, a Spirit of America show.

September 11th, 2001 was a Tuesday. Things were eerie around the company in the weeks prior. They often are as the summer begins to wane and missions slow down. As though unwitting characters in a *Twilight Zone* episode, soldiers vanish by twos and threes. A couple might be sent to the firing range, others to various schools, a handful volunteer for specialty platoons, and so on. It's all just ... eerie.

Almost overnight, that singular mission to which the company had, in its entirety, been zealously committed across the spring and summer months began to crumble. Even PT was unrecognizable, with platoon-level runs frequently replacing the squad-level alternative. These were typically organized by running prowess: (1) fast group, (2) medium group, 3) turds ... er, I mean slow group.

In truth, I sympathized with the slow group. They were generally the platoon's largest specimens, which made them invaluable during casket carries, but they were roundly ridiculed by many of the fast group, and even a few of the medium.

Tuesday, September 11th, 2001 was even more unusual than are so many September days in the Regiment. Nearly all of Second Platoon was tasked with some Spirit of America setup activity, or such is my recollection. This left only four of us behind for a very casual morning of PT—steel-lunged SSG Dussard, First Squad's respected Squad Leader, SSG Rivera, and a junior NCO.

Though the two squad leaders were E-6s, they allowed the junior NCO to lead PT for our small group, despite his being an E-5. As a private, I should've been silent as we went through our stretches. Instead, I decided to win-over the First Squad E-6 with laughter, just as I had done with Dussard.

Voicing sarcastic enthusiasm with every stretch command (thereby placing myself inside the inside joke), I made a mockery of the E-5's stretching regimen. As he spoke the words, "Our next stretch is..." for the thirtieth time that morning, I chimed in, "...the run itself!"

That did it. The E-6s were rolling in laughter, the E-5 powerless to stop them. I'd irritated one NCO, befriended another, and furthered my bond with Dussard. I thought all was going well.

I beat Dussard and the E-5 back to Myer, but lagged twenty or so yards behind the very fast SSG Rivera. Later that year, I would best him on an APFT two-mile run, but only just. He was a quick one, and represented another bar for me to surpass.

Runs of that sort didn't require us to re-group in the company quad. Instead, upon ascending CIF Hill, we jogged to the barracks and readied ourselves for the day ahead.

I had returned to the barracks by 0735hrs and was showered and dressed by 0830hrs. Whenever a spare window of time materialized between PT and 0900hrs, I permitted myself the luxury of a brief reading session or, if others had joined me in the room, a film.

On that morning, a few of my Second Platoon brothers came and went. Whatever nonsense had pulled them away from PT that morning, they still needed to eat. My roommate (now Drake) stopped in, as did Bradley. I spoke with Hoffman and put on a film for the sake of ambient noise whilst people went in and out.

Third Platoon, I should note, was practicing riot control techniques in the company quad. Full body armor, batons, masks, et cetera. Just the sort of thing one would never see at the height of summer season.

I was taking my time readying for the 1000hrs report time. There was to be an equipment draw, and a makeshift formation for the twelve or so of us not already in the confines of Conmy Hall.

Knock-knock-knock-knock-knock. "Mongilutz! You in there?"

It was the junior NCOIC. I knew I wasn't late for the equipment draw, as it was only 0915hrs.

Shit. Is he here for retribution? I asked myself.

"Yes, Sergeant," I responded as the door swung open.

"You hear anything 'bout what's going on in New York?"

"No, Sergeant."

"Better come downstairs. We're watching it in the dayroom."

Bravo Company's dayroom is perhaps a few hundred square feet in size, if that, and not well laid out for large congregations. It is L-shaped and freedom of movement is restricted by the presence of seating furniture and a large, fixed desk.

Being relatively short by Regimental standards and among the last to arrive in the dayroom, I was unable to see the large screen television set in one corner of the dayroom. But I knew I *needed* to see; that much was clear.

I lightly pushed past someone, and afforded CNN my quiet attention. Everything felt very real in that moment.

We watched what you watched: towers smoking, confusion on the streets, frantic reporting. We were, most of us, young and naïve. I doubt any one of us fully (or correctly) registered the geopolitical implications of what it was we were seeing. That changed almost immediately, as Second Platoon's brand new platoon sergeant entered from outside. He had been practicing ceremony with fellow senior NCOs. "Hey, uh, I think something just went off outside. Bomb, or something."

"It's probably just the Guns Platoon, Sergeant."

The Old Guard is home to a platoon of heavy gun specialists whose role is the ceremonial firing of sizable howitzers during certain, you guessed it, ceremonies. Think something along the lines of a twenty-one gun salute with far larger and far louder rounds being fired. Hearing the Guns platoon practice their rather precise craft was common. And as we all found ourselves firmly affixed to the television set while our nation's cultural capital was under attack, none among us suspected that our nation's *actual* capital had also been targeted.

It was not the Guns Platoon.

Someone in the dayroom spoke up, palpable certainty in his voice, "I think the Pentagon got hit."

Realizing the Pentagon, too, had been struck by a passenger-laden commercial airliner—foully re-purposed as a passenger-laden missile—took a little time. Several sections of Arlington National Cemetery are near the Pentagon, or near enough to render the massive structure visible from their location. I later heard that a pair of Caisson soldiers had been in one of those sections as the aircraft struck its target.

Too focused on a broadcast had we been to realize that tragedy had arrived in a fiery fashion upon our doorstep. And then it was made known to us via many sources.

Our eyes registered a smoke plume from what most of us recognized as the approximate location of the Pentagon.

Then came the flurry of spoken word reports.

"Did you hear? Did you see? Pentagon's hit. Fuckers hit it with a motherfucking plane. Motherfuckers! Fuck! Pentagon got fuckin' hit. It's on fire. Whole section, whole section gone. Gone. Motherfuckers hit us right fuckin' here! Fuck!"

A surfeit of largely pointless speech began a rapid-fire circulation throughout the barracks. Nobody afforded CNN another moment of time that morning. Whatever came next, we knew the Regiment would be playing a big part.

"Formation!"

Those three syllables have a compelling and universal effect upon soldiers of all ranks, regardless of their respective time in service or personality characteristics. Entire battalions of men have been witnessed to zombify upon hearing the word bellowed. They stop, take inventory of the situation, then robotically move towards wherever it is their formations take place.

Bravo Company was no different. Out we went into the quad. Uniforms were mixed, which is to say the term "uniform" was a misnomer in that moment. Most were in Class-B uniform, ten or so were in BDUs, and a couple were in PTs. On *any* given day in *any* given unit there are *always* at least two turds walking around in PTs during the duty day. *Always.*

We'd all be uniform soon enough. Come to think of it, even under those circumstances I suspect there were at least two turds still in PTs come nightfall. Otherwise, Bravo Company was in BDUs and soon would draw various weapons and protective gear … though not the sort of protective gear we would soon need.

"All right, I want all of you men to go to your rooms or, for you off-post guys, somewhere else, and call your loved ones. Let them know you're all right and ask them to pray for you. We're going to the Pentagon and we'll be there for a while."

These were our 1SG's orders. Triton had left the unit some months earlier. The new 1SG was a good man, and wise.

We went inside. We placed calls. I called home. My mother answered. I said … something, I'm not sure what. I recall asking that she turn on the television. I then drew my equipment and headed to the quad.

To its credit, the Regiment performed well that day. Our leadership at all levels had shifted gears from the mindset of the ceremony to the mindset of the tactical. And had done so quickly. At around 1200hrs the following day, maybe a bit later, Bravo and its sister companies had transportation lined up for a mass movement to the ferociously engulfed Pentagon.

As we made the short drive from Myer to the headquarters of the Department of Defense, our collective sarcasm had in no way been apprehended by the seriousness of those grave circumstances. There was shit-talking aplenty, some macabre humor, and an abundance of stock cynicism which comes to sharpen the wit of every TOG soldier within five weeks of finishing R.O.P.

It was Tim Pennartz (that team leader whose high standards had contributed to Third Squad's casket-bearing excellence) who spoke with maturity and a sense of solemnity.

"This shit's gonna be like our Pearl Harbor, guys. It's bad."

Normally a biting wit in his own right, Pennartz was looking to each of us with an element of poetry in his eyes. I'd never seen it in him before, and would never again see it at all.

For my part, I joked with Ebner.

"Hey, Ebner, do you see that apartment building over there?"

"Uh, yeah ... why?"

A long pause followed by a dramatic nod.

"Me too."

Good delivery coupled with Ebner's disappointment in my clarifying response led to a burst of laughter within the crammed Light Medium Tactical Vehicle (LMTV).

And then we were there. I'll note here that this arrival was followed by a shared sense of uncertainty. As far as could be discerned, there were no enemies at whom to take aim, and no task in desperate need of an infantry platoon's skillset. We were simply ... there.

It was the firefighters' show for many hours to come, naturally, as the structure was severely ablaze. I cannot know what it was each of my Battlehard brothers had expected to see in the way of damage, but my own prediction was incorrect. I had either overestimated the destructive capacity of a fuel-laden Boeing 757 or underestimated the resilience of the Pentagon.

Whether by design or by sheer happenstance, the airliner which had been repurposed as a kamikaze death instrument on September 11th, 2001 would cruelly collide with its target sixty years to the day after the Pentagon's construction was inaugurated.

Construction on the Pentagon broke ground on September 11th, 1941 and was the result of bureaucratic finagling stemming from what the United States Department of War saw as a problem of inadequate space for the housing of its innumerable functionaries. Space would no longer be a problem once the Pentagon was constructed.

Blueprinted by General Brehon Burke Somervell, the Pentagon's shape was originally intended to map the site of its chosen location—the roughly pentagon-shaped Arlington Farms. As so often happens in such cases, however, that site was removed from consideration. Hoover Field would end up being home to the massive structure, and despite that location not being pentagonal in shape, the structure's design went unchanged.

It was finished quickly. Over ten thousand laborers contributed to the structure's completion, so that by January 15, 1943, the Pentagon was armed and operational. Well, operational, anyway—thought a tongue-in-cheek Death Star reference would appeal to the Star Wars fanatics among you.

In sixteen months' time, the five million square-foot Pentagon went from groundbreaking to completion. Truly breathtaking.

Steel, I should note, was in short supply during World War II. This led to the Pentagon being designed as a relatively short concrete structure, rather than as a steel-reinforced building along the lines of a high-rise. Five sides to it, five stories above ground—the Pentagon is perhaps the most aptly named building this side of the Leaning Tower of Pisa. Though the White House is exactly that: a white house. The Pentagon is a pentagon. That's rather odd, all things considered.

It's also massive, which likely made a very easy target for the murderous terrorists who deemed its attempted destruction worthy of claiming their own lives, and those of the unwilling passengers on that tragic day.

Of course, nobody knew what to make of the circumstances as they played out before our eyes. It's interesting—the conflicts in Iraq and Afghanistan have metastasized so fully within our collective consciousness as to render alien the idea of the names "Al Qaeda" and "Taliban" being entirely nonexistent in public discourse.

To be sure, we men of Battlehard knew the United States was at war. Had it been just the Pentagon, or only one of the two World Trade Center towers, we might've allowed for the possibility of a terrible accident being responsible. But we knew of the World Trade Center, of the Pentagon, and later, of United 93.

What we didn't know was everything else, certainly nothing of the Taliban.

The Army's lower-enlisted soldiers did what they do well: they rumored amongst themselves. Blame was casually laid at the doorstep of every nation state and group. We didn't know anything.

And wouldn't for a time.

We were preoccupied with the blazing inferno that was the Pentagon's west side, and with an oppressive scent that would take up residence first within our sense of smell, and then within the deepest recesses of our memory. There was something about that scent…

Unsatisfied with the men of Bravo Company standing about, eyes affixed to the flames, our leadership tasked us with setting up a series of tents some hundred yards from where the inferno continued its consumption of all it could engulf. We would be taking up residence on the Pentagon grounds, at least for a time.

We made short work of those tents, and within an hour's time each platoon had staked out one of the General Purpose (GP) Medium tents for themselves. I made a point of placing my rucksack beside Sgt. Bradley's. He was looking after his team, proving himself every bit the leader we all knew him to be. I found myself looking to Bradley as a younger brother does to an older. I was glad he was there.

Hoffman, too, was the consummate professional. Fully capable of inhabiting a sillier persona, when a mission was at hand Hoffman assumed the bearing of a grim-faced warrior. Always a tad self-effacing, Hooph would deny every word of this. He was an example for soldiers both junior and experienced alike.

I saw very little of Roum during this time, though the three platoons were collaborative at every turn. A young Third Platoon team leader with whom I was entirely unacquainted offered me a handful of M&Ms one evening as a group of us sat awaiting orders. That's just how it was during our month of Pentagon recovery work. We'd shared in the work of showcasing the United States Army, a project which tends to become routine. Conversely, the seriousness of what had befallen the nation was binding Battlehard together in ways that, I'm reluctant to say, might never have been possible via ceremony alone.

It was all so … visceral. All of it.

We went in after nightfall on the first day. It was dark and had been since well before we entered the ruined structure. No. "Ruined" is too thin a term.

For that section of the Pentagon was a charred husk; a powder-burned and smoking wound; a passageway to what we immediately realized was nightmarishly authored destruction itself. It was murder thrust upon our national consciousness by a desire to kill for the sake of killing.

And that grotesque scent was overwhelmingly upon us. It had beckoned earlier and we had paid it a passing attention of sorts; perhaps hoping naively it'd make its exit prior to our entrance. If that hope had found purchase in the minds of any among our number, it was hope misplaced. The scent … it was, indeed, upon us.

Death.

The oppressive smell of jet fuel and of burnt wood (of burnt everything) accompanied the scent of death, but it was the latter that most ardently insisted upon being made known to we, its hapless visitors. We would come to know it all too well. I know it still.

Our mission was plain: empty the structure of all that lay within. Of *all* that lay within.

I won't allow this text to become an exercise in illustrating the macabre.

One-hundred-twenty-five Pentagon workers, a majority of whom were civilians, lost their lives that day. Aboard American Flight 77 were fifty-nine passengers, aside from the five hijackers. In all, there were one-hundred-eighty-nine human beings whose bodies had been overwhelmed by the forces of collision, of explosion, of flame.

All that lay within.

We were soldiers, all of us, and our mission was clear. Every man within a stone's throw of me had endured the hardship of Sand Hill, had completed the Bayonet. Each of us had been trained to push beyond our imagined limits, both physical and mental. Each had been trained to regard death as a secondary consideration, the mission being always first. Always.

And our mission was, indeed, clear.

The act of entering the wounded structure was surreal in a way that seems nearly fantastical as I recall it now. There was a darkness, but not the sort one experiences in entering a poorly illuminated room. It was a jealous and malevolent void, one capable of banishing from its province the intrusion of all outside noise.

When approaching the threshold, a large opening created by wholesale destruction, the sounds of ample human activity had populated our ears fully. In crossing that threshold, when making ourselves known to the void, those same sounds held no dominion. They could accompany us to the final step, but were forbidden from trespassing into a domain devoted to preserving a ghoulish absence of comforting ambience.

Where our ears wanted for more, our eyes perhaps wanted for less.

It was nearly impossible to envision that same void having housed a productive office environment but a day earlier. For what we beheld was a catacomb born not of careful human labor, but of merciless human barbarism. In the space of a single heartbeat, what had once been vital, organized, and cooperative was reduced to a foul crypt of wood and stone and blood and flesh.

We expended effort both optical and conceptual in attempting to correctly piece together what had once been, though we were each met with failure. Too distressed and mangled were the elements of life and architecture which had so recently known the invaluable blessing that is form.

The haunting void into which we men of Battlehard had stepped was otherworldly in its tormented echoes of that vitality which it had inadequately and instantly displaced. Our presence, the sights to which we bore witness, the scent we reluctantly registered, the very breath we drew—each of these was an affront to the rank grimness which sought to forever lay claim that structure.

I stood alongside Bradley for a time as we set ourselves to the work of moving … of moving *everything* from within the Pentagon to a designated area some short distance from the site of impact. We formed a human con-veyor belt of sorts—a technique which, though not taught in Basic Training, comes quite instinctively to infantrymen. We hadn't been instructed to carry out our grim task in this manner, we had simply set to it without uttering a word.

In re-connecting with Bradley recently, I was surprised to receive from him an apology. He recalled my having mentioned feeling sick, and him hav-ing responded with, "Let's just get this shit done."

Curiously, I do not remember anything of the sort, but I can imagine how it would've unfolded. Christopher Bradley stands over six-feet tall, while I was still an inch from what would amount to my present height of … less than that. I can also imagine looking up to Bradley (figuratively and literally), making that statement, hearing his response, and steeling myself for the mis-sion at hand, feeling miserable for having disappointed a leader I never deserved in the first place.

Bradley didn't owe me an apology. Not then, not now.

Besides, we all felt a bit sick, I would wager. It was sickening work, in sickening conditions. And our respective bodies were becoming rather inti-mate with whatever morbid toxicity was stewing in the air, on the surfaces we touched, and in the water at our feet. Even now, the feeling of moisture penetrating my footwear brings to mind those early days of Pentagon recovery work. Battlehard had immersed itself in the frontline residue of carnage and wanton destruction.

There would be more to come.

Work that evening ended, well, the next morning. Not at sunrise, mind you. No, Battlehard was released to its GP Medium tents perhaps an hour or so before dawn. And our days were anything but consistent from that point forth.

In exiting that toxic and vile cavern, it was as though we had reentered the Earth's atmosphere after having toiled solemnly in the emptiness of space above. Sounds and motion and fresh air—these joined together in a decidedly resuscitative manner, reigniting a sense of life within each of us.

Death, you see, tends to weigh rather cumbersome upon the psyche, as surely it did in that tragic void.

Like a nest of oversized caterpillars, we all laid on the ground within our tent, each of us in an Army-issued sleeping bag. Though we should've succumbed to exhaustion immediately, a pleasant round of interfamilial banter manifested. I recall Pennartz insisting that one of his soldiers, "…move the fuck over. I don't want you breathing on my face while I'm trying to sleep."

Williams, the Degree Four from Arizona, had us laughing with a few jokes about the curious accommodations. And they were curious. Not one of us, after all, had awoken two mornings prior with any notion of what sort of labor awaited us that night. Not one among us had any notion that the Pentagon grounds would serve as bed and pillow. Not one among us had fully come to terms with what it was we had seen firsthand during those preceding hours.

I remember saying something to Hoffman about war. He was characteristically dismissive, as neither speculation nor childish heroic ambition was of any interest to him. I remember saying something to Bradley about home, and I remember thinking about that scent. We had escaped its reach upon reaching the tent. I remember thinking of Rohde and of Naylor, and wondering if they'd be making their way overseas. I hoped they were doing well.

I remember thinking of the previous six months and of how committed I had become to the Regiment's mission, to my physical prowess, to my platoon, to my squad, and to my team. And I remember thinking briefly of Marysville, of my childhood, of our dogs, of my grandparents, of whatever came to mind.

And just prior to embracing my union with much needed slumber, I thought of that scent.

We hadn't slept long, but we were mostly rested. I'd wager we were eating breakfast chow by 1000hrs, having returned to the tent perhaps seven hours earlier. Whatever else was underway, two things were clear: (1) our leadership was uncertain of what was next, and (2) the country was standing united.

To the former point, there was a lot of standing around. Our commanding officer seemed frustrated by a lack of clear direction. Was Battlehard to remain on the Pentagon grounds all day? Would we be returning to Fort Myer? What the hell was next? That was for them to sort out. The platoons were still caught up in the enormity of it all.

The country stood as one. Countless civilians were manning various "Morale Tents" and food stands. It was as though a state fair had materialized on Pentagon property, and entirely overnight. A few major fast food chains were represented, with both McDonalds and Outback cuisine being made available to hungry soldiers and non-military relief workers. There were also medical tents, so-called "comfort stations" and prayer hovels where fatigued men and women were encouraged to collect themselves. Volunteers walked about with bottles of water, while others offered snacks and the like.

This had truly blossomed into an uplifting collective effort. It was enough to restore one's faith in humanity, a faith which had been harmed by the preceding day's ghastly attacks. Most of us were moved by what was a paramount outpouring of support, of concern, of patriotism.

And then we had our orders, sort of.

The Regiment had decided to implement a rotation system. With the various companies cycling back and forth from the Pentagon to Myer, Myer to the Pentagon. This would continue ... until it didn't. It wasn't the sort of question any of us thought to ask. We were simply relieved to be heading back to Fort Myer, as not one among us had been prepared for an extended stay on the Pentagon grounds.

Around midday, Battlehard boarded its transportation and made the short drive back to Fort Myer. We had been away for only a day's time, and yet our respective rooms held the feeling of entering a bygone era. There was something askew within the walls of those barracks. We had departed more than just the building that prior day; we had departed the pre–9/11 Army. The staleness greeting us was nothing if not an echo of an innocence we'd never again know in the flesh, merely within the imperfect and forever narrowing corridors of memory.

Not unlike the morning of a full-scale ceremony or a Regimental run, there was a good deal of activity in and around the hallways and in bedrooms that afternoon. The company's fractured state was no more—we were once again a single organism; each platoon an appendage of the company leadership and of its will.

The unit was under a rather strict lockdown in those immediate days following the attack. Soldiers who lived off-post were forbidden from leaving Fort Myer, which meant that team leaders, squad leaders, other leadership figures, and those guys who lived off-post for reasons of seniority and an absence of space within the barracks, would now need to find space within the barracks.

A couple of off-post guys slept in my room for a night or two. It was cramped quarters throughout Building 248. Not that any of us found the time to grow agitated, nor could we summon adequate energy to voice a complaint. Each company was tethered to a twelve-on/twelve-off schedule, which saw us laboring in the Pentagon recovery effort for twelve-hour stretches before returning to Fort Myer, wherein we ate chow quickly, slept deeply, and awaited our return to the frontlines of that intensive labor.

Days varied, but we often found ourselves standing by for perhaps two hours, maybe three, whilst construction teams worked to reinforce the structure's ruined (that inadequate word again) west side. The nature of our ongoing mission changed as the days turned to weeks. Several evenings, two-man teams were assigned to conduct guard duty *within* the vacant structure.

Those nights were strange.

Power to the damaged areas was initially absent, which meant we were "guarding" the interior of a scarcely illuminated structure with only flashlights and lanterns to guide us through the corridors. Within a building which had just found itself beset by unbridled carnage, and which still housed that scent (a cruel reminder, that scent), this all amounted to duty of a decidedly haunted sort.

Later that month, Second Platoon was involved in a couple of curious situations. In one instance, we were tasked with securing a section of the Pentagon road network while workers in white protective suits (think *X-Files*) sifted through debris which had been largely recovered by The Old Guard. In another instance, we found ourselves engaging in larger scale sifting. We didn't find occasion to don those white suits (the ones that get conspiracy theorists both excited and agitated at once) while sifting, at least not that I recall.

And speaking of protective gear...

I recall our having initially entered the Pentagon wearing BDUs, Kevlar helmets, and standard issue leather gloves.

This is not a criticism of our leadership, or of their leadership. They did right by us wherever they could and saw to the maintenance of our morale at every turn. That our initial foray into the impact site saw us immersed in a vile concoction of oppressive fumes while our feet were drenched by waters of questionable cleanliness should come as a surprise to nobody.

A day or so later we saw teams of Federal workers enter the building with respirators, waterproof boots, and white suits (probably Tyvek brand).

We eventually found ourselves donning respirators of our own, though these were prone to slipping about as their wearer engaged in heavy labor. Further layers of protective gear followed, and by the third day every TOG soldier entering the recovery zone was covered head-to-toe in watertight, hooded white suits, with thick yellow boots to keep one's feet dry. Bretty recalls each man having been required to seal via duct tape the sleeves and pant legs of their Tyvek garments, but that bit is entirely absent my own memory. It was surely the case, even if I am unable to coax its reality from the clutches of mental obscurity. There was also a decontamination tent on the Pentagon grounds by day three (or four, perhaps), in which each soldier was sprayed off prior to removing their outer protective layers.

In any event, the sifting team was similarly clad in Tyvek suits, though protective clothing was probably unnecessary beyond the limits of the Pentagon structure itself.

On it went. A week of gruesome, grueling work at the site of impact. A week or so of questionably necessary guard duty within the structure's damaged interior, a few days of either guarding said structure's road network or participating in the sifting underway within that makeshift perimeter.

Every night we would return to the barracks exhausted. I didn't see my dress blues once between September 11th and October 6th. For a soldier assigned to The Old Guard, this was highly unusual. And why shouldn't it have been unusual? It was *all* unusual.

Everything was unusual.

We didn't engage in physical training during that time. We trained for burials not once. We thought infrequently of Arlington National Cemetery. We saw Summerall Field while entering and exiting the barracks, but it too was a mere vestige of that inaccessible epoch with which we had mentally parted ways upon first bearing witness to the burning Pentagon.

Now in my thirty-fifth year, the passing of months is a rather quick phenomenon. The first of the month always seems like tomorrow, perhaps two tomorrows at best. September of 2001 was a lifetime unto itself. Curiously, things which happened prior to that month often seem more recent within my memory. It is as though the days separating 10SEP2001 from 07OCT2001 ventured off the timeline, electing to establish their own colony within my mind's framework. They are not past, nor present, nor future. They inhabit a space wholly removed from that linear arrangement into which all other life events have taken their place.

Some readers might be curious as to my thoughts on those conspiracy theories surrounding the 9/11 attacks. Did a missile hit the Pentagon rather than a passenger-laden 757?

Based on my earlier description of the attack, you know exactly where I stand on the subject. I will say nothing more

What I *will* say is that Second Platoon performed its duties with highly apparent competence, humility, and quiet professionalism throughout those four weeks. A full accounting of every soldier's respective contributions would constitute a separate tome of its own, but I will acknowledge a few herein.

Davidson and Drake, the "Bash Brothers," were a godsend. Both enormously strong and hardworking, they were happy warriors from whose presence the platoon benefited hugely. Always sensing when one of his brothers was struggling with the circumstances in which we found ourselves, Davidson would invariably extend forth his kindness, humor, and general goodness to see that soldier through the moment. Drake was committed to maintaining his trademark stoicism and, though a junior member of the platoon, carried himself as anything but.

Vinatieri (later changed to Slyder), a likable and goodhearted soldier whom I had met the previous spring, was diligent through and through. He worked hard and sought to elevate morale wherever he was able to do so.

My teammate Gonzales, a Spec4 with a heart of gold (yes, *actual* gold) was, by extension, the platoon's heart. He gave everything of himself and asked for nothing in return. I admired his quality then, and I admire it now.

I am told he also prevented a group of foreign diplomats from entering a closed-off parking lot. Bradley was proud of his soldier.

Palmer and Williams, those Degree Four gentlemen who had become a sort of Battlehard odd couple, contributed their collective sense of humor to the rather grim affair. Palmer is a bit like Alan Alda in his comedy stylings and could drive a knife-like wit into the ribs of even the most unimpeachable of men. During this time, he largely apprehended that characteristic and set himself admirably to the task at hand. Williams, who also contributed greatly to the recovery effort, is often devoid of anything even vaguely resembling an inner monologue. He was the platoon's unelected spokesman and reveled in bellowing out whatever cynical observations happened to read across the ticker-tape of his mind. This was met with hearty laughter, which meant a great deal for platoon morale. We were all fortunate for the combined presence of Bob Williams and Bill Palmer during that difficult time.

During an evening formation towards the latter half of our Pentagon experience, we learned that the headquarters platoon was to be excused from the duty rotation.

Williams' response of, "Oh, imagine that! The HQ turds have better things to do than join us in performing *actual work!*" was met with laughter. But one man was decidedly unamused.

"Williams, you'd better shut that motherfucking mouth of yours," came a cold whisper.

The company 1SG stood almost immediately behind Williams, which is to say, the very last person in the company Williams would've wanted behind him. From that point on, Williams was Bravo Company's "morale monitor." This was a position the 1SG had cut from whole cloth in order that he might accordingly punish his mouthy subordinate.

Either in response to that tasking or entirely of his own accord, Williams penned several messages to various tobacco companies in hopes of securing a few cases of cigarettes and chewing tobacco. In this he was successful, and a story was born. Soon, Williams was walking about dispensing cans of "dip" to any soldier interested in taking him up on the offer. If only I had possessed a taste for tobacco...

Swapp and Diller pushed themselves hard in doing good work for the platoon, with both men demonstrating a commitment to mission which impressed the lot of us. In particular, Swapp proved himself a tireless laborer throughout the recovery effort and earned a good deal of respect through and through.

Jason Barnett was a steadfast figure through it all. He smiled and asked after the wellbeing of his Battlehard brethren early and often, worked until his palms bled, and complained not once. *Not once.* He was among the very best Bravo Company ever did know.

Brady, the former carpenter, was both strong of body and logical of mind. He often took to directing work details and could be counted upon to exhibit mature, wise, and compelling leadership. I came to respect the man enormously, and respect him greatly to this day.

I've said all that needs saying about Bradley, Hoffman, and Dussard. They are among the finest of men; their guiding hands kept Second Squad intact physically and mentally throughout the Pentagon days.

Then it was over.

Being a lower-enlisted soldier, I was not privy to the official orders which ended those deeply consequential weeks of hard labor, of gruesome encounters, of pointless guard duty, of looking history squarely in the eye. But it ended, and I was changed.

Encapsulating that change via the written word could prove itself a rather lengthy (and self-indulgent) exercise.

I will summarize thusly: prior to that experience, I could almost always be found smiling warmly when being photographed. Since that experience, I smile very infrequently while being photographed, and seldom convincingly so. There are exceptions, of course.

On a calm October afternoon, Battlehard boarded buses and made the short drive back to Fort Myer. Our routine awaited us, as did another cold winter. There would be new duties which ensured our routine would be anything but.

And the winter was particularly cold.

Author (*right*) pictured alongside Bill Palmer, circa 2013, spring.

X

Returning to the Bravo Co. Grind

Timothy Joseph Maude was born on November 18, 1947, in Indianapolis, Indiana, which is to say, he was born just over six years after work on the Pentagon broke ground in 1941. As a lieutenant general, Maude was the highest-ranking soldier killed in that structure some sixty years after its groundbreaking, and fifty-three after his birth.

A Vietnam War veteran and soldier with over thirty years of active duty service to his name, Maude's laying to rest within the hallowed grounds of Arlington National Cemetery was fated to be an enormously well-attended funeral. Nearly the entirety of the 3rd United States Infantry "The Old Guard" would play a part in honoring the fallen general.

They numbered in the thousands, those many souls, both soldier and civilian, who came to bid Lieutenant General Maude farewell on October 6, 2001. That this would mark the Regiment's collective return to full-scale ceremonial duty could not have been any more appropriate. We'd done our part in the Pentagon recovery efforts, had stood up in defense of our nation's capital, had confronted a reality for which none of us were fully prepared, and psychologically marginalized the ornamental nature of our unit's primary mission while being thusly engaged.

The marginalization never fully subsided, not for those of us who had entered the abyss of a shattered national icon, a compromised symbol of strength, a structure whose occupants had no reason to consider their lives vulnerable in the seconds leading up to what was a monstrously violent demise.

Flag-folding, casket-bearing, the precision fixing of bayonets—reacquainting ourselves with those arts would take but an hour or so of practice; but affording them the luxury of undivided space within our minds would forever prove impossible. We had entered an abyss, and in doing so, had allowed its countenance a sliver of perennial purchase within that aforementioned space.

Somehow, in honoring Timothy Maude on that mild October day so very soon after our Pentagon experience had come to an end, we effectively bridged the aberration of that preceding month with our primary mission. The congruity was conspicuous, sacred, cathartic.

And in taking part in it to the extent that we did, Bravo Company, the second company to have reached Pentagon soil on September 11th, reached a shared peace with its pain, with itself, with its place in history.

Casket bearers are often relegated to supplementary roles during large-scale marching missions within the cemetery. Ushers, escorts, support— "supernumeraries" is the term generally applied. Such was the case for much of Second Platoon during the funeral of Timothy Maude, a state of affairs which allowed us to absorb a full visual inventory of that ceremony's sheer scope. I had never before seen Arlington National Cemetery's roadways so densely populated with foot traffic, and certainly have not since.

It was breathtaking.

I could certainly gather a very real sense of the funeral's larger significance. Yes, Maude's high rank accounted for much of that supremely swelled attendance. There was also a sense that this sacred gathering was extending itself outward, enveloping within its holy embrace the totality of lives claimed in the very attack which had taken Maude from his loved ones and from the Army to which he had dedicated his life. Unlike any other laying to rest in which I'd ever take part, this one suggested a grand and sweeping symbolism.

* * *

Davidson had jokes.

While he and I were working as ceremonial road guards (quite unlike the road-guarding undertaken by me and Rohde fourteen months earlier), many funeral attendees solemnly making their way through Arlington National Cemetery en route to Maude's final resting place took the time to thank us for our service. Some also had questions about the cemetery itself. To many of these questions I had perfectly useful answers. Others, however, were either far too specific for any soldier to know offhand, or had to do with different sites (Gettysburg, Mount Vernon, et cetera).

As Davidson was positioned around a quarter-mile up the road from my location, he saw fit to direct my way *every* inquisitive attendee. And as if this wasn't enough, he expended considerable lungpower and mental energy in heralding me as an expert in cemetery trivia. Thus, I found myself inexplicably (at the time) beset by the most esoteric of inquiries, and from such earnestly curious individuals as to have me feeling guilty in proving unknowledgeable on the topic of where some famous colonel's mistress's father-in-law was buried.

The inexplicable became very explicable later that day when Davidson, that genuine wanker, confessed. I couldn't help but laugh. It was a humorous scheme and was anything but irreverent, even under the circumstances. I like to think Timothy Maude would have chuckled in response to Davidson's trickery.

I hope.

What remained of 2001 would prove somehow interminable. Though we were a week into October, and November would be broken up by Thanksgiving, and most of us would take leave in late-December, the work days standing between Battlehard and 2002 may as well have numbered ten-thousand. I rank those three months as perhaps the slowest passing of time through which I've ever lived.

This was in part due to the expanded duties which became our charge. For as far as the Military District of Washington was concerned, the nation's capital and its surrounding metropolitan area ("The Beltway") amounted to a vulnerable and attractive target. The Old Guard, for its part, would see to the security of Fort Myer in a way that went far beyond the ceremonial.

In effect, the core companies (Bravo, Charlie, Delta) would become amateur MPs (military police) for some time. This meant that non–Primary weeks would see us pulling gate guard duty—checking vehicles for explosives, requesting identification from all visitors, providing additional armed presence for the actual MPs who took too much pleasure in having several 11Bs working in a role nominally subordinate to their own, and so on.

The days ran long. We were in a constant state of pressing our uniforms, performing funeral missions, running, and making our way to one gate or another for supplemental security duty.

* * *

A follow-up note on uniforms: the standard Old Guard uniform is the dress blues blouse, blue trousers with lengthwise gold stripe, cap, and steel-adorned shoes which create a formidable cl-clack, cl-clack, cl-clack with every step. However, there are two alternate uniforms whose usage is entirely weather-dependent—the overcoat and the raincoat. These replace only the blouse, with pants, shoes, and cap remaining. However, if the weather calls for a raincoat, the cap is then necessarily covered with a dark vinyl wrapping of sorts. And in very cold weather, a cold weather hat of a rather Russian appearance replaces the billed cap.

One challenge during the winter months is keeping all three uniforms in a state of equal preparedness, with the overcoat typically displacing the blouse entirely for perhaps a month or so. Neither the raincoat nor the overcoat require quite as much preparation and maintenance as does the blouse, as both are worn sans medals, badges, and the like. They are comparatively simple in appearance; less ornate.

Personally, I preferred the raincoat. It has a sort of sleek and elite appearance to it, while the blouse can look somewhat bulky by comparison. But that is neither here nor there. The point is that our busy winter days were compounded by the necessity of maintaining a trio of uniforms while hauling all three to every ceremony in the event of a sudden change in weather.

* * *

There was also an APFT to be taken, as most of us had not had our physical prowess tested since prior to the summer season. The Old Guard takes very seriously the maintenance of physical fitness, and always has. Regardless of our mission load, our gate guard duty, and all else underway, the APFT would be administered.

We took it. Most did well, though a handful of guys had managed to lose that edge during the preceding month-and-a-half. I scored around 315/300 and even made short work of the blasted sit-ups. God, how relieved I felt after achieving a maximum sit-up score. The 2/58 experience continued to haunt me.

I had moved off-post shortly after the Pentagon ordeal was behind us. This is yet another aspect of Old Guard service which can best be described as unique within the infantry, as Fort Myer has long struggled with the matter of space. There is inadequate barracks housing to accommodate every lower-enlisted soldier assigned to Fort Myer. The result is that soldiers are "encouraged" to "consider" finding civilian housing within a reasonable driving distance, and typically around their one-year mark.

There are other considerations, however, such as overall performance and the absence of any Uniform Code of Military Justice (UCMJ) action in one's record. For instance, a soldier with a DUI charge to his name is almost certainly ineligible for off-post housing.

Assuming you've done well ceremonially, have earned consistently solid APFT scores, and are regarded as being largely responsible, your leadership will likely endorse an off-post move. It clears up barracks space (always a problem) and encourages young soldiers to behave as self-reliant adults. But, really, it clears up barracks space.

My own situation was characteristically unusual, as very little happens to/for me in anything resembling a conventional manner. The fact is, I never formally requested an off-post move. And, in truth, Bradley or Dussard would've required that I complete a few pre-approval steps prior to doing so.

What happened was that a trio of Third Platoon soldiers (whose off-post housing had already been approved) needed a fourth soldier to occupy the four-bedroom Annandale, Virginia apartment they had secured for themselves. One lease split four ways would prove financially favorable.

The three men were Roy Gabriel, Brett Thurman, and my basic training comrade, William Roum. While Roum and I had seen little of one another since that past spring, Thurman and I had become fast friends over the summer. We shared several interests and were similarly motivated to prove ourselves as good soldiers. Thurman is a rare combination of tech-savviness, moral uprightness, and professional diligence. I'm honored and fortunate to know him as both friend and colleague.

I scarcely knew Gabriel, but he was willing to trust in the collective judgment of his two platoon mates. Gabriel was intelligent and very business-minded. It was he who, in his commendable cleverness, slipped my name to the training room guys as co-lessee with himself, Roum, and Thurman. Not thinking to inquire with my platoon leadership, the training room guys (who were probably in PTs; there are *always* guys walking around in PTs after 0900hrs) processed the paperwork as it was. The result was that I learned of my having been granted off-post approval around the same time Bradley, Dussard, and the platoon sergeant learned of it.

And no one knew quite what to do.

"Did you run this by anyone?" Dussard asked, a little irritated.

"Not exactly, Sergeant. By which I mean not at all." I was probably working to restrain a smile.

"Then how did you...?"

Dussard's line of questioning was cut-off by Bradley's perplexed voice, "How'd you get the CO's approval?"

"I believe my name was submitted in concert with those of my new roommates." I was no longer tempted to smile.

Dussard was back at bat. "Well," he said, while audibly sighing, "if the CO approved it, I guess there's no point in fightin' it."

That was where things were left. Anyway, if either Bradley or Dussard had genuinely harbored a desire to reverse the paperwork approval, their efforts would've been interrupted. All of this took place a short time prior to the events of 9/11, which created a problem all its own, as our lease was jeopardized by what became an extended recovery operation. Our move-in date came and went as Battlehard continued its Pentagon relief effort. I learned from Gabriel, who had (somehow) responsibly maintained contact with the leasing office, that our having missed the move-in date was in some way imperiling our right to the unit.

It was Roum and Gabriel who, during one of our evenings in the barracks, brought the weight of our circumstances to bear on the matter, thereby salvaging the lease. I was grateful for Roum's fiery resolve, and for Gabriel's business-minded doggedness. Lacking either, ours might've been a precarious situation once the Pentagon relief effort had concluded.

And so, within a week of our return to normal (or mostly normal) duty, the four of us loaded up a small truck and made our way to Annandale,

Virginia. Despite having been in the United States Army for well over a year by that point, I was only just becoming acquainted with the feelings of adulthood. Lower-enlisted barracks life coupled with my being an inherently imaginative kid had successfully tethered me to adolescence throughout those sixteen months. But having my name attached to a lease, well that was enough to…

No, never mind. I was still a kid. I was just a kid sharing a four-bedroom apartment with three fellow soldiers.

In its own way, this served to compound the busy nature of those early post–Pentagon months. After all, my commute had once consisted of a short walk downstairs to the company quad. It now consisted of a thirty-minute drive through Beltway traffic. Apart from Gabriel (the most responsible of us), we would all experience a few close calls where making first formation was concerned. This was not unique to us; not at all. I can recall any number of instances during which a soldier was reported as absent during formation, only to see that very soldier performing flutter kicks or mountain climbers in the barracks later that morning.

All in all, living off-post was very much a favorable change in circumstances for the four of us. Being released at 1700hrs on the Friday evening of a busy Primary week meant driving away from it all for two days' time. The autonomy (imagined though it might've been) was liberating. For a couple of days each week, we would live among civilians, in a civilian community, and engage in civilian activities. Whereas barracks life tends to evoke a constant sense of regimented existence, our Annandale apartment was suburban through and through. (A subsequent off-post residence of mine would roundly compound this characteristic.)

These feelings of liberation were, admittedly, fleeting during the latter months of 2001.

In contacting my Battlehard brothers while outlining this book, I'd often inquire as to what they most recalled about that period. Here I was occasionally guilty of leading the witness, though strictly in the interest of putting words to a sensation so many struggled to house within the confines of the spoken word. Once I articulated my own thoughts, the effect was often energizing.

"Would you say those days were surreal?"

"Yes! That's it—it was *such* a surreal time."

And it was. Surreal, that is. The days, the weeks, the autumn in its near entirety—it was simply surreal. None knew quite how to reconcile the events of September with the eerie calm that followed.

To be sure, we were busy. But all was, by comparison, relatively calm. There's also a sense that our part in the fight had concluded all too quickly, all too suddenly. We performed funerals by the dozens each month, but our minds were elsewhere. There was a war underway overseas and we of The Old Guard, trained infantrymen, were far from its reach. It had hit us in our backyard (quite literally) on September 11th, but since that time the blood-letting had been restricted to a battlefield some eight-thousand miles east.

We performed funerals, we did PT, we provided a presence at the gates, and we wondered about this newly minted War on Terror. I will note here that which may already have occurred to you: the 3rd United States Infantry Regiment (The Old Guard) was a non-deployable unit and had been since the 1970s. This would eventually change (sort of) during the Global War on Terror, but not immediately.

We moved through those eerie weeks in a shared haze. We all sensed that the world had become a darker place overnight, felt a bond with one another that stemmed directly from the inhumanity to which we'd been wit-ness, and the moving humanity of which we had been a part on September 12th.

Bradley was readying for a well-deserved honorable discharge by year's end. He had joined in the late-90s and had seen the height of his Old Guard tenure bridge one millennium to the next. He had performed hundreds (per-haps over a thousand) funerals in his time, had earned his EIB, had married and become a father, and had taken part in the Pentagon recovery effort in the second half of his final year with the Regiment.

His departure would hit the squad hard, though we each, to a man, wished him only the very best in life. I would miss greatly the man's tremen-dous leadership, his friendship, his example.

This period was also home to one of the more tumultuous of internecine conflicts ever to befall Second Platoon. On a cool, sunny, early-November day—Veterans Day—I joined several of my fellow casket bearers for an after-noon of buffalo wings and professional football viewing. Daman's was our choice of venue, as the restaurant boasts enormous television screens and very delicious wings, burgers, and (for those so inclined) beer. With two noteworthy exceptions in 2001, and perhaps three unnoteworthy ones in 2002, I've been a teetotaler for over sixteen years' time. On one occasion, prior to the Daman's outing, I had rather intentionally rendered myself utterly inebriated in the company of perhaps three or four platoon mates, a couple of guys from First Platoon, and an Echo Company soldier, Andy Graff, with whom my professional path would intersect later.

The second noteworthy exception was *far* less extreme. In any event—Daman's.

We numbered around seven or eight. There was Michael "Senator Fred" Thompson, Bill "Billy P" Palmer, Bob "Squirrel" Williams, Davidson, and a couple of civilians who were either friends or family members of the latter. And there was me. Though not a teetotaler, Michael "Senator Fred" Thompson

(AKA "Fred") was not drinking. Between the two of us, we probably consumed around six liters of Dr. Pepper that afternoon.

Everyone else imbibed, with Bob and Bill (the Degree Fours) doing so aggressively. The game that November 11th was between the Arizona Cardinals and the New York Giants, and this is significant.

Bob, being from Arizona, was a devout Cardinals fan; Bill, who was from New York, pulled for the Giants. These two were also off-post roommates. They had also been *on*-post roommates for a time.

Let's take a step back.

Bob had originally been paired with PFC Monte Swapp, as both were in Third Squad with Sgt. Tim Pennartz. This made perfect sense. Bill was paired with a young private named Edgar. None of this seemed to anyone within the platoon like the makings of a proverbial powder keg.

But the Army enlistment gods, dear reader, do laugh at us.

One weekend evening, perhaps during the mid-spring of 2001, Swapp and I were watching a film in my roommate's half of our shared space. Was it *Full Metal Jacket*? It might've been, as that was a platoon favorite. Somewhere around 2200hrs, the exterior door of our dwelling came crashing open, followed immediately by the interior door leading into the room where Swapp, myself, and my roommate were relaxing in peace while watching a film about war.

It was Bob "Squirrel" Williams. I came to learn something about Bob that evening, something I would remain familiar with for many years to come: He is notably articulate even when *clearly* under the influence of alcohol. He is also a bigger guy, perhaps 6'2" and, at that time, around 220 pounds.

In that moment, the man was standing over the three of us, and was directing a look of sheer hatred towards Swapp, his roommate. Bob was indeed drunk.

"Swapp, where the fuck is my pizza?"

It goes without saying that Swapp, myself, and my own roommate were rather astounded by this line of inquiry. In witnessing Bob's violent entry and his intensely accusatory gaze, I imagined someone had damaged his dress blues. But pizza? That hardly seemed to merit such raw hostility.

Swapp hadn't openly confessed to the larcenous transgression, but he had come near enough to doing exactly that for Bob's purposes. Shifting a bit from side to side in the manner of a person whose drunkenness was either just setting in or about to subside, Bob indicated that he'd like Swapp to order him a replacement pizza.

Swapp was unable to complete his counterargument, for Bob had come down in brutal fashion upon his reposed roommate, fists and elbows flying. Had Swapp thought to stand and face his accuser, the brawl would've taken shape quite differently. But between his size and having seized the initiative, it nearly became a completely lopsided affair.

Thankfully, Swapp was rather formidable and had proven himself a fit soldier. Even before those of us in the room could peel Bob away from his target, Swapp had worked to entangle his attacker's arms in his own. Unfortunately, Bob had managed to land at least one blow to Swapp's face with that first salvo, which meant there would be physical evidence of the ordeal come Monday morning. Even if Swapp had wanted to keep the matter contained, he'd be asked about his injuries in just over a day's time. And, understandably, would not lie to a commissioned officer.

Bob was punished at the Company level, which is to say, he was spared any serious repercussions. I know from having spoken with him on the matter that he regretted having lost the respect of our platoon leadership, but he remained adamant about being wronged by Swapp.

No matter. It was decided that Bob Williams and Monte Swapp would no longer live side by side. Bob would share a room with fellow Degree Four Bill Palmer, and Edgar would re-locate to Swapp's room. And when, a few months later, Bob and Bill undertook the off-post paperwork, they did so together. The universe had never before intertwined the fates of such a mismatched pair of souls.

While I was a casket bearer living in an apartment with three firing party members, Bob and Bill were two casket bearers sharing an apartment with a single firing party member—Brian Hett. Third and Second Platoon were more closely intertwined after hours then either was with First Platoon. Not exclusively, just generally.

And when, on the 11th of November 2001, Bob and Bill joined me and a few others for an afternoon of football spectating, wing consuming, and sarcastic bantering (and steadily realized inebriation for all but Fred and myself) they did so as off-post roommates. Please bear that in mind—the men *shared an off-post residence.* That information is germane to this anecdote.

In all, it was an enjoyable time. The wings were good, the game competitive, the banter humorous. Bob and Bill wore jerseys. Bill's Giants jersey was rather aged as I recall, while Bob's Cardinals counterpart was either new or very well cared for. As the game progressed, the banter grew less humorous. Bill, probably Second Platoon's quickest wit, knew how to dig his verbal rapier into Bob's abdomen. Bob, no lightweight with respect to wit, grew louder and (again, strangely) more articulate with every sip of beer.

Between myself, Fred, Davidson, and the civilians joining us, there was virtually no likelihood of things getting out of hand between Bob and Bill while the game was underway. We would've thrown ourselves in the middle immediately. As for after the game, those two had arrived separately and would likely return home separately.

The Giants won. The score was 17–10. Not a rout, but a respectable victory. Despite his team having prevailed, Bill insisted on behaving belligerently. Bob was surprisingly conciliatory, at least initially.

"Bill, *your* team won. I acknowledge that. Now will you please give me a ride back to the apartment we share?"

"Not while you continue to wear that losing team's jersey. No, I'm afraid not."

This was quite out of character for Bill, a typically reasonable (if endlessly sardonic) mammal. The alcohol was operating as puppeteer in this case.

"Bill, we *live in the same apartment*. Come on, man, just let me hitch a ride back with you."

"You have my answer."

While most of us were at least partially registering this exchange, there were still a few beverages to be finished and a tab to be paid. I imagined tensions would've eased by the time we departed Daman's. Fred and I would drive Bob to his apartment, the drunkenness would subside, and we would return to our casket bearing duties the following day.

Bill was a few steps out the door as Fred and I exited. Davidson and his civilian friends were handling their portion of the payment and would be at least a minute behind. Fred called out to Bill, I believe, something along the lines of, "Hey, Bill, you all right to drive?"

As he was asking that perfectly sensible question, Bob hurried past me. "Here, hold this."

He had thrust a wallet, watch, and keys into my hands so quickly that I dropped the keys. After picking them up, I stood and started to ask, "Bob, why did you hand m—"

CRACK!

I heard that first punch far more clearly than I saw it, but I believe Bob had spun Bill around by the shoulder before delivering a solid fist to the man's eye.

And they were off.

Having seen Bob like this once before, and noting that Bill seemed to be holding his own reasonably well, I decided to let the drunks have at it for a moment. Fred was of the mind that Bill had brought this on himself, and he had no interest in intervening.

I looked on passively and in mild amusement as the fight unfolded. Drunkenness had compromised coordination in both men, but their tolerance for pain was astronomically high. The result being that more punches were thrown than did connect, and those that connected did little to incapacitate their recipients.

It was only when a car was placed at risk that one among our number decided to intervene. The fight had seen Bob and Bill roll somewhat clumsily atop Davidson's hood, and the latter wouldn't have it. He threw his sizable frame in between the two pointlessly belligerent belligerents and shoved Bob towards me. I held him back as he went after Bill yet again, while Davidson effortlessly kept Bill at bay.

With some strain, I managed to drag and verbally cajole Bob over to Fred's Chevrolet Tahoe. As we were placing him in the vehicle, Bill materialized quite suddenly and attempted to rekindle their combative flame. Standing between the two men, I took a step towards Bill.

"Bill, get the fuck out of here. If you'd like to continue this stupidity, do so in your goddamned apartment. Get the fuck out of here."

And he was gone. Had I been thinking clearly, I wouldn't have allowed him to drive at all. In that instant, I was focused solely on getting Bob *back* in the Tahoe ... and keeping him there.

As we left the parking lot, Fred, via inquiry, made note of an observation: "Did you see Bill's face?"

I had. It was in horrible condition. Bob, I then noticed, had worn his class ring throughout the brawl. In much the same way as our leadership had learned of Swapp's encounter with Bob because of the wounds he bore, so too would they learn of Bill's encounter by way of the same.

Bill, I later learned, had driven himself to an emergency room which he soon realized was closed. He did eventually find medical help before returning to the home he shared with his attacker. As I understand it, both were too exhausted to continue what they had started hours earlier.

The following day, we returned to the cemetery and to our routine. Bob had been reprimanded to some degree, but little came of it this time around. Bill healed quickly and the two would remain close friends for years to come. And yes, there would be more brawls.

Bravo Company had re-entered its funeral grind in fine form. It was the laying to rest of Timothy Maude that had pulled us back into the ceremonial mindset, and rightly so. War now raged beyond our borders, security was now heightened throughout the Military District of Washington (MDW), and our shared sense of mission had begun to change in ways not yet clear to all.

There were other considerations, too. EIB would be conducted somewhat differently this time around. There'd be more prerequisites than had historically been the case. These would be spaced out during the coming months, with their completion being mandatory for a chance at those daunting lanes.

We were also due for a couple weeks of leave in December. I do not keep orders or documentation of any sort, but I believe most of us signed out on or around the 20th. Prior to taking that leave, however, there was to be a mandatory Christmas party.

Now, please understand, I loved my Battlehard brothers. I love them still. But it had been a very long three months since September 11th, 2001, and most of us yearned for an escape from Fort Myer, from Arlington, from uniform, from any reminder of our being soldiers.

And mandatory *anything* typically sucks.

This sucked.

There was terrible karaoke, the food was miserable, and one of the Third Platoon soldiers tried his hand at stand-up comedy ... with predictable results. When at last we were released, I returned with Roum and Thurman to our Annandale apartment. Gabriel had driven separately, or had hitched a ride with another Third Platooner.

The following day, it was Gabriel who drove me to the airport. I believe he had a flight the following morning or later that evening. Either way, it was a kindness I did appreciate. Having experienced Sand Hill and Airborne with Roum, and having forged a strong friendship with Thurman throughout the spring and summer of 2001, Roy Gabriel was a comparative stranger when I was enlisted to join in their off-post move. We did, however, become close that year and are forever bound by the shared Pentagon recovery experience.

When I took my seat on the aircraft around one hundred days after 9/11, I remember thinking that the attacks seemed long ago. So very long ago. Events which preceded it by weeks and months seemed nearer my mental reach. Even certain high school memories proved clearer, more accessible, more *palpable* than those events of just a few months earlier.

I hoped Rohde and Naylor were doing well.

I didn't dwell on these thoughts for any great length of time, for I was soon asleep. In some ways, it felt like the first rest I had experienced in a very long time.

XI

Polk, EIB and
the Musketeers

The sense of the surreal was not bound by geography. It accompanied me to my beloved Washington and to my hometown of Marysville. Still, the leave was cathartic and I cherished every moment spent with friends and family. I spent considerable time with my sister and Travis. They were not yet engaged, though we all knew that much was soon to follow. I also spent time with Geoff and Andy, my childhood friends with whom I had been in very limited contact since having enlisted eighteen months earlier.

Whereas during HRAP, and while home that past June for Megan's high school graduation, I'd found myself feeling restless at times, such was not the case this time around.

With HRAP, I had been eager to make the acquaintance of that storied unit whose ranks I would (quite unexpectedly) soon join. That past June, I knew my every day spent on leave was one in which my platoon mates were hauling caskets around as I took in the comforts of hearth and home. The leave request had almost been denied, in fact, but Dussard thought it important I be present for my sister's graduation. The "Bash Brothers" were fully trained by then, which put Second Squad over-strength; still, I did not want to miss too much.

But this time, I was experiencing neither eagerness nor any sense of missing out. The previous three months had been difficult, and the winter ahead would be challenging in its own way. Every day spent in Marysville was a day of restoration both physiological and psychological. Having a very good idea of what the next six months would entail, I brooked no dissent within my inner monologue as to the importance of this personal time.

The day of my departure, I took a few moments to voice a "farewell" to my parents. My mother, who had been in tears two Novembers prior, was calm. I spoke for some time with my dad (though our stepfather, Megan and I had known him as our father since a very early age; we had never known his biological counterpart) and spent a few moments petting Patches and Cinnamon, our dogs.

It was then back to Seattle-Tacoma International Airport. All was heavier, more solemn. Leaving for Fort Benning had been the journey of a wide-eyed boy; leaving for Fort Myer had been much the same; returning from my sister's graduation had seemed perfunctory. This time, however, I was returning to an Army at war, to a unit which had found itself swept up in the winds of history. Much of our collective sarcasm, a hallmark of Old Guard experience, had been tempered by pervasive melancholy.

Much, but not all. We were still a cynical bunch across the board; we had come face to face with a degree of monstrousness our youthful minds had been reluctant to process as being real ... as being upon us.

Thus, I did return to Fort Myer with the mindset of a young man making his way to stand atop a wall, rather than to strictly carryout funerals in honor of those who, in previous generations, had stood atop their own walls in ways legendary and enduring.

Plus, we had EIB prerequisites to think about. I say "we" because several of my close friends would also be working towards the badge that winter. Brett Thurman and Jason Barnett were motivated to earn that long rifle, as were James Taheny and Michael "Senator Fred" Thompson.

Taheny and I had not yet made one another's acquaintanceship, as I recall. Or if we had, it'd been in passing. He was a First Platoon new report from the Bay Area and would ultimately become, along with Thurman, a brother in as real a sense of that term as can be applied in the absence of a consanguine connection. A cerebral individual, Taheny is something of a Renaissance man, with interests ranging from architecture and ballistics to endurance racing and outdoor adventuring. Keeping pace with his mind has enduringly made for an intellectual odyssey of a rather high order.

Things were off those first few weeks back in the unit. Just bloody off. There were funerals to be done, of course, and the gate guard duty was still in play. But it was EIB prerequisites that'd most complicate matters. That surreal pall continued to blithely haunt Myer and Arlington National Cemetery alike. It was all so ... off.

EIB the previous year had been a very consolidated series of events. The land navigation, the APFT, the lanes, the road march—all of this had been carried out within the space of a couple weeks' time. One exception was the M16 expert qualifying, which had been conducted one week prior.

Those days were prologue. The Regiment was now frontloading the APFT, the M16 expert qualification, four rounds of land navigation, and the twelve-mile forced march. By "frontloading" I mean, having these things done weeks and months prior to the lanes getting underway. They were also carried out in something of a piecemeal manner, with little done at the company or platoon level. Instead, multiple iterations of each event would be made available to Old Guard soldiers throughout January, February, and into the first week of March.

A soldier might qualify expert with his M16, achieve the necessary APFT score, then return to Fort Myer for two weeks of funeral duty. He'd then make his way back to Fort A.P. Hill along with fifteen other soldiers from throughout the Regiment to complete the land navigation stages.

Leading all of this off for many of the EIB candidates that year was, oddly enough, the twelve-mile forced march. I say *oddly enough* because that forced march was traditionally completed in a capstone capacity; the final EIB test. Now it was a box to be checked.

We did the forced march in January. Setting aside the soldiers who already held EIBs, those who were on medical profile (usually one or two), and those who were otherwise mission critical in the cemetery that week, Bravo Company sent its EIB hopefuls to Fort A.P. Hill a week following our return from Christmas leave.

None of us were as ready as we would've liked to have been. Though the platoons had prioritized PT once the Pentagon recovery effort was complete, and though we had maintained a high mission load throughout October, November, and December, none of us had found much time for road marching.

What saw us through the twelve-miler's completion was nothing other than muscle memory and the grit accumulated throughout our respective Sand Hill experiences. Though it didn't help that I broke my left foot around the seven-mile mark. As a result of an ingrown toenail which had plagued me since Benning, I took to walking on the outside of that foot in order to mitigate the pain, in order to continue the march.

Continue I did. Continue, that is, until—

Crunch.

And there it was. Something had broken inside my boot. Fortunately, the boot was laced tightly. Fortunately, the march was more than half complete. Fortunately, I was marching with Jason Barnett. Broken foot or not, I would not fail my friend and fellow casket bearer. I didn't say a word to him about what I had felt (and heard) within my left boot. I did the best I could to disguise the limp and carried on for those remaining five miles.

I expect that had this twelve-miler come to pass during that chapter of my TOG tenure in which VanMeter and I were road marching on our own, it would've been less taxing on my body. As it was, it had come to pass following a long stretch of time in which I had road marched not at all.

And the broken foot didn't help.

While I still rank that Sand Hill twelve-miler as the single most difficult road march of my Army enlistment, the latter half of this EIB version stands as a close second. It's a photo-finish, really. After we finished—with mere minutes to spare—I unlaced my left boot completely and wrenched from it the swollen appendage it only just barely contained.

The break, though not unsightly, had caused my foot to visibly swell. It was perhaps twenty percent larger than its counterpart. While I should've been concerned about receiving medical treatment, what most worried me was the idea of forgoing EIB this year due to injury.

To be sure, the lanes were manageable with a broken foot. Not with a broken hand, as nearly every task required considerable dexterity and the manipulation of weapon systems or field gear of some sort.

That was neither here nor there. What the broken foot would prevent me from completing was, of course, the land navigation phase. To say nothing for the APFT.

Fuck. I thought to myself while viewing the x-ray. The foot was plainly broken. I wouldn't be able to participate in the following week's round of land navigation trials, nor the APFT which would follow in February. It would be at least...

"Eight weeks, private."

The aid station medic spoke with the indifference of an automobile mechanic delivering bad news about a faulty fuel injection system. He could've cared less for my EIB plight.

"How about six?" I asked, as though it were a negotiation.

The medic raised his eyes and looked directly into my own. "*Eight.*"

While returning to the barracks, my foot in a ridiculous boot-cast, I ran a few calculations and found reason for hope. March was seven weeks away, more or less to the day. The EIB lanes would be underway perhaps around the tenth, maybe later. If I kept up a solid push-up and (of course) sit-up regimen while healing, I could certainly make short work of the APFT in late-February. Once it was clear my recovery was complete, I would be sent to Fort A.P. Hill for the land navigation trials. From there, it would be a matter of qualifying expert with my M16; the Lanes would follow.

"But I will need to remove the boot in six weeks' time, not eight." This I recall mentioning to Barnett, the goodhearted friend who had risked failing the twelve-miler in order to walk across the finish point at my side. He hadn't realized my foot was broken.

"Hell, Mark, I thought you were just bein' a pussy, or havin' a bad day. Why didn't you say nothin' 'bout your foot breaking?"

"I didn't know with certainty, and there was nothing to be done ... aside from finishing the road march."

"Well, I sure am glad you made it. And with a broke foot, man. Damn."

"Thank you for sticking by me, Jason. There was no need to risk your own time."

"Hell, I knew we was gonna make it. But we sure did cut it close, didn't we?"

"Indeed. The break cost us a quarter-hour. More."

"So you're just gonna cut that bitch off your foot two weeks early?"

"I don't know. Maybe. Yes. I have to do exactly that. EIB waits for no man." (Was I always so damn dramatic?)

"Well, there's always next year, brother."

"No. I fucked up last year, and on a goddamned anti-tank mine. I'm getting my EIB in March, even if it means land navigating on a broken foot."

I spent the rest of that evening in one of the A.P. Hill buildings purposed as an administrative center. Unlike the previous year, the collection of barracks and office-like structures which we'd inhabited for EIB's three-week stretch of time were now in a constant state of use. This stemmed from the ongoing rotation of TOG soldiers cycling down from Fort Myer to complete various EIB prerequisites.

I hope they'll still be hanging around in late-February. I must've thought while my foot was still in the third hour of its healing process.

Soon, I found myself distracted by Richard Donner's 1987 film *Lethal Weapon* which was playing in the administrative building. Also watching were a couple of medics, a soldier from one of the other companies, and Barnett. Once it was over, I hobbled (as gracefully as I could manage) over to the barracks with Barnett, changed into PTs, unrolled my sleeping bag, and fell soundly asleep. The following day, I returned to Fort Myer and prepared for a trip to Fort Polk, Louisiana. Bravo Company was slated for a few weeks at the Joint Readiness Training Center (JRTC).

I had mixed feelings about this trip, which is not to say I had a say in the matter. Whether incapacitated or not, I'd be joining my company to Fort Polk for all that JRTC had to offer.

"What the hell am *I* going to do there, Sergeant?" I asked this of the team leader under whose leadership I had incidentally fallen in the wake of Bradley's departure.

"We'll figure something out for you, Private. Just follow the packing list like everyone else and we'll see about finding you a job down there."

The packing list was easy enough. And anyway, we were in a constant of packing/unpacking between the various EIB prerequisites and increased time on the firing ranges. This latter development was, I suspected, a direct result of the 9/11 attacks. If I was correct in that suspicion, I never had it confirmed officially.

So I packed and, along with the rest of the company, awaited our transportation to the airport. We'd be flying commercial to Louisiana. And why not? Civilian airlines are perfectly efficient providers of air travel service.

As we had a flight time of somewhere after 2300hrs, there was a good deal of milling about the barracks prior to our departing from Fort Myer. True to my commitment, I worked hard to maintain my physical strength while unable to run. This I would achieve by adhering to a strict push-up and pull-up regimen, along with sit-ups and flutter kicks. I would also re-engage with my weightlifting regimen once in Louisiana.

Still, I was concerned. The idea of losing every bit of running ability I had cultivated over the preceding eighteen months plagued my mind daily. Even if I managed a suitable APFT run time, the land navigation trials were also timed.

In all, I would estimate that just under one-hundred Bravo Company soldiers made their way to Fort Polk that February. Not the whole company, of course, as many were attending schools or had obligations keeping them on base. But I'd wager it was around eighty-percent of Bravo.

Of those, there were six who were medically unfit to participate in the role reserved for the soldiers of the 3rd U.S. Infantry Regiment during their JRTC rotations—that of Opposing Force (OPFOR). In effect, this meant that The Old Guard fulfilled the role of "enemy" against other units visiting Fort Polk for purposes of tactical training.

Unfortunately, it was a role of which we (me and five others) had no part. One of those five was Robert "Squirrel" Williams, that friend of mine who had engaged in brawls with three of his roommates. He had undergone knee surgery some weeks earlier and was experiencing a slow but steady recovery.

As the senior soldier among us, Williams was tasked with designing a schedule for the truly pointless duty that was our charge. Bravo Company's 1SG, not wanting six of his infirm men to sit idly by in the barracks whilst our brothers trained in the so-called "box" of JRTC, had decided that we'd instead sit idly by alongside a six-ton steel arms room.

Truly.

The arms room door belonged in a medium-sized bank. It was solid, heavy, and situated within the secure borders of an Army fort. It was surely safe.

We six men of the cast, crutch, sling, and splint would render it safer still, and merely by virtue of our combined presence. And by "combined presence" I mean two of us at any given time. Bob had authored a schedule for each pair to "guard" the arms room door for twelve hours' time, after which that team would enjoy twenty-four hours of off-time as the other two teams completed their respective twelve-hour shifts.

This odd arrangement had us working from midnight until noon one day, then from noon until midnight twenty-four hours from the completion of the former shift. Needless to say, any semblance of a circadian rhythm was entirely absent from our respective organisms throughout those three weeks.

The duty was painfully dull and sublimely devoid of challenge. Having no sympathy for the former aspect and resenting the latter, it was Bill Palmer who deemed our decrepit crew the "Shammer Knights: 2002" or "SK2K2" as it would come to be endearingly known throughout Bravo Company.

Bob and I (paired with one another) made interesting use of those three weeks. Cabin fever became a way of life, as did the card game, Spades. We viewed five films three times each. I read a good deal, and the two of us visited the Fort Polk gymnasium during each of our twenty-four-hour periods of off-time. Like myself, Bob was unable to run during the SK2K2 stint. Unlike myself, he seemingly reveled in that fact.

I could go on about the absolute insanity that overtook me and Bob during our "guard" shifts. There were arguments, oddly dramatic reconciliations, innumerable Spades games, more arguments, pizza orders, and a weird instance in which we each retired to one corner of the room to compile a complete list of the other's flaws. That was surely the nadir of our bizarre bout with sustained cabin fever.

Indeed, we often found ourselves running the full spectrum of human emotion within a given shift. From close friendship born of shared military experience to abject hatred following a petty disagreement. In the space of four hours' time, we might enjoy a healthy round of laughter while rendering impressions of company leadership, only to engage in the venomous hurling of insults thirty minutes hence. These were often followed by sincere apologies and assurances of our having been anything but serious when impugning the other's quality. An hour's time later, another round of impressions, a game of Spades, an argument, a reconciliation, a film-viewing and the shift was over.

Cabin fever is a potent toxin when visited upon the psyche. What surely did not help matters was Bob's rather temperamental disposition and my own immaturity.

I will prioritize a story which will render the quality of my judgment highly questionable to even the most charitable of readers, as Bob and I set ourselves to executing perhaps the single most foolish prank we could've possibly undertaken, and took complete leave of our senses in so doing.

It happened around Valentine's Day of 2002.

Bob and I were viewing the duty schedule. There was talk of a shift-swap or some such. While looking at the days ahead, one of us noted that February 14th (Valentine's Day) was nearing. We lamented the absence of any women within the unit, and the fact that we had seen not one while visiting Fort Polk. That line of conversation somehow—and I truly don't recall how—led us to conceive of the worst idea either of us would ever voice or endorse.

The plan was simple: we'd visit Fort Polk's nearest PX, which is essentially an on-post K-Mart, during our next twenty-four period of off-time. While there, we'd purchase Valentine's Day-themed gifts, chocolates, and cards to comfortably fill the confines of a handbasket.

And then ... well, then things got interesting.

As a lower-enlisted soldier and an E-5 buck sergeant, the two of us were outranked by no fewer than a dozen soldiers within the company. It was four of these higher-ranking soldiers who would find themselves swept up in our truly idiotic scheme.

In Second Platoon, there was our platoon sergeant, Sergeant First Class Boorman and our platoon leader, First Lieutenant Wainwright. At the company level, there was our first sergeant, 1SG Cantor, and the company commander himself, Captain Ferrer.

As far as Bob and I were concerned, these guys were the Joint Chiefs of Staff. Of course, they were nothing of the sort, but we liked to imagine we had set high our proverbial sights.

Regarding those sights...

We included a singing rose. You've seen the sort, a foot in height and, when activated, spin around while spewing forth a hideous version of some well-known romance ballad.

We were idiots who knew precisely the rooms the four recipients of that Valentine's Day bounty occupied throughout the duration of our JRTC stay. We had the night off, as one would expect given the sublimely favorable guard shift schedule Bob had authored.

Under the cover of relative darkness on the evening of February 13th, Bob and I made our way slowly (broken foot, recovering knee) to the rooms where our platoon sergeant, platoon leader, 1SG, and company commander were soundly resting.

I'm not certain as to who among those four received the singing rose, but I do recall that Bob had thought to knock prior to our hobbling away. My insistence that he was venturing onto the terrain of sheer stupidity with that idea kept him from doing so. Perhaps I realized then that the undertaking was stupid. In confirming as much, I would be guilty of revisionist history, or at least wishful thinking.

We made our way back to the barracks, and set an alarm for prior to first call. Given the nature of our temporary duty, we weren't expected to attend first formation, nor did first call have any meaning for us. However, it stood to reason that whatever reaction we hoped of our moronic prank would manifest shortly after first call ... after one of the recipients stumbled upon their gifts.

At 0550hrs, no more than six hours after our foolish scheme had come to pass, an alarm sounded in our room. Bob and I sat up immediately and, like a pair of unruly schoolboys, went to the window, crouched low, and peered down on the formation area. Scarcely contained anticipation was enough to have my heart audibly pounding within my chest. Our eyes suggested an element of glee which, given the repercussions that might well have followed, was profoundly misplaced.

Bravo Company began to form-up. Eagerly, Bob and I observed. What was it we hoped would follow? Neither of us had thought that far ahead. We had parted ways with anything resembling a reasoned thought process. And now we waited, curious as to what our idiocy would yield in the way of short-lived entertainment value.

Then it happened.

1SG Cantor approached the formation, singing rose in hand. SFC Boorman followed behind, also holding one of the gifts. They were nearly a hundred yards from our concealed position. Little was clear.

It was Boorman who leveled a charge. "Pennartz, I'm guessing this was your bullshit. Was it?"

Pennartz looked genuinely confused. And why wouldn't he? He'd been wrongly accused of a prank of which he legitimately had no knowledge. I was concerned. What the hell had we done? We certainly couldn't allow an innocent man to take the fall for our brazen misdeed.

There was a brief round of "whodunit?" before the 1SG, apparently disinterested in pursuing the matter further, readied to call his company to attention. Bob, too, was readying for something.

"Company! Atten—sh—

Bob yelled out from our second-story hiding place. "*We* did it!"

—un!"

Bob's bizarre confession overlapped with the 1SG's call to attention. If anyone had heard the *mea culpa* as it was voiced, no heads turned our way to suggest as much.

It was what Bob did after the fact that most appropriately capstoned our exercise in unbridled insanity. The man (twenty-five years of age at the time) leapt into bed and hid under the covers, as though in doing so he would effectively stave off whatever UCMJ action might have awaited us.

Cabin fever had consumed the better part of our collective judgment.

Fortune smiled upon us, as nothing was ever said of the mysterious Valentine's Day gifts. Some weeks later, we divulged to Pennartz the details of our superhuman idiocy. He laughed and credited us with possessing considerable boldness. Exchange "boldness" for "stupidity" ...

That was the SK2K2 experience for myself, for Bob, and for four other invalids. While I cannot speak for the group in its entirety, Bob and I exercised with considerable intensity throughout those twenty or so days. And while I'd been unable to run, I was confident my overall fitness level would see me through the land navigation and APFT prerequisites.

The JRTC excursion concluded a few days short of my self-imposed six-week deadline. I had favored that left foot carefully since the broken bone had been set. Meanwhile, the boot-cast performed nicely in keeping any stress or hard impact from reaching the healing bone.

Once those few days passed, I decided to take what I hoped was my healed foot for a test run. Removing the boot-cast, I gingerly slid the foot into a running shoe. While I thought I felt something akin to a strange inter-locking sensation, there was no pain and I was indeed able to support my full weight.

"Let's go," I said aloud, as though addressing the foot itself. It had perhaps become something of a stranger to me since the injury.

I ran. Not far, not fast, and not in a stride I would've called familiar. It was perhaps a mile-and-a-half, at about an eight-minute pace, and my gait was off. Still, I was grateful for what had, apparently, been a swift healing process. The EIB lanes were fast approaching and I had three prerequisites to complete, two of which required two healthy feet.

It was Monday morning, first formation, and I was restless. Dussard knew I'd been wallowing in a mist of paranoia since the moment I viewed that x-ray.

"How's the foot?"

"It's fine. I ran on Saturday. It's perfectly fine."

Dussard looked at me with some suspicion.

"All right. Keep up on this day's run, and we'll see to it that you make those prerequisites."

Now I was nervous. Dussard meant to take us on a long route, and the pace would be quick. My brief jaunt two days earlier may as well have been a casual jog 'round the barracks.

Formation behind us and a few stretches completed, we then ran.

When I took the lead, I did so without so much as betraying the effort involved. I ran as though mine had never been a broken left foot. I was as determined in that moment as ever I could recall having been, apart from during the twelve-miler.

As it happened, I returned to Fort Myer well ahead of the next man behind me. After cresting CIF Hill, I walked the remaining quarter-mile to the barracks. While doing so, I thought of McGuinness, that gifted runner whose example I had decided to emulate during my first morning with the Regiment. I was grateful to the man for the high standard he had so effort-lessly embodied.

I thought of the coming land navigation trials and recalled with some fondness a night in which, while struggling to find an elusive checkpoint under pitch black circumstances, I had stumbled upon a First Platoon soldier by the name of Brian Carroll. As we were each seeking the same checkpoint, we decided to do so together. And while unsuccessful, we had reveled in the shared misery, the disappointment, the darkness. Carroll is a good man and had proven himself an excellent soldier in the year or so that I had known him. He was a skilled marcher through and through, and represented much of what is good about The Old Guard.

As for my audition run and its swift completion, I came across Bill "Billy P" Palmer. He'd been moved to the Full Honors casket team, which meant his PT was as likely to consist of heavy weightlifting as it was a mid-distance run on any given day. It had been the former on that given day.

"Even in your weakened state, you're able to outrun your whole squad?"

It's important to note that Palmer very rarely voiced compliments of any sort. I swelled with pride in response to his rhetorical inquiry.

"Dussard laid down a gauntlet. I passed his test. I'm getting my fucking EIB this year." (Was I always so dramatic? Probably.)

"Don't you have something like *everything* left to do?"

"I do, yes. With the obvious exception of the twelve-miler."

"Godspeed, Markington."

Already in BDUs, Palmer was off.

I ate breakfast alone and returned to the barracks to find half the squad in my room. They were watching a film, Dussard included, and had cartons of McDonald's cuisine in front of them.

Dussard looked me in the eye and smiled. "Smartass. All right, get to the training room and have those dipshits schedule your range time."

I did immediately, and before I had time to fully adjust from the much too easy SK2K2 mindset, I was beset by an onslaught of activity.

Later that very week, I found myself at the M16 range. I had qualified expert before, and doing so again was simple enough.

The following week, I joined a handful of soldiers from throughout the Regiment for an APFT. That's one thing worth noting about the Army: at least a couple of times each month, there is an APFT being conducted somewhere on every post and duty station, both in the Continental United States (CONUS) and outside the Continental United States (OCONUS). Someone always needs one for promotion purposes, to make-up for one they had missed due to being on leave, or to qualify for a school of some sort. In my case, I was catching up with what every other Bravo Company EIB candidate had completed weeks earlier.

The intensive PT I had committed myself to during JRTC/SK2K2 while at Fort Polk certainly yielded dividends. I coasted through the push-ups and sit-ups with minimal effort and achieved a two-mile run-time a few seconds short of my best to date.

If any of this has yielded the impression that I was feeling highly confident in that moment, allow me to assure you otherwise. The Lanes continued to plague my psyche. And besides, I had the land navigation trials to complete.

While there had been two trials (day/night) in 2001, this time around it was to be four. Two phases, each to be conducted during daylight and after nightfall. The first was a map/compass phase; the second would replace those ancient artifacts with a cutting edge global positioning system. And by "cutting edge," I am referring to a four-pound box far less reliable than the Google Maps application.

Much like the APFT, I was attached to a hodgepodge group of soldiers from throughout the Regiment when heading back to Fort A.P. Hill for the land navigation trials. The bus we occupied could comfortably seat around forty men; we numbered well under half that. In most cases, those with whom I'd be completing this task had missed out on earlier opportunities for reasons of injury, leave, or because they were new to the unit. There was not a Bravo Company soul to be found aside from myself, but knowing that my dear friends Barnett, Thurman, and "Fred" had all qualified for the lanes provided me with a vague sense of having those excellent soldiers being present in spirit.

What followed was a long and tiring couple of days. As expected, I completed the trials and qualified for a second attempt at the Lanes … those bloody Lanes. My stride had returned, in large part, though every now and again I would feel or hear the slightest "click" when stepping too forcefully during an ascent.

Strange, that click.

In hindsight, I rather prefer having completed the land navigation trials separately from my Battlehard brothers, if only because the inevitable quips regarding my having abandoned my—what was it, again? Oh yes, my assigned weapon. The quips regarding my having abandoned an M16 whilst negotiating the Day Land Navigation portion a year ago would surely have placed me in a rather foul humor.

As it was, not one of those strangers I'd visited Fort A.P. Hill this time around had any knowledge of that miserable error. Small miracles, and what have you.

With the land navigation trials completed, I returned to Fort Myer knowing that the Lanes would soon follow. The Lanes were underway the next week.

It was also during this time that brotherhood of a rather enduring and multi-platoon sort began to take shape. Williams had once characterized the Bravo Company platoons thusly:

Third Platoon, the Firing Party, is a bunch of skinny turds who are prone to UCMJ action of one sort or another. First Platoon, the Marchers, is a bunch of tall, skinny kids who behave like a wannabe frat house. Second Platoon,

Caskets, is where all the older, bigger guys end up. It's also the smartest platoon.

Now, perhaps, he was speaking unfairly of our Firing Party and Marching colleagues. I had come to know many within both platoons and count them as dear (if distant) friends to this day. Carroll (Marcher) and I had endured the hardship of a hopeless night land navigation quest. Brian Hett (Firing Party) was a running phenom and hyper-professional soldier. Matt Genkinger (Marcher) was that rare sort of person who is both disciplined and kind in spirit; he is pure of heart, and I will forever remain grateful for having known the man.

But Bob was also right in many respects. Third Platoon guys seemed to cross paths with the Military Police and were typically smaller in stature than most others in the company. First Platoon was almost solely comprised of stubborn, juvenile soldiers; even their team/squad leaders appeared a bit too youthful in relation to the authority they wielded. And Second Platoon did indeed seem to be a bit older on average. We had several Degree Fours and guys like Brady, Hoffman, and Pennartz brought the average up by a couple of years or so.

We also seemed to be a bit more erudite, man for man. Which is not to take away from the cleverness and raw intelligence exhibited by several soldiers within the Firing Party and Marching platoons; rather, there was simply a good deal more academic engagement amongst we casket bearers. In that way, I was very much at home. As for height/build.... I surely should've ended up in the Firing Party.

In any event, while I was very close to, among others, Williams (SK2K2), Palmer, Hoffman, Barnett, and "Senator Fred" within Second Platoon, right around EIB II (as I occasionally referred to it), a trio of us began nurturing the seeds of camaraderie which would blossom throughout the years ahead.

Though Roum was (and is) very much like family to me (Benning, TOG, roommates), and though Gabriel and I had shared in a few post-9/11 adventures (so surreal, that autumn), it was with my roommate Thurman that I would forge a most enduring bond. We were similarly eccentric in our media tastes and took every opportunity to train with one another on our own time. As many of our Battlehard brethren would agree, Thurman was perhaps the most driven soldier of us all. I was a better man for knowing him, a better man for serving with him, a better man for laboring to match his quality.

That covers Second and Third Platoon where this trio of musketeers is concerned. Who was the First Platoon representative? It was the recently arrived (November 2001) James Taheny, a kindred spirit, expert shooter, lifelong reader, and avid athlete who would intertwine his TOG experience with that of myself and Thurman.

I'd go through the Lanes with neither Thurman nor Taheny. The three members of my EIB II group who could accurately have been described as friends of mine were Jason Barnett, Jake VanMeter (Inauguration Day, R.O.P.), and Adam Behrens, a First Platoon kid with whom I had overseen a rather unusual C.Q. shift some months earlier.

The three of us entered a mindset of rather severe interdependence during those ten or so days. We authored an informal pact that committed each of us to ensure the others' success. There was no doubt of it—I would be earning my EIB this year.

I feared that anti-tank mine to a hugely irrational extent, if for no other reason than because the fatal wound it inflicted upon my EIB candidacy the prior year had been so entirely unanticipated. The others were paranoid in regards to entirely different stations. Behrens, for instance, was inconsolably nervous over the gas mask station, an admittedly tricky task that, though not complicated, could trip up even the best of soldiers. It was a closely timed event.

Barnett was troubled by one of the weapons stations. There was a function check that consistently plagued the man, who was otherwise in very high spirits. Palmer was also pursuing his EIB, though he and I suffered from the same handicap—we crippled our efforts by way of overthinking every step of every task.

As for the "Musketeers," we were inseparable during those afterhours training periods. Though moving through the Lanes in different groups, we often gathered following dinner chow and supported one another's efforts as best we could. I recall sympathizing with Taheny, as he was as new to the unit as I had been when experiencing EIB in 2001.

And so it went: Barnett, Behrens, VanMeter, and myself by day; Thurman, Taheny, and myself by night. After, to once again borrow from Dennis Brady, "eating, breathing, and shitting" EIB for the second time, I very nearly messed up again. Yes, I became a bladerunner on Day Two of the Lanes testing, which meant Day Three would have me on tenterhooks. It wasn't due to the anti-tank mine, which I bested with ease this time around, nor the grenades, which claimed the candidacies of so many soldiers every year. It was range estimation (a task of medium difficulty) and one of the more technical stations, but the truth is, I immediately purged that much from memory upon completing my final station and, indeed, earned my EIB.

Like a small child, I ran to where I knew John "Hooph" Hoffman was milling about and informed him of my success. What I had feared was a doomed effort upon breaking my foot, was instead an unlikely victory.

Hoffman did the honor of bestowing the badge (a long rifle; a musket) upon my chest. It was a rare moment in which I felt something resembling unmitigated pride. I hadn't exactly covered myself in glory the previous year, and matters seemed bleak following the twelve-miler. In truth, the badge belonged as much to Hoffman and to those two groups (one day, one night) with whom I had trained throughout the preceding days, as it did to me. It also belonged to Bradley, my friend and mentor whose absence stung sharply during such times.

But there were casualties. Palmer, my friend and brother, suffered the very fate which had befallen me a year prior, as did one of the musketeers— Taheny. For Palmer, the pain ran deep. Always sharp of tongue and highly committed to his work as a casket bearer, he had longed for an element of tactical credibility which always seemed out of reach.

Taheny's failure was one of bad luck (grenades), nothing more. The experience left him jaded. He'd never again try for the badge, feeling as though he had earned it once, only to be robbed by the cruelly indifferent EIB Gods. I tend to agree—he had essentially earned it, for all intents and purposes.

I hope, given the circumstances, I was as good a friend to both men as I could be. So inward were my thoughts, I couldn't keep from recalling the moment my foot had snapped within a tightly laced boot. We humans are so often prone to bouts of self-absorption, soldiers or not.

That my friendships with both Palmer and Taheny have carried on to this day is a testament to anything other than my tacit lack of empathy for those men on what I know was, for them, a dark day...

...and a long ride back to Fort Myer.

XII

Driving, Crashing, Moving

An informal tradition, EIB is usually followed by a long weekend. Based upon when the Lanes have concluded, it might be a Friday-Sunday stretch or it could be Saturday-Monday, or, as was the case in March of 2002, the company returned to Fort Myer on a weekend day. Though not ideal, as there was no likelihood of our leadership extending our time-off two days into the business week, the 1SG was indeed adamant about his men having Monday to themselves.

There was, however, a caveat.

"Any of you decide to fuck-up this weekend, get in a bar fight, beat up your roommate, or put your drunk ass behind the wheel of a car, let me just say this—I'd better not hear about it. And I'd damn sure better not hear about it from an MP."

There was no mistaking the 1SG's tone. He was deadly serious.

"Because if you decide to fuck yourselves, you'll also have fucked your battle buddies. Roger?"

As one voice, we responded, "Roger, First Sergeant!"

The four of us inhabiting that Annandale apartment had all driven separately to Fort Myer prior to boarding the buses for Fort A.P. Hill. There was occasional carpooling, particularly with the other three, as they were all in the Firing Party, which meant their schedules were even more closely aligned with one another.

I'd purchased a car from Bradley a month prior to his departure. It had been his wife's car, and like the car I had left with my sister over a year earlier, it was a Honda Prelude. This one was a bluish-purple hue which earned the car an endearing moniker about a year after I purchased it.

Whatever it was any of the men of Bravo Company had planned for that day off, none of those plans came to pass. While men like myself, Thurman, Roum, and Gabriel were neither married or had children, many of our Battlehard brothers did and had surely been looking forward to seeing their families.

It was with them I'd most sympathize on that oppressively glum morrow.

My mobile phone rang between 0600 and 0700hrs. Which is to say, it rang two hours earlier than I had planned on waking up on that overcast morning.

It was Hoffman. "Hey, dude, you gotta get into Myer right away."

Imagine my thought process. Hoffman had worded the statement in such a way as to have me wondering if the recall was unique to my person. We were a mere six months from the Pentagon recovery effort; the possibility of subsequent attacks had been on the minds of us all. Lastly, I was still fairly exhausted from the weeks ... months leading up to that very moment.

"What's going on, Hooph? Is it anything serious?"

"Someone fucked up."

That was all that needed saying. We knew our 1SG well enough to know that his were not idle threats. If one among us fucked up, we would all be made to pay.

Gabriel was already awake and dressed in BDUs. Being a good friend, he reminded me to shave before heading in and asked if I wanted to ride with him. I noted that Thurman was at about the same point in the process as I, and decided to carpool with him.

"Thanks, Gabriel. I'll be there soon enough. If you see Dussard or Hoffman, let them know I'm right behind you."

Gabriel was off.

Surprisingly, and unlike Thurman, I didn't have BDUs in the apartment that morning, having changed in the off-post room the evening prior. I'd report to Bravo in civilian clothes and perhaps find time to change prior to formation.

The mood in Bravo's barracks was grim, ugly. Had we returned from Fort A.P. Hill with the expectation of coming in the following day, there might've been a bit less raw anger populating the hallways and rooms. That we had been granted a day off only to have it rendered forfeit because of a fellow soldier's mistake—that was enough to incapacitate company morale.

It was Palmer.

My close friend and Second Platoon's sharpest wit. Failing to earn his EIB had run roughshod over the man, and his better judgment had suffered because of it.

Driving under the influence of alcohol is not smiled upon by Virginia law enforcement, nor by the United States Army. And in driving as such, Bill had run afoul of both. While Virginia law enforcement had been content with limiting its punishment of the man to the man himself, Bravo Company's 1SG and company commander were more inclined to spread such things around.

Selfishness would not do.

Perhaps had I been a better friend to Billy P during and immediately following our return, he wouldn't have behaved with such rank recklessness. But I hadn't, and so he had ... and there we were, in the barracks on what was supposed to have been a much-deserved day off.

The 1SG was energetic. It's as though he saw the need to compensate for what would, of course, be a deficit of energy amongst his one-hundred-twenty soldiers, not even the most patriotic of whom had any interest in cleaning weapons that day.

Cleaning weapons is exactly how we spent our time. It was the work we had planned on completing at some point later that week, rather than twelve hours after our return from EIB. Even the elation of having earned the badge was insufficient where maintaining my own morale was concerned. This was a shitty set of circumstances.

Above all, I was worried about Bill. With Bob and Bill, I had formed the most unlikely of connections that previous year. Both were college educated, and quick to remind others (and one another) of their verbal prowess. That we would form a trio was perhaps inevitable, despite the fact that I (a) was indeed a teetotaler, (b) was several years younger, and (c) was not given to the general debauchery in which they occasionally reveled. In effect, I was the kid brother of the group.

Thus, I was worried about Bill, as he'd become a widely-detested figure within the company that day. While his reputation would recover, he was despondent. There was allegedly a platoon sergeant (Firing Party?) looking to visit violent retribution upon Billy P, though the two didn't cross paths that day.

Characteristically, Bob elected to, under the circumstances, take advantage of Bravo Company's "Open Door Policy," which in theory allowed for any soldier of any rank to at any time enter the company commander's "open door" in order to voice a concern. This policy existed for the sake of keeping congress people (and their constituents) happy, but was generally understood as a non-option option. Using the "Open Door Policy" was an exercise in futility, as company commanders were rarely inclined to do anything other than politely listen for perhaps forty-five seconds' time prior to politely asking the soldier to get the fuck out of his office. Unless, that is, the soldier had a *legitimate* concern to voice.

Bob was not in the least discouraged. As I understand it, the conversation between Sgt. Bob "Squirrel" Williams can best be paraphrased as follows:

"Sir, I think it's unfair that you have chosen to punish the company in its entirety for the actions of one man."

"That it? Okay, thank you for your concern."

Again, this is a severely truncated rendering of that ill-advised exchange (as reenacted by Bob for his platoon mates' amusement), but it succinctly captures its essence and outcome. Only Bob would've possessed the monolithic gall to do as he'd done.

We were released around 1600hrs, and our collective spirits had recovered to some degree. There's something soothing in the phenomenon of shared misery. None of us had any interest in cleaning weapons for eight hours' time on what was supposed to be a day away from it all. But if weapons were to be cleaned, we were happy to be doing so alongside one another.

To his incalculable credit, Ebner had hosted perhaps ten or so soldiers in his room and played a couple of films for the group as weapons components, strewn about his floor, were slowly cleansed of their carbon residue. He was a model of human decency on that day, and on countless others.

Admittedly, the spring/summer omens didn't appear overly favorable for Bravo Company, not if our first day following EIB was a reliable indicator. Regardless, the mission tempo was poised to accelerate within days, and we all had dress blues to press and overhaul for the months to follow.

As I think on it now, I was rather eager for the old routine to materialize. The rhythm of ceremonies, PT, and occasional range time looked attractive by late-March of 2002. September 11th, 2001 had brought the previous year's summer season to a devastating halt, and the fall/winter that followed had been rather trying. All that stress and uncertainty fed immediately into EIB prerequisites, my injury, and the Lanes themselves.

In what was yet another departure from standard TOG duty, Bravo Company was tasked with providing MP support on the Army installation that is Fort Belvoir, VA. Located thirty minutes south of Fort Myer, Belvoir is an odd base. Home to several units and agencies, it houses hundreds of military families. Among those on Belvoir was Hooph.

Our bizarre mission was similar to the mission in which we'd been participating since October—providing a "show of force" presence in support of Belvoir's MP gate guards. It ran about a week. A bizarre week.

And when it ended, we were eager for our return to Fort Myer.

The spring and summer routine was looking mighty attractive. As was so often the case, I had no idea what was coming. When serving in the Armed Forces, one mustn't make the mistake of mistaking oneself as the puppeteer of one's own life; we are, to be sure, the puppets.

It was now June of 2002, and the preceding April and May had played out very similarly to their 2001 precursors. Primary weeks saw us performing as many as twenty-five funerals; back-up weeks, perhaps a third of that. We made good use of our non–ANC days, with visits to the range, supplemental PT, and even a few "hooky" excursions, which saw Dussard running us to Georgetown for mornings at a coffeehouse.

We'd trained ourselves into a state of elite funeral performance, with

Second Platoon's three squads dedicating a solid week to rehearsing ad infinitum flag folds and casket carries. Soon, we were performing as though the preceding six months had been a mere six days of leave. I was now the default "Present" man and regarded the role as both sacred and worthy. I cherish those days closely.

Afterhours, I lived something resembling a civilian life. The apartment, though very much a bachelor's residence, was certainly not the barracks. I was finding far more time to engage with the written word in those months than I had in a very long while. In short, all was going well on The Old Guard front.

Until one day I was tasked, for the first time since reporting to the unit, with Staff Duty. This was a Regimental equivalent of the company-level CQ assignment. A staff sergeant from one of the companies would be assigned to the Regimental Headquarters desk and would have from his own company a lower-enlisted soldier to serve as a runner. You will recall that upon reporting to the unit over eighteen months earlier, it had been SSG Saxon and Specialist Paxton (with their game of Risk™) who had been running the Staff Duty desk. Because they were from Bravo Company, they'd called their CQ counterpart to retrieve me from their charge, Nelson had eschewed the "next 5 to alpha" dictum three days later, and the rest was history.

Now, I was in the Paxton role of Staff Duty runner. Risk™ was nowhere to be seen.

When serving in a line company, the average lower enlisted soldier tends to very rarely cross paths with senior leadership figures within the Regiment. It is generally perceived as a benefit of the obscurity which comes from being both low in rank and sufficiently busy with missions.

However, the Staff Duty desk is a veritable freeway of high-ranking individuals bustling to and from here and there. Captains and 1SGs cross paths with Majors and warrant officers, SFCs come and go with various papers to be signed and processed, and, of course, the Regimental Commander and the Regimental Command Sergeant Major sit in offices no more than ten paces from the desk.

There is no obscurity for those working Staff Duty during the daylight hours.

"I can't tell if you got a big head or if it's that spiky hair."

I knew the voice. It belonged to Command Sergeant Major Aubrey Butts, the highest ranking enlisted man in the Regiment and a very respected figure in the Military District of Washington. The non-inquiry inquiry he'd made was indeed directed at me, though it took me half-a-second to register as much.

"I think it's the high-and-tight, Sergeant Major. Nobody looks good with this haircut."

"I don't know. It might be that head. Could just be a big head."

"No, Sergeant Major. I'm proportionate. It's the haircut."

"Whatever. Have a nice day."

I had just experienced a mild disagreement with the Regimental Command Sergeant Major ... and I had neither stood nor gone to the position of parade rest, both of which are expected of *any* soldier when speaking to a man six ranks (or one) higher on the food chain. When speaking to an officer, the position is that of attention. Either way, I should've certainly been on my feet. The CSM's conversational tone had seemed to invite a more casual exchange. And besides, he hadn't ordered me to my feet.

"That was weird."

A few days later, along with twenty others, I was being awarded an Army Achievement Medal.

Okay, so I was being awarded an Army Achievement Medal. I believe it was APFT-related, but that might not have been the case. It's also irrelevant. When Command Sergeant Major Butts pinned me with the medal, he also elected to lean in very close.

"Who's your 1SG?"

"It's 1SG Carlson, Sergeant Major."

"Good, you tell Carlson you'll be reporting to Headquarters on Monday to be my driver."

And that was it. No official orders, at least none to which I was privy. I was simply to tell my company 1SG that I'd be leaving Bravo Company as a result of the CSM's whim.

I imagine there were probably at least thirty soldiers in 3rd U.S. Infantry Regiment who would've leapt at the opportunity to serve as the CSM's driver. It was regarded as reasonably easy duty, and it meant no time spent on Summerall Field, in ANC, and likely very little on the range. It was, in other words, a cake assignment.

But to me, it was a death sentence. I loved Bravo Company. I love her still. I had fully embraced our return to fine ceremonial form. The camaraderie, the PT regimen, all of it; I was perfectly content with the idea of spending my remaining twenty-four months with Battlehard. Driver assignments tended to run long. Perhaps a year; perhaps more.

"Blast."

While walking down Sheridan to the barracks following that fateful award ceremony, I thought of ways to extricate myself from this miserable assignment. Cut up my driver's license? Tattoo my face Mike Tyson–like over the weekend? Egg the CSM's office window?

"Or, I could ask the 1SG if he has any suggestions. Yes, that's it. Brilliant!"

Ask him I did.

"Sorry, kid. Better pack-up your wall locker. Give Butts my regards."
That obviously didn't work.

Had I been departing at any other point, and with a bit more notice, there might've have been something of a sendoff. As it was, I emptied my wall locker on a Friday afternoon, said farewell to my brothers, and reported to Headquarters & Headquarters Company (HHC) on a Monday morning.

Upon reporting to the S-1 shop, essentially the unit's version of a company training room, I was told CSM Butts wanted to see me at 0900hrs. It was 0615hrs.

Feeling understandably pensive, I elected to take in a brief (three miles) run, then spent twenty or so minutes with a pull-up bar. I thought about joining Second Squad for breakfast chow, but ultimately ate alone. At 0900hrs, as instructed, I reported to CSM Butts' office.

"Good morning, Sergeant Major." Unlike what had transpired during our exchange two weeks prior, I now stood firmly at parade rest.

"Good morning. At ease. Sit down."

I'll admit that this seemed like a ploy. Sit down? What the hell was going on here?

"How's your morning going, Private?"

"It's been a bit unusual, in truth." I was taking a seat while responding.

"Yeah, I bet. Do you know why I selected you to be my driver?"

"I haven't the faintest notion, Sergeant Major."

"It's because when I talked to you at the Staff Duty desk, you didn't get nervous and start fumbling around for your words. You talked to me like a normal person."

"Truly." Was very possibly my one word response. What the man said was, indeed, true.

"Right. And that's what we need up here. There's two other drivers: one for the Regimental Commander, one for the Deputy Regimental Commander. But sometimes, you'll be driving two of us, sometimes all of us. Means you have to be able to feel at ease with top brass."

"Roger, Sergeant Major."

"Okay. That's all I have for you right now. Why don't you get down to the drivers' office and meet the other two? They'll get you squared away."

"Tracking, Sergeant Major."

I was *not* tracking. I wanted nothing to do with what I regarded as a wholly demeaning position. I had trained as a casket bearer—I wanted to bear caskets.

And I missed Battlehard. Specifically, my fellow casket bearers.

While I'd see many of them from time to time, and had become roommates with three of them in May, I wouldn't return to Bravo Company for fifteen months' time. And even then, it would be under the strangest of circumstances.

As I made my way downstairs to the drivers' office, I thought about recent experiences

My time cohabitating with the Third Platoon soldiers had come to end. Circumstances had conspired to have me move-in to a brilliant Fairfax townhouse with Mike "Senator Fred" Thompson, Tim Pennartz, and Travis Smith. It was this residential scenario that would most closely tether me to Second Platoon during my fifteen months away. If I wasn't outwardly grateful for that tethering at the time, I am very much so now.

It was a beautiful home. Billy P would remark that it was by far the best off-post residence he had personally visited since reporting to The Old Guard. There were surely many officers and senior NCOs who lived in larger and perhaps more pleasant homes, but only by the narrowest of margins. We had done well for ourselves.

Fairfax was miles away and far from mind ... and I had reached the drivers' office.

The senior driver was on his way out of the Army, which meant the orientation process was left largely to PFC Daniel Johnson, a very tall kid who had been plucked from Echo Company. Echo was also known as Honor Guard Company, as it was home to the Regiment's tallest soldiers and (arguably) its best marchers. I'd wager that Bravo's Marching Platoon was commensurate in terms of discipline and precision of movement, but they were shorter man-for-man by around one-two inches. And mind you, within Bravo Company, First Platoon tended to run rather tall.

I liked Johnson immediately. He was the sort of person who belonged in the Command Group driver role. Courteous, responsible, and content with the job and all it entailed. He couldn't understand my being unhappy with what he regarded as an enviable duty. It is to his credit that Johnson doesn't allow such things to rankle him. Unlike a great many within the Regiment, he was uniquely averse to cynicism. I would wager he still is.

Drivers were charged with pressing the uniforms of those they were tasked with driving. So, I spent a great deal of time doing exactly that. I came to know CSM Butts' dress blues and Class A jacket as well as I knew my own.

Drivers were also expected to drive their drivees to and from, well, everywhere. This meant driving CSM Butts to various offices and ceremonial sites throughout Washington, D.C., Arlington National Cemetery, and to the Pentagon. I also drove him to both Fort Belvoir and Fort A.P. Hill on a couple of occasions.

During a trip to the Pentagon, I had dropped off both CSM Butts and the S-3 (Operations) Sergeant Major, and was waiting in the vast parking lot for their meeting to conclude. Because of the lot's curious arrangement, making my way back to the pickup location required my re-entering the large road network that encircles the great structure. It's a bit like one of those roads which surrounds and intercuts a sizable airport.

While looking for the turn-in, I noticed a bus to my left and rear. Not realizing the bus had gained on me, I began to change lanes and, in so doing, placed the driver-side panels of my hapless minivan squarely in the path of a hefty oncoming land vessel.

The crash was deafening.

If forced to wager it, I'd estimate the bus had been moving at a speed of twenty-five miles per hour when it struck the left flank of my van. Though the impact was largely limited to the sliding panel door, somehow my own window was destroyed. I was fine, at least in body. Psychologically, I would rather have run back to Marysville than to the pick-up point where I knew that very moment two Sergeants Major were awaiting me ... awaiting me and a functional, undamaged van.

Rather than running three-thousand miles due west, I reluctantly made my way on foot to CSM Butts and Sergeant Major Todd Hunter. They were plainly confused as to where I had left the van.

My explanation was either nonsensical or inadequate. I'm not certain what I expected would happen in that moment. Would either of the E-9s—one a Sergeant Major, the other a Command Sergeant Major—see fit to drop me then and there? As in, right *on* the Pentagon grounds?

No, in fact.

Both were expected back on Fort Myer within the hour, so alternate transportation took precedence over the meting out of my punishment. Hunter, with whom I was only scarcely acquainted, placed a call on his mobile. Within fifteen minutes' time, another driver arrived.

I stuck around for legal reasons. There was, after all, a crash to be investigated. After providing my statement and assuring the investigating authorities that my van was insured by John Q. Taxpayer, I secured a ride back to Fort Myer.

I had no idea what to expect upon returning. Was CSM Butts upset? He hadn't indicated as much. Sergeant Major Hunter had seemed irritated, but certainly not angry. Might this result in my return to Bravo Company, and to the way of life I had come to so proudly inhabit? Had I subconsciously destroyed a Command Group minivan to achieve that outcome?

The answer, of course, was no. I had simply been distracted when changing lanes. Admittedly, the nature of my circumstances had lent itself to looking inward than was normally the case. After all, I was mere weeks into the job and not yet warmed to it.

That said, there was ample silver in the lining of that otherwise dark cloud, though I was rather blind to it in the moment. For one, I'd soon plant the seeds of an unlikely professional connection with Sergeant Major Hunter, even if there was another hurdle to overcome on that front. And secondly, I learned a great deal from CSM Butts during my short tenure as his driver.

Short, because he'd soon leave the Regiment. Senior leadership assignments tend to run two years in duration, and Butts' two years were upon him.

Still, I continued driving for the man throughout the early summer, and came to know him rather well during that time. The role of Command Sergeant Major—and it *is* a role; there is a good deal of pageantry involved—tends to render its occupier somewhat remote, even inaccessible to the very soldiers whose wellbeing they're charged with overseeing.

This is rarely by design.

Rather, lower-enlisted soldiers (and most NCOs) tend to avoid figures of such high rank and great standing within a given unit. The risk of being scolded for an infraction of some sort was too great. Even the most well-intentioned of CSMs are plagued by undeserved reputations for gratuitous fuckery.

Butts was no exception.

The man demanded excellence from his subordinates. Privates got off easy; NCOs were walking bulls-eyes. I'd come to know Butts as a real flesh-and-blood person. The massive rank disparity eventually became a matter of negligible importance, and Butts took to speaking with me as does a man to his protégé.

Often while on an extended drive (A.P. Hill, Belvoir), we would mutually philosophize on any number of matters. Butts drew a very stark line between his early Army career, during which he insisted he had been "dumb," and his later career, when he became a reflective thinker and a close student of leadership psychology. He dedicated considerable energy to the sharpening of a mind which he imagined himself to have wasted during his youth.

One morning in late-June, Butts informed me that we'd be taking a trip to Fort A.P. Hill. Delta Company was running a firing range, and their Command Sergeant Major had every interest in ensuring the training was being conducted properly.

We arrived around 1100hrs, if not earlier, and observed Delta Company on the firing line. They were firing the M249 Squad Automatic Weapon (a favorite of mine), and suspended training for midday chow shortly after our arrival. Butts walked in and around the dining platoons, me a step to his side, asking after the men in a manner that was clearly sincere.

Having seen enough, Butts suggested we make our way north, back to civilization. While walking towards the van, a tall and burly E-5 (likely a casket bearer), who was seated on a large ammunition can, put an odd question to Butts.

"How you doing, Sergeant Major? I thought I heard a cough there. You doin' all right?"

Butts stopped. He had been a half-dozen paces past the man when the inquiry was voiced. First turning only partway around, he observed the tank-like buck sergeant with the scrutinizing eyes of a physician examining lab results.

"What was that?"

"Said I thought I heard a cough, Sergeant Major. Hope you're feeling good."

Another heartbeat of scrutiny.

"Stand up."

The seated E-5 jolted upwards and went to firm parade rest. Butts looked at the now nervous man for perhaps five seconds' time, scanned the area around him briefly, then turned and walked towards the minivan.

After a moment of thick silence, Butts spoke to me while looking straight ahead.

"Mongilutz," he let out a heavy sigh, "everyone's a bullshit artist."

I'm not certain what it was about the CSM's words that struck me, but strike me they did. He'd put words to an ugly aspect of the human condition, and had ignored the fact that I was a mere private, while the man whose actions he had tacitly impugned was, indeed, an NCO. It was, in its own curious way, significant.

We stopped at a convenience store just outside of Fort A.P. Hill, as Butts often liked to do. He purchased soda and a few snacks for the two of us, and insisted we quietly enjoy both prior to making our return drive. Whatever resentment and insolent self-pity had accompanied me from Bravo to the drivers' office, they did subside on that day. I had learned a great deal from Command Sergeant Major Aubrey Butts, and ultimately came to admire and respect the man to a far greater extent than would've been possible had I known him strictly as a remote and inaccessible senior leadership figure.

I daresay that when he left the Regiment around three weeks later, we parted ways not as private and command sergeant major, but as friends, of a sort.

Following Butts' departure, Sergeant Major Todd Hunter was named interim CSM while an official replacement was vetted and ultimately hired. Hunter, as mentioned earlier, oversaw the S-3 Operations office, and would be returning to it once the new CSM was identified.

My time as Hunter's driver lasted six weeks, and as had happened when driving for Butts, we eventually behaved more as mentor and protégé, less as low-ranking soldier and high-ranking senior non-commissioned officer. We ran together once or twice, took a few trips to Belvoir and A.P. Hill, and conversed on topics ranging from fitness and nutrition to war and something known as "The Old Guard Twenty."

As for "The Old Guard Twenty" …

While driving down Sheridan with both Sergeant Major Hunter and the Regimental Commanding Officer, the RCO noted that a soldier walking towards Hotel Company looked rather … *thick* in the middle, shall we say.

"Sir, I don't know what it is, but a lot of guys put on weight after their second, maybe third year in the Regiment," SGM Hunter responded with a sigh.

Seemingly having lost interest in the topic, the Colonel abandoned it entirely. I'd continue to explore it myself in subsequent months.

Eventually Butts' replacement was named and Hunter readied for a full-time return to S-3. Sensing that I wasn't overly committed to the driving role, Hunter asked if I had any interest in joining him in Operations.

Now, if the decision had been between Operations and Bravo Company, there would've been no decision at all. However, the good Sergeant Major had provided me with a choice between Operations and continuing to work as a driver. I decided to join Sergeant Major Hunter in the S-3 shop, and in so doing, would embark upon a unique Old Guard experience.

XIII

S-3: "Nobody knows what to do with these guys!"

The Regiment's Headquarters & Headquarters Company, HHC for short, is The Old Guard's cerebral cortex.

In mid–2002, as I was moving up to S-3 Operations with Sergeant Major Hunter, the Regiment was home to Alpha Company (18th century colonial costumes); Bravo, Charlie, and Delta (the Regiment's backbone); Echo Company (the Presidential Honor Guard); Hotel Company (the specialty platoons); and HHC (headquarters).

I had officially moved to HHC. For administrative purposes, the drivers fell-in with S-1, also known as the Regiment's DMV. Those guys handled paperwork of all sorts for over a thousand soldiers, working closely with each company's training room to manage documentation, orders, records, and financial materials in something loosely resembling an effective manner. Loosely.

As for the other S-Shops...

S-2 is the intelligence group. I believe they numbered three souls, if that.

S-3 is the training/operations group. It's about the size of an under-strength platoon, but a platoon in which privates are swapped out for lieutenants, captains, and senior NCOs. And a platoon in which the platoon sergeant is in fact an E-9/Sergeant Major, while the platoon leader is a field-grade officer, an O-4/Major. Lower-enlisted soldiers are very much the minority in S-3, which was a state of affairs I'd come to appreciate.

My time in S-3 was hugely educational; I learned a great deal about the Army, about bureaucracy, and about operations. Far more did I learn in my first three months in S-3 than ever would've been the case had I remained on the line.

S-4 is supply and logistics. Drivers, mechanics, quartermasters. Plenty of turds in this group, though there were also a few diamonds in the rough, so to speak.

S-5 is a myth.

S-6 is communications.

So, what was it I'd be doing in S-3? What did a shop replete with skilled, senior, knowledgeable, tenured, Army careerists need with a Spec4 only just then entering his third year in uniform?

In a word—drafting.

Midway through my time in S-3, I lobbied for a switch to "draftsman," but the movement never gained traction. And anyway, it would've amounted to a lateral move, as it was no more descriptive than was "drafting."

I regarded my joining Sergeant Major Hunter in S-3 as a high honor. I had not made an overly strong first impression upon the man (wrecked van, and what have you), and I had behaved rather awkwardly when first serving as his driver following Butts' departure. I overcame both the shitty first impression and my palpable awkwardness, enough so to showcase for the Operations E-9 my wit and devotion to both physical fitness and to the Regiment's mission; both resonated closely with Hunter. Had they not, I would surely have remained a driver once he returned to the S-3 shop.

As it was, on a hot August day, Hunter told me, in the casual and charismatic tone which was his trademark, that I'd be following him upstairs to S-3, to the Regiment's engine.

It was early September when I officially reported to the S-3 office. I couldn't so much as walk two steps without bumping into a senior NCO, nor three steps without encountering a captain. This would normally have had the average lower enlisted soldier feeling overwhelmed or a bit uncomfortable. But this is where my education truly began. None of these men had the time (nor the inclination) to fuck with lower-ranking soldiers.

S-3 was all business. Necessarily so, I'd learn. There was too much to be done on any given day for boot camp-style idiocy. Sergeant Major Hunter was certainly not interested in fostering a Benning-style atmosphere upstairs, and his boss, the Major, was motivated solely by mission, and by its flawless execution.

The shop was a collection of knowledge and experience which committed itself to the daily fulfillment of training and operations across the full breadth of the Regiment. The drafting team was the physical manifestation of the shop's will.

The staff officers and NCOs were hands-on to varying degrees, but this wasn't entirely without its limits. After all, senior rank and officer status carries with it the implication of keeping one's uniform unruffled, at least while in garrison.

Thus, the grunt work fell to the four-man drafting team. As lower-enlisted soldiers, we had no business rubbing elbows with some of the

Regiment's top brass. But so long as we were there, we'd make damn certain to earn our keep.

Our mission was, on the surface, rather straightforward. Simply put, we were charged with setting the proverbial "stage" for large-scale ceremonies on Fort Myer and throughout Washington, D.C.

Our team sat in a small walled-off corner with a pair of E-6 staff sergeants, an E-7 sergeant first class, and an O-3 captain. This group was responsible for generating mission orders, among other things.

There were three drafting guys on the payroll, and I made number four. On that particular Monday, only one of them was present. Andy Graff.

Plucked from Echo Company, Andy and I had crossed paths over a year earlier. He had, in fact, witnessed my one instance of drunkenness. Struck by that memory, he found my subsequent teetotaling to be quite odd.

"Promoted for crashing a van," Graff said. "You're a lucky man."

"Promoted?" I asked.

"Yeah, man. You'll see. Nobody really fucks with you, as long as you're getting the missions set-up without any mistakes."

Graff took me out to see a vehicle I'd come to know very well over the next year. It was the Drafting van, a maroon(esque) full-size van which could comfortably seat nine occupants, including the driver. In the back were two crates of equipment, though this was not the entirety of the Drafting arsenal; it was merely what was kept handy for purposes of exigency.

A couple of very large tape measures, a few dozen thin rubber squares (marks), several boxes of chalk, and more rolls of tape than could be counted.

"Is there a guide? I mean for setting up the fields and C-Hall?" "There's a notebook upstairs. We'll go through it later. But you'll just learn it by watching us. It takes like three or four missions, but you'll have it down in a couple of weeks."

Every ceremony involving groups of soldiers organized into lines and rectangles requires sets of marks to serve as guides for said soldiers. This ensures that platoons and columns of marchers turn where necessary, conduct their "eyes right" movement at the right time, and ultimately end up parked in perfect alignment with the men and platoons to their left and right.

This is true whether it be a marching parade or a smaller version on the Pentagon's ceremonial grounds. There was also the indoor Conmy Hall whose floor required fresh coats of deep-blue paint prior to *every* ceremony held within its confines. The National Mall, which sits in that lengthy stretch between the Lincoln Memorial and the United States Capitol Building, is also home to various public events in which The Old Guard plays a part.

Most common is the Twilight Tattoo, a routine show which features patriotic music, Drill Team displays, a marching number, and even a bit of historical reenactment. These are limited to the summer months, and had concluded when I was reporting to drafting.

Graff was dressed quite unlike any other soldier in the Regiment. Well, aside from the other Drafting guys, wherever they were. He wore a pair of tan slacks, a brown belt, running shoes, and a blue polo shirt with the Regiment's insignia emblazoned over the left breast. Within two days' time, I would join Graff in that resemblance.

One of the senior Drafting guys, a gentleman named Sean Levitt, had shown up one evening to a late spring ceremony. He and another Drafting team member had setup the marks earlier in the day, rendering his presence that evening necessary only for the removal of the marks upon the ceremony's completion.

For reasons which were never made clear, Levitt didn't arrive in uniform. Instead, he wore clothing almost identical to what Graff was wearing the day I reported to S-3.

At some point following the ceremony's completion, the Regimental Commanding Officer noticed Levitt and approached him. Following a brief conversation, it was decided that Levitt's choice of clothing would become official Drafting uniform.

This amounted to one of the more controversial elements of the already lightning rod-like nature of that peculiar assignment.

Lightning rod? Doesn't that contradict Graff's statement about people leaving us alone?

Graff was mostly correct in his assessment. But there were a couple of older, stodgier NCOs within the HHC corridors who took exception to a group of soldiers milling about the building (to say nothing for Myer and D.C.) in what was, without question, non-martial attire.

Polo shirt aside, there was another risk for conflict inherent in our role. Our work saw us intersecting routinely with NCOs and officers throughout the Regiment. We'd oversee the coordination of ten-man work details, liaise with team and squad leaders, and often found ourselves orienting decidedly disoriented officers when the need arose.

A few layers of defense shielded us from the sort of, "Hey, lock it up" fireworks so often associated with garrison life, particularly in the infantry. The uniform was one such layer. It was utterly devoid of any rank insignia. Junior NCOs couldn't discern whether we were of equal rank to themselves; junior officers thought we might be fellow lieutenants.

In my case, it was wholly ineffective with Bravo Company, whose leadership figures recognized me as a Spec4.

Another layer was that of the men for whom we worked. Simply because of the way we carried ourselves, it was presumed that whatever we were doing was, well, important ... and was being carried out by order of either the Major (who outranked every company commander) or Sergeant Major Hunter (who outranked every company 1SG). Even if some hotheaded buck sergeant was tempted to place one of the Drafting guys at parade rest for a dose of ass-chewery, none wanted to risk inviting the scorn of Hunter upon themselves.

Mind you, this risk was only implied. We never once (*not once*) articulated it in the slightest. Let the hotheads cultivate their own paranoia.

Still another layer of protection was the absolute necessity of our work. Nobody wanted to mess with guys who appeared to be conducting complex calculations while running lengthy tape measures from one end of a field to another. It's possible we played up the complexity to some degree, but only for a laugh here and there.

Lastly, was a layer of protection that wouldn't materialize until my third month with Drafting.

That weird DMZ we of the Drafting cloak inhabited was best summarized by a senior NCO who once lamented, "Nobody knows what to do with these guys!"

The outburst was in response to a situation in which the man had desperately wanted to exert a helping of drill sergeant-style lunacy upon a couple of Drafting guys, but realized their mission was too necessary and too urgent to be delayed. He was forced to let them complete their work before watching as they casually strolled to the maroon(esque) van and drove off to their next assignment.

Truly, nobody knew what to do with (or make of) Drafting. And the uniform didn't help.

"Yeah, just get with S-4. Tell them your shirt size and they'll have two for you in a couple of days. The slacks, belt, and shoes are up to you."

I confess that leaving the beautiful Fairfax townhouse I shared with Thompson, Pennartz, and Smith on a Thursday morning while wearing civilian clothes seemed a bit, well, civilian. Of course, there were plenty of mornings I left wearing the same PT uniform assigned to all Army soldiers, but even in this regard Drafting was prone to deviating from the standard Regimental schedule. Often, the mission necessitated reporting to Headquarters ready to depart for a mission setup at some early hour.

We typically found time during midday for a short run or a few rounds of pushups, but morning PT fell upon the sacrificial altar of mission precedence. Which meant that the 2002–2003 timeframe was as close to civilian life as ever I'd know while serving in uniform.

Lower-enlisted soldiers were wildly outnumbered in the S-3 shop. Whenever there was a detail to be done, a last-minute tasking, an APFT to be proctored, et cetera, Drafting was called up to cover down, and not always with an over-abundance of notice.

That was a small price to pay for what ultimately amounted to an educational experience unlike any other I'd know. My time in S-3 was in some ways more formative than my time in Bravo Company, if only because the responsibility that accompanied the role generally exceeded what was asked of most team leaders in the line companies. We were certainly expected to embrace a diverse set of skills and bases of knowledge in order for our work to meet the Regiment's high standards.

As for those standards, I'd soon come to ask more of myself than I'd thought possible, and for reasons having everything to do with the people for whom I worked, rather than with the specific operations role I inhabited.

XIV

The Earning
(and Occasional Abuse)
of Trust

"You guys are basically NCOs. That's honestly how I see you."

Those were the words chosen by SSG Kevin Silvis in explaining to me the often-controversial Drafting role.

Like me, Silvis had been pulled-up from Bravo Company, though he hadn't made his way to S-3 via the Command Group driving team, nor was he a Drafting professional. He, along with another E-6, was charged with "cutting" missions orders for our Regiment.

Nothing in the Armed Forces moves forward without a clear set of orders. Nothing.

Well, a few things. But only a few.

Almost everything requires official orders, if for no other reason than the documented accountability they yield. Bureaucracies breed paranoia of a rather notable pathology. Thus, S-3 shops cut orders for small groups of soldiers to visit firing ranges, to undertake minor work details, for individual soldiers to visit the Capitol Building.

Orders.

Orders.

Orders.

SSG Silvis was a good hire for the role he held in S-3. Detail-oriented to the highest degree, he was the consummate professional and regarded his work as being very important. Despite the pencil-pushing stigma which often accompanies administrative assignments of the sort Silvis held, he was no mere pusher of pencils.

His work was far more keyboard-clacking in nature than it was pencil-pushing. But more importantly, he held himself to a commendable standard in terms of physical performance. He made time each week for a lengthy run, but cherished his weightlifting hours. The evidence was clear—he was built like an off-season bodybuilder and maintained that size without compromising his APFT output.

There was also Silvis' E-6 counterpart, SSG Smith, a taller gentleman who, like Graff, had been pulled up from Echo Company. There was E-7/SFC Coburn, the senior NCO of that S-3 subsection, and Captain Matthews, the subsection's presiding commissioned officer.

Aside from me and Graff, there was Specialist Levitt (to whom we owed our civilian uniforms), and Specialist Ivan, a former Charlie Company soldier. These were good and reliable men, which went a long way towards explaining their having been selected for the peculiar role that was S-3 Drafting. I'd come to know them all very well in the months ahead.

None of the NCOs within that S-3 subsection took it upon themselves to directly manage Drafting. We were often left to our own devices, and our work benefited for it. The role required an autonomous mindset; had any of the NCOs decided to arbitrarily switch into drill sergeant mode, that mindset would've been the first and most consequential casualty.

Three of the four Drafting guys needed no guidance or oversight in the way of PT. Ivan was, like Silvis, an avid lifter. Levitt was a natural athlete with a strong sense of discipline and clean living. I had my hills and my ropes.

Graff was, by no means, in poor physical condition. He loved to get by, and was good at doing so. I often marveled at his indifference with respect to Army priorities. He marched (so to speak) to the beat of his own drum, and was also given to prank-style comic antics. We got on well, with the exception of one falling out which had everything to do with my short-fuse.

Because Silvis and every other human populating S-3 were extraordinarily busy every weekday of every given week/month, he relied on Drafting guys to behave a rank or two above their respective paygrades. He asked that we regard ourselves as NCOs, conduct ourselves as NCOs, and perform work to the caliber expected of NCOs. There is no way of concisely articulating the favorable effect this leadership approach ultimately yielded.

In asking that we ask much of ourselves, we found ourselves doing precisely that.

I hadn't known Silvis well during our overlapping Bravo Company days. He was in the Firing Party, was an NCO, and had little reason to speak with a Second Platoon private. We crossed paths on a few occasions during the Pentagon recovery effort, though the details of each crossing are, like so much else from that experience, rather foggy. We also had a conversation regarding the benefits of weightlifting in readying for an APFT. Possessing a notably scientific mind, Silvis had made a compelling case for heavy lifting in order that it might provide one with a sense of their body seeming "light" by comparison to the weights they had been moving. Months later, I would employ that strategy in keeping myself in shape while my foot healed (SK2K2).

So here we were, in S-3 together, each cognizant of being under the microscope of Regimental senior leadership as we carried out our piece of the Operations mission. Silvis, above all, wanted us to do well. He empowered us to that end and entrusted us with responsibility beyond that which would normally be entrusted to lower-enlisted soldiers in the line companies. Whether we registered it at the time, we were in his debt.

His counterpart E-6 largely left us be, as did Captain Matthews, though the latter would periodically implement accountability measures for the sake of reminding us that we were, indeed, soldiers. I respected him greatly and admired his leadership. (Seven months later, he'd host a *Star Trek* viewing party at his home. Thurman and I attended.)

SFC Coburn also left us to our own devices, because the man was severely overworked and had neither the time nor the energy to do anything but leave us alone. I had met Coburn over a year prior. He was overseeing a painting detail in Conmy Hall, a detail which ten Battlehard soldiers (myself included) were charged with carrying out. Recognizing in me a somewhat sly—if not outright irreverent—soul, Coburn humored me in a manner far more lenient than he should've.

To my surprise, Coburn recalled the Conmy Hall painting episode and was happy to have me in his corner of the S-3 shop. I learned soon thereafter that Coburn was due for a PCS, which is to say he was due to leave the unit. This meant S-3 would have another job opening within a couple of months' time.

At present, things were as they were, and I had a notebook full of ceremonial setups to learn.

Graff was right—they were best learned onsite. The diagrams contained within the notebook were certainly helpful, but it was in setting up Conmy for the first time that I came to understand just what Drafting did, and how they did it.

It was all in the first measurement.

So much so, that a second was rarely necessary. Graff and Ivan taught me well, even if I had proven a bit stubborn. Once, Graff had me run the measuring tape out thirty yards, only to insist that I had gone astray from the reference point we had been using for purposes of maintaining our bearings. Irritated at the (correct) accusation, I became needlessly recalcitrant.

Youth makes fools of us all, as did that measuring tape.

Graff was right, I was wrong; the line was off.

Still, these minor impediments to learning the job came and went quickly. Soon, I was as knowledgeable as any of those three with respect to mark placements, measurements, alignment points, and even the eyeballing technique which we necessarily employed at a couple of specific ceremony locations.

I enrolled in a college course around the time my S-3 tenure was getting underway. Many soldiers, both enlisted and commissioned, took advantage of the Army's tuition assistance program while on active duty.

Not that my community college bill was exorbitant. It wasn't. Nevertheless, I appreciated the help greatly and was happy for the nine credit hours I earned. They'd ultimately prove the first of those achieved in pursuit of my dual-B.A.

There was at least one officer, a young lieutenant, who was using his time with the Regiment to work towards a master's degree. A lot of those guys plan on resigning their commissions in pursuit of work for the State Department or one of the many Federal agencies. Graduate-level coursework is helpful for the purpose of distinguishing one from one's peers.

U.S. Army Drill Team performing in Conmy Hall (3d U.S. Infantry Regiment, "The Old Guard").

I took an English class at Northern Virginia Community College. Coburn, though experiencing a bizarre combination of both "short-timer" syndrome *and* work-related stress, was vocally supportive of my efforts in that regard. As was Silvis, himself a learned man.

I managed to maintain close contact with many of my Battlehard brothers. My Second Platoon roommates—Smith, Pennartz, and "Senator Fred"—helped see to that. And my friendships with Billy P and Bob arguably grew stronger following my departure from Bravo Company. They'd come to spend a good deal of time at the preposterously gorgeous townhouse.

Still, it was with Thurman and Taheny that I'd spend most of my post–Bravo off-hours when I wasn't on campus. But off-hours were rare in those days. Drafting had a lot on its proverbial plate, and we'd soon find ourselves working for a man who demanded excellence at every turn.

By every conceivable measure, the move to S-3 was a turning point. Regardless of those for whom I directly worked, I would not fail Sergeant Major Hunter. He and I had started out on as bad a foot as one could imagine, and I had managed to secure a role in Operations under his leadership.

I would not fail Sergeant Major Hunter.

* * *

A few observations about life in The Old Guard circa 2000–2004:

1. There was a good deal of guilt in the air after war was declared in 2001. This stemmed largely from the Regiment being non-deployable. Many of us struggled with the idea of our fellow grunts braving the hostility of Afghanistan while we tended to the dead in Arlington.

2. Tactical training became a greater priority beginning in 2002. Regimental recruitment literature suggested that it *always* had been a priority, and that was true. But the very real possibility of TOG soldiers finding themselves at war should they re-enlist and make their way to a line unit rendered the maintenance of tactical proficiency a veritable mandate.

3. Soldiers reporting to the unit in the months and years following 9/11 were viewed a bit differently than those who had reported prior to or shortly after. The difference? They had joined a wartime Army, and we respected that greatly ... in most cases. Occasionally, they were verbally needled for having required the impetus of a war to enlist at all. I never witnessed as much, but have it on good authority that such criticisms were leveled.

4. Soldiers reporting to the unit months and years following 9/11

viewed those of us who had taken part in the Pentagon recovery effort with more reverence than most of us felt we deserved. We did what had been asked of us—full stop.

5. Prior to Operation Enduring Freedom (and Iraqi Freedom, which would soon follow), an overwhelming majority of the funeral missions saw us laying to rest veterans of World War II, the Korean War, and the Vietnam War. Beginning in mid–2002, ongoing combat overseas saw an import of coffins bearing the remains of casualties far younger than those we were accustomed to honoring. The Regiment began sending casket bearers to Dover for the express purpose of receiving the remains of recently fallen warriors. And all too often, I am saddened to note. All too often.

6. Rumors ran rampant. Everybody had a scoop of some sort: "We'll be invading Iran next year"; "Did you hear Bush is gonna implement the draft?"; "Saddam Hussein has nuclear weapons"; "Saddam Hussein doesn't have nuclear weapons"; "The Old Guard is gonna be replaced by a National Guard unit while we deploy." Actually, that last one would prove partially true. About fifty-percent true.

7. The Beltway sniper attacks created tension throughout the Washington, D.C. area. It was all very small in scale by comparison to what we had experienced a year prior, but paranoia nevertheless took root.

8. Around 2002, the U.S. Army initiated a partnership with the National Association of Stock Car Auto Racing (NASCAR), a partnership which would come to involve S-3 and Drafting. Several of my Battlehard brothers were fans of the sport. By early-2003, I even found myself pulling for a driver. Hope you're doing well, Bobby LaBonte.

9. The so-called "Old Guard Twenty" was a very real phenomenon. Many soldiers in their mid-second year with the unit would often start to pack-on pounds, though generally keeping it sufficiently under control to avoid being flagged and forbidden from performing funerals/ceremonies. Taheny once calculated that this was the case for around seventeen percent of the Regiment, or nearly one-in-five.

To their credit, most of those who accumulated those additional twenty pounds typically did so at a slow enough rate so as to accustom themselves to maintaining a passing APFT without losing much in speed and muscular endurance. If anything suffered, it was the buttons holding together those straining blues; but even that could be addressed by way of clever tailoring. It was a Hotel

Company soldier suffering from the "Old Guard Twenty" who had so visibly troubled the fitness-focused Sergeant Major Hunter during my final week of serving as his driver.

10. Lastly, the Regiment performed marvelously during my tenure, as surely it had done every year prior to my arrival, and has done every year since. The line companies (Bravo, Charlie, Delta) carried the bulk of the funeral load and did a fine job of it. Alpha Company wore their wigs with pride. Echo continued to set the standard for marching excellence, particularly the Continental Color Guard. The Tomb Sentinels continued to set the standard for us all. And the specialty platoons of Hotel Company (Caisson, Drill Team, Guns) exemplified the very essence of Old Guard brilliance.

Throughout my year with S-3 Operations, I'd come to understand the Regiment in a, well, operational context. I would also observe the other companies in action from an excellent vantage point. It was during this time that the supreme standards to which Tomb Sentinels hold themselves became known to me. Likewise, the Drill Team, who train themselves to the point of robotic precision. Caisson soldiers are hardworking and humble to a man.

A well-trained Tomb sentinel performing his sacred duty on a uniquely beautiful day.

But it is the Continental Color Guard I found most remarkable. The degree of skill, discipline, uniformity, and strength those guys achieve throughout their superhuman training regimen is truly the stuff of legend within the Regiment.

Drafting, for its part, was far more of an unknown quantity.

XV

Twenty-Five-Hour Days, a Promotion Board and a Rumor

Coburn was gone just over a month after my reporting to S-3, and there were tears.

What?

Not *mine*.

His.

The man wept. He bloody wept. He was a man in his late-thirties and had said goodbye once too often to one too many colleagues when moving from duty station to duty station every two years' time. It was with Silvis' fellow E-6 who Coburn had grown closest, and the two hugged not twice, but something like ten times.

To a certain extent, I could relate. Leaving Bravo was challenging. I certainly would've preferred staying put, at least at the time. Which is to say, that while I sympathized with Coburn's emotional outpouring, I suspected the change was a healthy one. Even necessary.

Admittedly, I've lost sight of the important role change plays in keeping minds strong, agile, and dynamic—it is a lesson which bears learning again and again. Perhaps I have been wiser at times than at others. In that moment, I felt wise—I was happy for Coburn, not sad.

As I had said farewell to Bradley, to Dussard, and to Butts, I said farewell to Coburn.

The person who would be summoned to replace Coburn was not so much a man as a reputation. Well, of course, he was a man, but that reputation of his...

This was the first of two instances in which I would find myself helping to manage the arrival of Sergeant First Class Scott Taylor. In the former instance, he was unknown to me on a personal level; in the latter, it was quite the opposite.

Towards the end of my time with Bravo Company, a ceremonial force of nature began to make himself known throughout the Regiment. He belonged to Echo Company, though he *never* once referred to it as anything but Honor Guard Company, at least not to my knowledge. This was understandable, certainly as he ran things. Though not the company's 1SG, Taylor essentially took upon himself the task of Echo—uh, I mean Honor Guard Company's marching training. And made for himself a reputation in the process.

While on Summerall Field, Taylor could be heard forcefully voicing corrections and various commands, even from fifty yards off. He demanded excellence from all under his charge, and settled for nothing less.

He looks a bit like John Travolta. Difficult to say just what it is, but the resemblance is there. I wasn't alone in noticing it. Once, as the various companies were making their respective marching passes in Conmy Hall, Billy P noted that "Evil John Travolta" was right royally taking his men to task, ostensibly for poor marching performance.

Little did I know that "Evil John Travolta" and I wouldn't merely cross paths in S-3, but share a path for well over a year's time.

Some twelve years later, when Scott Taylor flew out to Arizona (my present home) for a concert I was hosting, I reflected on that day in C-Hall. Billy P had us all in stitches with the apt moniker—I, of course, had no way of knowing that he was speaking of a future colleague.

Graff and I were braced ... no, *I* was braced (Graff could care less) for a decided switch from Coburn's entirely hands-off leadership approach to, well, that of "Evil John Travolta" himself. If things were going to take shape as such, I'd prefer they do so straightaway

The S-3 shop provided its mostly higher ranking men with the luxury of an adjoining shower and locker room. It was immediately adjacent to the offices of the Major and the Sergeant Major, and made for a much-appreciated convenience. It was there that I'd first speak face-to-face with SFC Taylor. If things were poised for a descent into Benning-style regimentation, best it happen then and there.

But that first exchange, it was so very ... tame, civil, polite.

"What's up, Sergeant?" I asked.

"Not much, man. What's going on today?"

Okay, he's going to change gears momentarily. Keep up the casual tone, that might get the bull charging.

"A few things," I said. "We need to get C-Hall painted. I think Charlie is sending a detail, but Graff and I will grab the paint."

"Cool. You guys need anything from me?"

What the fuck is going on here? Why am I not performing flutter kicks? This is "Evil John Travolta" himself.

"No. We have it."

"All right, bud. Let me know if anything changes. I'll be meeting with the Sergeant Major."

That was it. We each closed our lockers and headed out. He went to the right, I continued straight ahead.

"Did you talk to Taylor?" Graff was more curious than I imagined he'd be.

"I did," I said.

"Was he a prick?"

"Not at all. I guess a part of me has been missing the line company atmosphere. I was hoping for a smoke session, or a chewing out. But we spoke like adults, and that was it."

Graff and I did whatever it was we had on the docket that day, and wondered what the coming months had in store for us.

Later that week, Taylor asked the lot of us if we were available during the afternoon. I couldn't recall ever having been asked about my afternoon availability by a senior non-commissioned officer. Generally, such men could be counted upon to simply inform us as to whether we were available during a given time.

As it happened, the Draftsmen … er, Drafting had little on the schedule after 1300hrs. Taylor requested we join him in a room for a conference. We agreed.

While Ivan, Levitt, Graff, and I sat, Taylor stood. The meeting saw us touch upon a few topics.

"All right, guys, I know you've got a system up here, and I don't wanna mess that up. But I do wanna make sure you're developing as soldiers while working in this role."

At this, we were entirely silent.

"Ivan, you're coming up on gettin' out, right? Have you considered re-enlistment?"

"On and off, Sergeant."

"All right, get with me later," Taylor said. "We'll look at some options."

"Roger, Sergeant."

"Graff, you're getting out in the spring, right?"

"Yep. That's right, Sergeant."

Graff—being Graff—was casually conversational, even by Drafting standards. Taylor didn't seem to have interest in recalibrating Graff for Army service.

"All right, there's probably no time to get you to the board. Mongilutz, when are you getting out?"

"I've the better part of two years, Sergeant."

Taylor's eyes widened as he nodded. "All right, bud, be ready to start looking at that promotion board in a few months. How long have you been a Spec4?"

"Not long. Butts pushed the promotion through before he left the unit."

"Got it. Okay, it'll probably be a few months, but I wanna get you promotable sooner than later."

In truth, this had never occurred to me, not really. Coming off the 1990s and the pre–9/11 aughties, quite a few TOG soldiers were leaving the Army as Specialists. Making E-5/Sergeant in four years was certainly achievable, but doing so required a good deal of shepherding by one's immediate leadership. The more I thought on it, the more promotion seemed worthy of my pursuing.

I left the meeting in a very different state of mind than the one I had been housing at its outset. Something about Taylor's tone, his message, and his willingness to develop his men—it had resonated. Perhaps it was my understanding of what Taylor was capable of—his reputation, and what have you—that reinforced the larger meaning underlying his words. Though I was likely unaware of as much in real time, my Old Guard experience had taken yet another turn; the third in five months' time, by my count.

The holidays were fast approaching, but this did little to diminish the Regiment's workload. Funerals were underway with predictable regularity. Larger ceremonies were now held in Conmy Hall, the indoor answer to Summerall Field, and there were missions on the docket in and around Washington, D.C.

I came to learn a good deal about my Drafting colleagues during this time. Levitt was several years older than Ivan, Graff, and myself, and was far more mature in many ways. Ivan was nearing the end of his enlistment and had developed a sense of "Hooah" once Taylor took over for Coburn.

"I mean, the guy is a tabbed Ranger and went to Malaysian Tracking School," Ivan said. "I feel like I've got a lot more tactical ability than I ever knew."

Graff was unchanged by Taylor's arrival, for the most part. He did begin cloaking his person in a veneer of blatant recalcitrance soon thereafter. It was effectively his way of communicating complete indifference regarding Taylor's interest in developing his men. Whatever comes to mind with the term "short-timer," Graff embodied it through and through. Spring was still six months away, but he was engaged in the steady work of checking out.

The Regiment had plenty on its plate during the fall and winter months. The mission load had slowed just enough to allow for slightly increased range time and the like. That being the case, even Drafting guys were occasionally ordered to the firing line for a day.

It was also a good time to get caught up on PT records. The Regiment does a good job of keeping its men physically fit during those incredibly busy summer months, though the mission load itself plays a big part in achieving that end. Yes, the "Old Guard Twenty" tends to manifest regardless; but only about one-in-five soldiers struggle in that respect.

Drafting would take an APFT along with the rest of HHC. This would be a good time to demonstrate for Taylor my worth … a worth I had strived daily to cultivate; a worth I had jeopardized only twice in my nearly two years with the unit.

On a cool October's night, shortly after 1700hrs, I went about my pre–APFT ritual like a man possessed. Likely by accident, I had discovered that preparing for the APFT was best done in reverse order. This meant putting my body through numerous CIF Hill sprints, following that with several sets of sit-ups, and finishing with as many rounds of push-ups as I could manage prior to reaching muscle failure.

Whatever level of intensity my previous rounds of preparation had reached, this one exceeded them. Paranoia had taken root, and the possibility of producing anything short of a maximum score drove me to perform beyond my imagined physiological/psychological threshold.

The work proved worthwhile. I scored well over 300 on the APFT three days later and provided SFC Taylor with good reason to believe that I did not regard my Drafting tenure as a respite from Army standards. Even Graff managed within five-ten points of 270. He was a better soldier than he let on. Always.

Taylor was sufficiently satisfied with respect to our physical fitness…

…And the work of ceremonial drafting could now be seen to without fear on his part that his men's soldiering aptitude had been compromised as a side-effect of our decidedly civilian attire.

Graff, along with the other two, had acquainted me closely with most of the work that was Drafting's charge. There remained several ceremonies that needed to be learned on-site, which typically relegated them to the realm of mystery until said ceremonies came to pass in an official capacity. Once they did, Drafting would make its way to the site and apply its touch. I learned largely by way of observation in most cases, but Graff held my feet to the fire at times.

One such ceremony was a Tomb of the Unknown Soldier wreath-laying, which saw that sacred site populated to capacity with Old Guard soldiers, observing civilians, government officials, and foreign dignitaries. These missions invariably required an early first call for all involved. The reasoning was simple: on-site rehearsal was essential. There is simply no other structure or setup quite like the Tomb and its massive staircase, which meant marching elements needed to be reacquainted with the ascent hours prior to each such mission.

President George W. Bush along with several senior government and military figures attend a Wreath Laying Ceremony at the Tomb of the Unknown Soldier in May of 2003. Setting up the marks for such ceremonies was a fixture in the Drafting schedule (3d U.S. Infantry Regiment, "The Old Guard").

Which meant Drafting needed to arrive earlier still, with an 0330hrs wake-up call.

A positive aspect of this early-rise was a near total absence of traffic heading into Arlington from my beautiful Fairfax community. Meeting Graff at HHC around 0415hrs, we had only an hour until the companies would make their way to the Tomb. Our job was to ensure those men knew where to end up after they had ascended that sacred staircase.

I remember experiencing an all-too-familiar feeling when first chalking up those stairs. It had struck me over a year earlier, when I took part in the 2001 Memorial Day Weekend flag placement process. Each year, the Regiment sets itself to the large-scale task of emplacing a small American flag before every headstone in Arlington National Cemetery. This amounts to well over two-hundred-thousand flags emplaced approximately one foot from the headstone itself. The "one foot" in question is quite literally the soldier's boot-clad foot, which he positions against the headstone, toes first, planting the flag just behind his heel.

Suffice it to say, I was slightly troubled by what seemed an intrusion upon the hallowed soil atop each soldier's remains. Granted, the way the sausage of The Old Guard is made requires intrusions of that sort on an hourly basis during the duty day. After all, our ceremonial carrying of caskets from curbside to gravesite meant walking directly across graves and barely missing headstones at times.

But it troubled me, nevertheless.

This I carried with me when setting up ceremonies at the Tomb of the Unknown Soldier, even if the Sentinels themselves were always understanding of our mission.

A spell of necessary haste one morning as we were applying chalk marks to that area *immediately* adjacent to the Tomb Monument itself saw me pass too closely to the three marble grave slabs beneath which rest the Unknowns themselves. Though I hadn't intended to tread thusly, an ass-chewing followed, courtesy of the Tomb's NCOIC. As had been the case when emplacing flags during previous Memorial Day weekends, I found myself regretting the necessity of working at such close range to sacred ground; it's all too close.

And as for the Tomb Sentinels themselves, I respected those guys and their mission to an impossible degree. I always felt a bit odd engaging in drafting work whilst they observed, but was happy to answer their questions about our niche role in the Regiment.

Mercifully, most of the Drafting missions took place on non-sacred ground. Often ceremonial ground, to be sure, but not hallowed. Summerall Field, Conmy Hall, Whipple Field, the White House, the National Mall, the Capitol Building, the Pentagon, and a few lesser known sites.

When I look back on the late fall of 2002 and the early winter of 2003, it seems that most of our time was spent in Conmy, at the Pentagon, and only infrequently elsewhere.

Christmas came right on time during that stretch. I spent it with Thurman, Taheny, and Taheny's girlfriend, whose father was an Air Force officer and had politely offered to host us for dinner. It was my second Christmas away from home, though not consecutive, as I had returned home during that surreal (yes, surreal) winter following 9/11.

However, I felt surrounded by family that evening. Thurman and Taheny had become brothers in a very real sense, as had "Senator Fred," though he was in Texas.

Drafting would usher in calendar year 2003 rather memorably, with a trip to San Antonio, Texas. Our reason for visiting the Lone Star State during the New Year and throughout the days that followed? The U.S. Army All-American Bowl, an annual high school football game held on January 5th that year.

In the interest of affording ourselves ample site-preparation time, those of us from S-3 who were tasked with seeing to the event's pre-game ceremonial setup arrived nearly a full-week prior. We were sufficiently early to celebrate the passing of 2002 and the inauguration of 2003 in and around San Antonio's famous River Walk.

So, what is the U.S. Army All-American Bowl, and what role does The Old Guard play? It is a high-profile athletic contest in which the nation's most promising high school football players convene in San Antonio for a nationally broadcast and heavily attended East vs. West matchup. Each year, the All-American Bowl hosts dozens of athletes who ultimately end up playing in the National Football League.

As for the Army's part in all this? It's all a bit incongruous as it's unfolding. Few, if any, of those players participating in the game have any interest in joining the Armed Forces, and the military pageantry that plays out prior to and during the game is sort of tacked-on.

In one notably awkward scene during the 2003 iteration of this tradition, a few TOG platoons performed a pass in review for a field-grade Army officer (which is common) and a high school football player, who seemed terribly confused as to why he was being honored by active duty infantrymen. The field-grade officer was wearing crisp Class As bedazzled with reams of well-earned ribbons and badges; the high school kid wore jeans and a loose-fitting jersey.

Incongruous in the extreme.

But my opinion on the matter counted for approximately nothing. The Army had decided it had an interest in football players, and so the interest became manifest. Drafting's part was easy, and we were grateful for the change of scenery. Even given the wide-range of ceremonial sites we frequented in and around Washington, D.C., that canvas was all too familiar.

My first visit to San Antonio, known as "Military City USA" to many, was enjoyable in the extreme. Of course, we had plenty to do there, but our leadership saw to it that we had a few hours each day to tour the historical sites, the River Walk, and the local community. For a twenty-year-old kid who had, prior to enlisting, spent very little time outside of Washington, a week visiting Texas was eye-opening.

I love culture, and always have. Whether immersed in it abroad or stateside, the experience of acquainting myself with a distinctive way of life is enriching.

The football game was enjoyable, and we of the S-3 cohort found ourselves caught up in its nearly every play. Though it was ultimately a rout (East defeated West 47–3), the athleticism on display was nothing short of impressive.

Things got going a week following San Antonio. By "things" I mean the steady progression of Drafting labor. Summerall Field and C-Hall ceremonies were effectively weekly or bi-weekly fixtures on the schedule, with Pentagon missions materializing monthly. Our steady, reliable, and nearly flawless completion of each mission had the incidental effect of earning Scott Taylor's near-total trust.

Which is not to suggest that the man didn't double-check our work whenever time permitted, but he relied *very heavily* upon us to perform with something like total autonomy. Alongside Sergeant Major Hunter, there was nobody I more feared disappointing.

During this chapter of my TOG experience, I daily learned something new and noteworthy about Army operations:

1. Every S-3 shop in the Army is characterized by a breathtaking intersection of knowledge, experience, diligence, and quiet profes-sionalism. Grizzled senior NCOs, sharp-minded officers, ambitious mid-level NCOs, and a few lower-enlisted soldiers self-consciously hoping to prove themselves useful—these combine to render S-3 the most effective collection of human bodies and minds under any single roof within any given battalion, regiment, division, et cetera.

   Simply breathtaking.

2. Company commanders and 1SGs are often as misinformed regard-ing mission details as are those under their leadership. In as many as thirty instances (by my nearest estimation), an O-3/Captain in command of one of the companies, an O-2/1LT operating as XO for one of the companies, or an irritable company 1SG approached me with any number of questions. "Where are we supposed to put our guys?"; "Is there a chow truck coming or are we doing MREs?'" "Did the report time change?"; "Why are those guys in BDUs? Are *we* supposed to be in BDUs?"; "How is ammo being disbursed?"; "Are we in the right spot?"; "Can you tell me where we're supposed to drop our rucks?"

   This phenomenon I invariably found gratifying.

   For one, these guys seemed to have no interest in rank disparity when putting voice to such inquiries. They knew we were from S-3, which meant we probably knew things they didn't.

   Secondly, when a man is placed at the mercy of misinformation, humility and irritation are soon to follow. Suddenly, they care not as to the *source* of the correct information; they care only for the *acquisition* of said correct information. That fact alone often placed Drafting in the role of S-3 intelligencer.

3. No operations hub in existence (military or otherwise) can func-tion as anything other than a collection of competent professionals. Rank is almost an afterthought in the S-3 shop. I'm not referring to Drafting, specifically. I'm referring to everyone else. There's a

Major and a Sergeant Major, and their word is law in the shop. But the mood is not one of said Major and SGM walking about placing men at attention or parade rest; nor do captains and lieutenants waste time with regimented discourse and behavior. One competent, patriotic professional looks to another professional and communicates a message. That message is received and acted upon, with any difference in rank between them amounting to a secondary (if not tertiary) consideration.

I found this fascinating.

Lower-enlisted men know very little about how the Army works. This is also true of many mid-level NCOs. It would've been true of me had I served the entirety of my enlistment in a line company. An offshoot of this maxim is the fact that many mid-level NCOs don't know how to work the Army.

First, this is how the Army *works*. Any given military unit is essentially a multi-faceted, complex engine organized around a primary mission statement. Infantry units are required to close with, engage, and kill the enemy. Medical units are required to treat the injuries of wounded soldiers. Intelligence units are required to overcome the oxymoron that is "military intelligence." And so on.

Needless to say, the effective operation and managerial oversight of any such organization is labor-intensive in the extreme. It requires a good deal of mental prowess and leadership acumen. A lower-enlisted soldier doesn't have visibility into the clockwork of their respective unit's S-Shop machinations to understand the administrative intricacy by which said unit is characterized. Spending a bit of time in operations is essential to garnering any such understanding.

Second, *working* the Army. You see it from time to time—a battle-hardened, badge-heavy, long-tenured NCO who's seen his advancement through the ranks conspicuously arrested at SSG or SFC. Nearly as often, you'll see a soldier with far less in the way of apparent accomplishment who has ascended to the rank of 1SG or SGM.

Any organization of humans numbering more than two provides suitable soil for the cultivation of a political harvest. Which is to say, the Army, like any other aggregation of ambitious souls, is as much an arena of realpolitik jockeying as it is a (partially) blind meritocracy.

During my time with the Army, I encountered types at both ends of the spectrum. Those of the former category typically trust that their efforts, their worthiness, their skill, and their time in service will inevitably see them through from one promotion to the next. What this interpretation fails to recognize is everything else that matters. For instance, much of the Army's promotion system is predicated on the non-commissioned officer evaluation (NCOER) report. The NCOER is an annual review generated for purposes of documenting each NCO's individual performance throughout the preceding year.

And their importance cannot be overstated.

Simply put, when serving in garrison (particularly during peacetime), NCOERs are best understood as the rungs of a promotion ladder. Average or (worse) negative NCOERs are fatal to one's promotion prospects. And far too often, the NCO being evaluated fails to take a hand in the authorship or revision of his NCOER, thereby dooming himself to an incomplete, inadequate, or misrepresentative report ... and, by extension, to promotion stagnation.

Those, on the other hand, who know how to *work* the Army, are inclined to take a firm hand in the generating of every NCOER bullet-point, ensuring no deed or achievement goes unmentioned ... thereby ensuring their promotion prospects remain healthy and well-nourished.

This division between those who know how to *work* the Army and those prone to being *worked by it* leads to a larger division between what a wise NCO once described to me as the "Grunt Army" and the "Political Army." From the outside looking in, one might mistake that division as one which separates the officers from the enlisted.

It is not.

Within both the commissioned and the enlisted ranks, there exists "grunts" who set themselves to the work of carrying out, well, work, and those others who set themselves to the work of constructing a successful career. I don't fault either for the way they order their respective priorities; I merely noted midway through my TOG tenure that there are, indeed, two armies within the U.S. Army.

Those who seem a bit old for their years and light in rank are those who are committed to work for its own sake—let the promotions come as they may. Alternately, those who appear a bit youthful in relation to the rank they wield are, naturally, those of the political Army. May they both go with God in their every endeavor.

We had returned from San Antonio, various missions followed, Taylor came to regard Drafting as a trustworthy extension of his will, and the shop was running well. The 9/11 attacks were a year-and-half past by this point, and the Regiment had returned to a business-as-usual operating model.

A testament to this was EIB itself.

While EIB had come to pass the year prior, it was a distinctive experience from its 2001 predecessor. Echoes of the Pentagon recovery effort had continued to make themselves heard, and uncertainty as to what wartime service in The Old Guard might look like tended to cloud matters from day to day.

March of 2003 looked far more like its 2001 counterpart than it did 2002. I remember regretting (much to my surprise) that I wouldn't have the opportunity to serve as EIB cadre. Doing so would have comported well with my fondness for teaching, as I had, the year prior, developed a couple of useful memory tricks and training measures in helping soldiers from both of my groups with the successful negotiation of certain tasks. That had made for nearly as rewarding an experience as earning the badge itself.... Nearly.

It was a non-starter: drafting numbered four men, and Taylor wouldn't risk sending men to A.P. Hill for the better part of two weeks only to find himself shorthanded. Though I regretted not participating in 2003, I nurtured the idea of perhaps serving as cadre during EIB 2004, which would be leading up to my exit from the Army.

"Mongilutz, Graff! You guys up here?"

The voice belonged to the HHC 1SG, under whose leadership Drafting nominally fell. We worked so close with SFC Taylor, and within the powerful orbit of Major Smith and SGM Hunter, as to have our bureaucratic placement within HHC amount to little more than an afterthought. But as active duty soldiers, we were necessarily accounted for on an organizational chart—that of HHC, in this case.

"Yes, First Sergeant," I replied for the both of us as our notably tall 1SG turned the corner into our section of the shop.

"You guys both got your EIB?" This was a bizarre hybrid of statement and question. The tone suggested both, and I had a sense that he already knew the answer.

"Yes, First Sergeant."

"Good. HHC needs to send a few extra guys down to help as cadre."

Graff immediately looked to Taylor's desk, which was utterly devoid of the man's presence.

"First Sergeant," Graff began, "there's only four of us. I think Sergeant Taylor s—"

"It's not up to us. This is coming down from Regiment. Make sure you've got your shit packed for a two-week stay; we're going down a couple of days ahead."

Conflicted is how I immediately felt. I hadn't considered, when lamenting my impending non-participation with EIB 2003, that I was, indeed, taking night courses at Northern Virginia Community College ... some fifty minutes' drive from A.P. Hill.

My concern was an exercise in wasted energy. I approached SFC Taylor and informed him (a) of my eagerness to participate in EIB as a cadre member, and (b) of the two mid-term examinations I was certain to miss while participating.

"You tell whichever station NCOIC you fall under that *I* said they gotta find a way to get you to class. I'm not gonna have you missing those exams if it can be avoided."

Turns out the word of an Operations SFC carries a good deal of weight. Arrangements were made to allow for my leaving A.P. Hill when necessary.

That aside, working as EIB cadre was rewarding and an otherwise welcome disruption to the Drafting grind. I was assigned to work with the Regiment's Field Medics and would be demonstrating the correct life-saving treatment of various battlefield wounds. This station hadn't been a problem during my own EIB candidacies, and I was acquainted with the NCOIC, SFC Timmons. He was a good man. I couldn't have asked for a better set of circumstances.

With one exception.

The mornings were cold.

Cold to such an extent as to place it at odds with the season and with our location, as EIB was not held in Siberia at the height of winter. The chill cut mercilessly through our clothing, then settled icily upon our bones until, at last, the sun had fully risen. Each morning was an exercise in attempting to keep warm.

Teaching came easily to me. Passing on memory markers and time-saving task measures was nothing if not reflexive; intuitive, even. Most candidates took to my teaching style. Although there was one SSG who found my approach all too conversational given our rank disparity. My response was one of indifference. Drafting had that effect on us all.

When it was over, I took considerable pride in shaking the hands of those who had earned their badges. It was a rite of passage I regarded as pure and worthy.

The April-August timeframe is arguably the Regiment's busiest. There is a case to be made that increased tactical training coupled with more or less steady funerals render the year evenly active. But that case is bollocks. There is more happening on any given spring/summer day than on their fall/winter counterparts, full stop. Drafting (well, S-3 in its entirety) would certainly contribute to the Regimental mission, and often in ways that went entirely unseen.

* * *

I've long been of the mind that every person houses within their heart and their mind a period which, were it an option, they'd gladly have embalmed for purposes of eternal preservation. For many, it might have been the days of high school athletic glory and carefree partying. And some might guard closely memories of having felt important, loved, or useful—these memories are of days which I believe those who lived them yearn to once again inhabit. I wish for them the fruition of that for which they yearn.

I do.

Had I the option to re-visit any single chapter of my life, that might very well be the one. The spring and summer of 2003. It has a close contender or two, but it's very much in the running.

We of the Drafting Order were operating above our paygrade on a nearly daily basis. What business did a couple of twenty-year-old kids have making visits to the White House for purposes of mission set-up? We operated with sublime liberty and were entrusted by men we respected. If there is a more enviable fate, I'd rather not know it for fear I might prove unworthy of its grace.

In my off-hours, I was still living in that beautiful Fairfax townhome, finishing up two courses at NVCC, had taken to rock climbing with Taheny on a thrice weekly basis, and would soon prepare for my promotion board.

There was also the Taylor factor. I have extolled the goodness and greatness, and various other nesses of many men. My drill sergeant, SSG Spencer; my 2/54 brothers; Bradley, Dussard, Hoffman; CSM Butts and SGM Hunter; and many others.

What I have written of each I will stand behind until I draw my final breath.

Such is the same for Scott Taylor—mentor and friend and father figure during two significant periods of my TOG experience. In Taylor's absence, I'd very likely have foregone the opportunity for advancement to E-5/sergeant. I would likely have not come to regard myself as a true S-3 professional, as the role invited a sense of levity which conflicted with as much. I might not have returned to Bravo Company the following September as an NCO capable of leading a deployed fire-team.

What I learned from Taylor I learned far more from the man's example than ever I did from his spoken words. He is the very embodiment of selfless work, competence, discipline, and mission-focus. He is savvy, formidable, fearless, and frank.

And above all else, he was everything an Army non-commissioned officer should be—selflessness was (is) the foundation of the man's being. Mine was a humbled soul under the direct leadership of so worthy a figure.

That we would form a friendship beyond the walls of HHC was purely a product of our being S-3 colleagues. Such would (*could*) never have been the case had I been one of his Echo Company marchers.

* * *

Scott and I had also become (along with Jamesy) climbing buddies, and routinely visited our local rock gym.

Fortunately, there was no time for nepotism to manifest while I was on the clock. While we were often working in Conmy Hall, Summerall Field, at the Tomb, or at the Pentagon and the White House, the most prominent fixture on our schedule was the Twilight Tattoo.

I came to learn the specific Tattoo schematics mere weeks prior to Graff's departure from the unit. Though we had graduated from Basic Training/AIT in 2000, Graff had enlisted for three years, which meant he'd be discharged a full year prior. Levitt had also left the Regiment, the Drafting uniform having been among his most (though not his only) noteworthy of contributions to the cause. Ivan had re-enlisted and was heading to another unit.

I'd soon need help, and would be the senior Draftsman ... er, Drafting professional.

One of the replacements, Tiller, had been plucked from Delta Company. The story on that was never clear to me. Even Scott is uncertain as to how it all came about.

As for the other two, I knew the story well. Futrell had been one of Taylor's Echo Company soldiers and was well-regarded for his staunch loyalty. Graff, though well-liked, had been rebellious—managing that characteristic required energy Taylor couldn't spare. Futrell was anything but rebellious, and he'd taken well to Taylor's strict training style. Futrell possesses a kindness of heart rare within our species. I never once heard the man speak negatively of another soldier—never once.

As for the final replacement, I had a hand in making that selection ... though there were other factors in play.

One of the musketeers, my former roommate Brett Thurman, had been making a name for himself as a board soldier. Which is to say, Thurman was participating in a series of highly competitive evaluations which pitted his Army knowledge against that of our fellow soldiers.

And he was winning ... routinely.

This placed Thurman on SGM Hunter's radar, which made my case for his joining the Drafting Team rather defensible. Besides, Taylor took immediate note of Thurman's quality and was happy to welcome him aboard (if you will forgive the pun).

Following Graff's departure, that was the lineup—Tiller, Futrell, Thurman, and myself. We would throw ourselves fully into the operations role, even if I was somewhat apprehensive about leading those guys through a summer season. During the busiest of fall and winter months, I had three senior Drafting professionals to my left and right should matters become less than manageable.

Almost overnight, I had graduated from being the most junior Drafting professional to most senior. It had not been entirely unforeseen, it was simply sudden. In such cases, much depends upon one's leadership. Thankfully, by the time I found myself at the Drafting helm, I had established pristine rapport and immeasurable credibility with SFC Taylor, who trusted me closely with the careful oversight of every high-profile ceremony setup and operational task for which on-site labor was necessary.

Drafting was a living extension of Scott Taylor's will. We recognized that for what it was and cherished its significance closely.

At least whenever we found a moment in which to do so.

A given Drafting day might look a bit like this:

Thursday
0530—Report to Myer. Secure our orders and the equipment unique to that morning's mission
0540—Depart for the White House
0610—Arrive at the White House. Yes, it takes a while. D.C. traffic, and what have you
0630–0800—Setup series of marks for White House State Dinner
0830–1000—Execute "Operation: McDonald's Breakfast." Two Draftsmen … we're going to stick with that term … exit the White House grounds with a handful of ones, fives, and tens. Those gentlemen enter that convenient McDonald's nearest the White House and proceed to order their combined bodyweight in McMuffins, McGriddles, McPancakes, McSyrup, McHashBrowns, McMilk, McEverything. Those Draftsmen then return to the White House and bestow upon their fellow professionals a McFeast of infinite McWonder and profound McJustice.
1000–1200—Observe the State Dinner rehearsals, talk-throughs, et cetera
1200–1300—Reset the marks where necessary
1300–1400—Battle D.C. traffic in returning to Fort Myer
1400–1430—Drafting Special (brief two-mile+ run near the base perimeter)
1540—Race back to the White House while hoping Taylor did not witness us departing around fifteen minutes later than he would have liked for us to depart
1610—Reach the White House *just* in time … for some reason
1615–2000—Do little of anything whilst the State Dinner unfolds
2000–2100—Retrieve marks and return to Myer
2215—Seriously, that Fairfax townhome is likely worth well over a half-million U.S. dollars. When I entered it that evening, it was worth under four-hundred-thousand, give or take ten-thousand.

Variations on that schedule played out daily, but what I've provided above leaves you with some sense as to how the Drafting role often took shape.

Jamesy and I (as well as Scott) would maintain our rock climbing routine. I'd also spend time with my former Second Platoon brothers (Billy P, Matt "Bacardi" Lemon, Hoffman), and on weekends, the coursework I was pursuing, and my impending promotion board...

It was perhaps the best five-month stretch of time I'd experience while in uniform. I have missed those days many a time since.

There was a peculiar intersection of NASCAR with both S-3 and the Regiment at large.

My roommate Mike "Senator Fred" Thompson was an avid racer and (by extension) a devout racing fan. And while few of his fellow casket bearer colleagues could say the same of themselves, many of us took a liking to the sport. Not a single weekend passed during the 2003 Winston Cup (now Sprint Cup) season in which either (a) Fred didn't host a NASCAR viewing party, or (b) we didn't attend the race in person. While I attended only a couple of races during those days, that number would balloon during my S-3 tenure.

The Old Guard began, in 2003, to showcase the Army prior to the start of NASCAR events. This meant marks which needed to be emplaced by Drafting. And as it happened, Scott Taylor, my boss and friend, was also an avid NASCAR enthusiast. It all made for a curious case of confounding congruity. Which is to say, it all came together nicely.

S-3 had a hand in setting up nearly ten NASCAR/Old Guard events. This saw Scott traveling with the Drafting team and several operations personnel on a semi-weekly basis.

During one such trip to Michigan, Scott and I ended up making the airport-racetrack drive in his rental car. Upon the race's conclusion, we took that same car for a wholly unauthorized drive around said racetrack. It was a truly grand time. I rarely saw Scott happier.

About a month later, following considerable preparation, I attended the promotion board in hopes of earning my NCO stripes. Taylor had invested of himself greatly in my professional development.

But there were other factors in play.

Promotion boards consist of the unit's command sergeant major and several company first sergeants. Had I attended the board a year prior, the CSM would, of course, have been the estimable Aubrey Butts. In the summer of 2003, the CSM was Hank Winchester, a hardened, grizzled, extremely respected warrior who, interestingly, had developed a close friendship with Scott Taylor throughout the preceding year. Like all senior NCOs, Winchester hadn't initially known what to make of Drafting.... He seemed trigger happy, as though an old-fashioned smoke session was in order.

Soon enough, he came to appreciate the novelty of having a few E-4s milling about the S-3 shop, which he visited perhaps twice each week. As Hunter was the S-3 SGM, there was no need for two E-9s to spend much time within the same space. We are territorial creatures, after all.

That said, whenever Winchester *did* visit, it was to our corner he was drawn. Often, he'd hand me or Thurman a twenty-dollar bill and ask that we pick up doughnuts and coffee for the shop; or for our section. In a grab bag of requests one's CSM might make of oneself, a request of that sort is certainly preferable to two-thousand alternatives.

Truly, the Drafting job made strange bedfellows of grizzled lions and growing cubs.

Command Sergeant Major Winchester came to understand and respect the necessary work undertaken by Drafting, and would often put questions to us regarding that work. He was as much a friend to our section of S-3 as we could have hoped for. Between Winchester's general support and the excellent in-shop leadership of the Major and SGM Hunter, Drafting was doing well for itself.

E-4/Specialists, such as I was in August of 2003, are accompanied by an NCO within their company when attending the promotion board. In my case, it was SGT Mintner, a former Echo Company team leader handpicked (like Futrell) by SFC Taylor. Also like Futrell, Mintner was a loyal and good-hearted soldier. He worked side-by-side with Silvis in generating orders and occasionally joined Drafting on an outing of one sort or another. He was my backup on the day my person and record were to be subjected to scrutiny by a group of men whose collective military experience numbered the better part of one-hundred years' time.

The term "sponsor" is reasonably apt, I suppose, but misrepresents the role. Essentially, the accompanying NCO sits in a corner whilst his charge (standing directly before the board) endures an interrogation. If necessary, one's sponsor will provide the CSM with supporting documents pertinent to his charge's service record. These range from counseling statements and various certificates to APFT cards and official school records.

None of it proved necessary in my case.

To Winchester, I was a known quantity, which set me apart from most (if not all) of those who had preceded me in being board-evaluated that morning.

I had studied thoroughly for over a week's time and brought three years of (admittedly uneven) Army experience to the table. My APFT record was beyond reproach, I wore a couple of respectable badges (EIB, Airborne), had at least one AAM, and knew The Old Guard history from start to finish.

That last point bears mentioning as it has to do with the first question asked of me.

CSM Winchester asked that I walk the board through Regimental history to the best of my knowledge.

I spoke uninterrupted for nearly three minutes' time on The Old Guard's enormous, consequential, and complex history.

When I had, at last, finished speaking, Delta Company's 1SG asked me, "How long did you spend studying our unit's history, son?"

To this I had nothing at all in the way of a precise response. I presented the man with a figure plucked cleanly from the branches of thin air: "Around two hours, First Sergeant."

His response was blunt and was spoken not to me, but to CSM Winchester: "I got no questions for this soldier."

Rather than thanking the man verbally, I nodded in acknowledgment of the courteous gesture. One fewer 1SG from whom to field inquiries.

All that followed fell largely within my knowledge base. At least one did not, for which my response was something to the effect of, "I haven't an answer for the question, First Sergeant, but will research the topic at a later time." This was apparently satisfactory, as it elicited a muffled "All right, soldier," response.

CSM Winchester asked if I had any knowledge of California's gubernatorial recall election.

"I do, Sergeant Major."

"And can you tell me which celebrity is running for that office?"

The good sergeant major was clearly thinking of Austrian-born bodybuilder and film star Arnold Alois Schwarzenegger, as the man's candidacy had generated considerable media reaction throughout the preceding weeks. However, a day or so prior to the board, I learned that *Diff'rent Strokes* actor/icon Gary Coleman had also thrown his name in the ring. That knowledge had failed to make as broad an impression upon the national consciousness as had Schwarzenegger's bid, but Gary Coleman was a celebrity and he was, indeed, seeking gubernatorial office in the Golden State.

My answer should have surprised nobody. But, in fact, surprised everybody.

"Yes, Sergeant Major. Actor Gary Coleman has announced his candidacy for that office."

A collective response of, "What the fuck?" mixed in with a wry chuckle overtook the room. Winchester looked to one of the 1SGs and asked, "Is that true?"

The man gave a response in the affirmative, and Winchester looked to me and said, "All right, Specialist Mongilutz, I think we're about done here."

"Roger, Sergeant Major," I responded while preparing to exit. "Thank you all."

I learned from Mintner an hour or so later that mine was a score of one-hundred-forty-nine out of a possible one-hundred-fifty. It was allegedly my former Bravo Company 1SG—First Sergeant Carlson—who had docked me the single point, though I never confirmed as much ... nor did I confirm the rationale underlying that docked point.

Also in attendance for that board was Thurman's promotion packet.

His promotion packet had been presented to the board and would earn the man a perfect score. Yes, I was bested by a packet of paperwork. Thurman had earned as much. He had won something like six consecutive Soldier of the Year boards by that point, which meant doing the same for promotability purposes would've amounted to little more than a formality.

I was proud of Thurman, and of myself.

"A tapestry of error which I labored mightily to beautify with the occasional triumph...." You may recall that passage from the foreword. I recall it often.

As modest as the successful completion of a mere promotion board might seem to many, I regarded it as a triumph. Whatever my failings, errors, and embarrassments throughout the preceding thirty-seven months' time, I was now promotable to E-5/Sergeant and would likely be pinned by October 1st. (Fun fact: It was a month later.)

That I would not be pinned in S-3, or even in HHC, was yet unknown to me. On that day, I was certain I would complete my TOG journey in the employ of SFC Taylor, and that I'd do so as a non-commissioned officer.

Mortals do make their plans, and the gods ... well, the gods do laugh.

And it all started with a rumor.

XVI

Left Bravo a Private,
Returned an NCO (Almost)

I had asked Scott if a week or so of leave was possible once the final Twilight Tattoo had come to pass. Indeed, I was anything but optimistic. As Drafting technically fell under HHC, Captain Branson and 1SG Wallace were technically our approving authorities where leave and passes were concerned. Neither of those guys cared much for Drafting. Something about our uniform and our falling under the umbrella leadership of the Major and SGM Hunter. They never seemed overly warm to the curious grey area in which we lived, worked, and politely bucked authority. Politely, mind you.

For which reason Scott's solution amounted to more than mere earthly music; it was, to my ears, an angelic choir.

The leave was approved.

Apparently, the good Major and equally good Sergeant Major agreed with Scott's assessment—I had earned a round of leave. It would be my first visit to Washington since before my S-3 tenure got underway. I had thought less of home while in Drafting than had been the case when bearing caskets with Bravo. Homesickness does diminish as one advances in years, to be sure, but there was something else to it.

Perhaps it was nothing more than the feeling of having inhabited a unique niche, and having found a second home, of sorts. Surely the sense of being useful in a way both esoteric and necessary provided me with a sense of purpose. What better remedy for feelings of longing than feelings of belonging?

Washington was exactly as I had left it. Mount Rainier, the state's crowning jewel (geologically speaking), had not relocated to, say, Oregon. The Space Needle sat where the Space Needle sits, and Safeco Field was its monolithic self. I was happy to see them all, to a one.

Of course, there were other matters on my mind. Shortly after the board but prior to signing out on leave, there'd been talk, all of it rather secretive.

Mind you, command meetings are generally closed-door gatherings, but additional layers of shroud and fog had descended upon the Regiment.

This rumor carried with it more credibility than do so many others of its species. In the absence of cloak-&-dagger behavior on part of Old Guard senior leadership, hearsay would've found scarce little purchase in the minds of the unit's more discriminating soldiers. But there seemed to be enough unusual behavior afoot to suggest a coming revelation. Just what was anyone's guess.

I was in my beloved Washington and appreciating my every breath of Northwestern/Puget Sound air. I made no mention of any rumors and, in truth, spoke very little of my Army experience. The novelty of my serving in uniform had diminished once I entered the second year of my enlistment ... and I was in my fourth. It was simply my job, and rarely came up in conversation.

This was the last time I'd see our family dog, Patches, in his native Washington. My parents would soon leave the state, which is to say Patches would pass away elsewhere a couple of years later. That knowledge weighs on me to this day.

Leaving home this time around was a mixed experience, psychologically speaking. Saying goodbye to my home state invariably leads to feelings of somberness. But I was eager for my return to S-3, the shop in which I imagined I'd finish out my time with the Regiment.

Mine were excellent leaders, the work was fulfilling, I knew the job, and the long days were giving way to productive weeks in smooth, sustained fashion. If anything, I was dreading the prospect of my discharge date materializing too suddenly.

* * *

It happened sort of like this, kind of. We two Spec4 (promotable) soldiers stood at parade rest two paces from Winchester's reach. "You boys both came from Bravo, didn't you?"

Thurman and I answered as one. "Yes, Sergeant Major."

"Well, I'll put this simply—do you wanna go to PLDC or do you wanna go to Bravo?"

The "PLDC" to which Winchester referred was the Primary Leadership Development Course. This was the month-long training program which either shortly preceded or shortly followed one's promotion to E-5/Sergeant.

I answered for the both of us, "Sergeant Major, I've never really thought of those as being diametrically opposed options."

"You're a fucking smartass, Mongo." (I hated that moniker and had occasionally battled its usage since Basic Training. Usually, a firm "That is not my name." was enough to retire its being spoken.)

"Yes, Sergeant Major," I replied, while tightening up my parade rest stance in a way both visibly detectable and mildly uncomfortable.

"I'm asking because Bravo's got something comin' down the pipe that I don't think you're gonna feel like sittin' out."

So, there was truth to the rumor, after all, and it had to do with Bravo Company.

Thurman leapt at this, knowing full well he spoke for the both of us. "We'd like to go back to Bravo, Sergeant Major."

"Yes, Sergeant Major. No question of it." I contributed.

Winchester grinned that ancient grin of his and nodded in approval. "I'll talk to Taylor and see about getting you your orders. Either way, plan on reporting to Bravo on Monday."

In perfect synchronization, "Roger, Sergeant Major."

"And, boys," that grin had fled the man's weathered visage, "keep your mouths closed about all this. You know more than most of the men in my regiment, and I aim to keep it that way for a while longer."

That was a strange order, given that Thurman and I didn't regard ourselves as being particularly well informed as to what was in store for Bravo Company. Nevertheless, we were obedient.

Much of what happened in the days thereafter aggregates within my memory as a sort of punctuated blur. I don't remember speaking with Scott regarding my departure, certainly not immediately. Thurman and I went to lunch with our fellow Draftsmen, Futrell and Tiller (now completely trained), and told them scant little as to the nature of our departure. By the end, they knew only that we were returning to Bravo Company, not that CSM Winchester had presented us with an unexpected ultimatum.

I suppose they knew as much as we did.

I remember cleaning out my HHC locker later that week. This I hadn't expected to do until the next spring. Instead, here I was in August of 2003, loading my uniforms and gear into the trunk of that Honda Prelude. I realized they'd likely remain there for a few days' time. I didn't yet have a wall locker assigned in Bravo Company. It was a strange sense of limbo of which I was curiously fond. It was as though I had somehow managed to graduate myself to a still higher plane of independence within the unit, Drafting having planted the seeds of rebellion within my mind ... or nurtured those already present.

Orders were drawn up later that week and Thurman and I found ourselves saying farewell to the S-3 Shop we had come to know closely.

We wouldn't be sent-off quietly, however. SGM Hunter would see to that.

If Hunter did anything notably well, it was his exhibiting of sincere appreciation for those over whom, with whom, and for whom he worked.

This went for the Major, whose farewell party Hunter hosted in his own home that summer, and for a very humble and soft-spoken SSG whose presence in S-3 often went unnoticed, but whose departure Hunter made certain to acknowledge by treating the shop to a lunch in the man's honor.

Though we were among the lowest ranking lifeforms assigned to the shop, Sergeant Major Todd Hunter scheduled for me and Thurman a large luncheon which was attended by field-grade officers, senior NCOs, and various figures from throughout HHC. For those two mildly nerdy soldiers who had bonded in Bravo Company over the spring/summer of 2001, endured the Pentagon recovery effort, shared an Annandale apartment, and maintained a friendship thereafter, this amounted to an enlistment high-point neither of us could've predicted.

Curiously, my mind wandered to thoughts of Ariel Denton during that farewell luncheon, and to the Pilchuck High Homecoming '99 dance. I often wondered then (and often wonder now) about a life devoid of military service, a life spent within walking distance of everything I had known since early-childhood. I often wondered if Ariel ever thought of me...

I thanked SGM Hunter for his leadership, his mentoring, and for the wholly unexpected decision he made in moving me to S-3. I thanked every officer and NCO for their patience with my slightly-too-familiar tone in speaking with them throughout the previous year. I also thanked Futrell and Tiller.

And I thanked Sergeant First Class Scott Taylor, who had become to me a friend of the highest order in a very short time. It was he who was most reluctant to see us go; it was he who had most readied us for the leadership roles awaiting us in Bravo Company.

When the luncheon was complete, I returned to that beautiful Fairfax townhome and enjoyed a weekend of climbing, reading, and wondering about what was to come.

On a warm September morning, I awoke around 0500hrs so I might arrive to Myer well before the 0630hrs first formation awaiting Bravo Company. I was quick in leaving the townhome and the traffic was cooperative, the combined effect of which saw me entering the Bravo Company command hallway at 0610hrs.

The company 1SG arrived minutes later and ignored me. Allowing thirty or so seconds to elapse, I stepped into his office.

"Good morning, First Sergeant."

"What are you doing in my company?"

This was perplexing. Surely the man knew Thurman and I were returning to Bravo with the CSM's blessing ... and with official orders.

"I'm reporting for duty, First Sergeant."

"No you ain't."

"I can assure you I am."

"Who sent you? SGM Hunter?"

"In effect, yes, I suppose, but it was Sergeant Major Winch—"

"They want your ass back in *my* company?"

"Truly."

Whatever I had expected my initial returning moments to Bravo Company might look like, that certainly wasn't it. Nevertheless, I'd been exercising largely on my own or with the Draftsmen for a year's time. I didn't have any objections to doing so this morning.

As it happened, while walking up the short staircase that led from the command hallway to the rear of the barracks, I encountered Sgt. Joshua Robinson, a highly competent and professionally minded soldier whose acquaintanceship I'd made during my tenure as a Command Group driver. Originally from Alpha Company, Robinson had transferred to S-3 a year earlier and would visit the drivers as a sort of refuge.

"Hi, Robinson," I said. "Just saw the 1SG. He's in no mood for visitors."

"Fuck it. I wasn't planning on reporting until 0900hrs, anyway. Let's run."

*Shit. Robinson is fast. **Really** fast. I'll agree for the sake of my pride ... but this will surely be a test of will.*

Robinson was feeling good that morning. He thought it best that we run bridge-to-bridge, because, well, of course he did. I kept even with the man from first step to last, and nearly overtook him when bounding up CIF Hill. It was the most difficult run I had endured since reporting to HHC. What better way to inaugurate my return to the line?

Robinson still had a wall locker in HHC, and peeled off towards that august structure following our run. I continued towards Bravo in hopes of tracking down a familiar face...

"Hooph!" I had seen Sgt. John Hoffman, my friend and former team leader, coming in from PT with Second Platoon.

"Did you get yourself fired from the shop, man?"

"Nearly, at least once or twice. But, no, I asked to return. Are you heading to the DFAC?"

"Yeah, in a few minutes."

And off to the DFAC we went. In a sense, it was as though I'd never left. Time has a curious way of folding on itself when closely familiar activities are reenacted. Hoffman and I had made the DFAC stroll perhaps two-hundred times prior to my leaving Bravo Company. A similar phenomenon is known to materialize during leave. Somehow it feels closely linked to previous visits, regardless of how much time has elapsed from one visit to the next.

Hooph caught me up on Bravo Company politics, promotions, UCMJ actions, new arrivals, recent departures, et cetera. Some of this was known to me, as two of my three roommates belonged to Bravo, but I appreciated the conversational foyer Hooph had constructed for my benefit.

After returning to Bravo, I made my way down to the command hallway and entered the Second Platoon administrative office. SFC Boorman, who had become the platoon sergeant just prior to 9/11, was exactly where he was when last I had seen him. The role of platoon leader, however, had been turned over to Second Lieutenant Cesare, a motivated young man of perhaps twenty-six years.

A brief hello, an awkward introduction, and I was off.

The Training Room was (is) exactly eight paces from the Second Platoon office. I covered this distance quickly and walked in to greet "Senator Fred," my roommate. Fred knew my orders, as we had discussed them in the Fairfax townhome.

"Fred."

"What's up, Mark?"

"Second Platoon needs an E-4(P) in its ranks," I said.

"They do?"

My eyes met Fred's and channeled paramount resolve. "*Yes*, Fred, they do."

"Ah. Top didn't assign you yet, did he?"

"Afraid not."

"Well, just fall-in with them during our 1000hrs formation. I'll get you on the roster."

So, I fell in with Second Platoon under an hour later, and trusted that Thompson had handled the necessary paperwork. The Army is, above all, a bureaucratic juggernaut.

In the interest in doubling down on my gambit, I fell in not just with my old platoon, but with my old squad. I found myself standing mere inches from the precise plot of ground on which I had stood hundreds of times throughout my first eighteen months with the Regiment. I'm certain the 1SG directed a look of disapproval my way, but on a long list of matters in need of attention in that moment, the defiant behavior of a single Spec4(P) was categorically minor, to be sure. He let it be, and tacitly permitted my assignment to Second Platoon for whatever awaited.

Prior to the 1SG calling us to attention, there was a good deal of milling about. We were awaiting the CO, Captain Travers, who was nowhere to be seen at 1000hrs. And as always happens when too long a period passes, the formation began to deform itself. The three platoon blocks drifted first apart and then into one another. This reliably predictable phenomenon placed me in the orbit of both Thurman, whose presence of course did *not* surprise me, and Taheny, whose presence *did*.

Taheny had put himself forth as a Continental Color Guard candidate. I respected him hugely for having done so. Every bit as skillful and ceremonially elite as are the Regiment's finest marchers (if not more so), CCG professionals are a rare breed within the ranks of The Old Guard.

Because of the visible/central parade position which is their high responsibility, CCG holds itself to an exacting standard of marching (and wheeling) excellence. It was always my understanding that the so-called starring roles (those who bear the U.S. and Army flags) are almost invariably populated by soldiers recruited from Echo Company platoons, as stature was an essential ingredient of the CCG recipe. Those riflemen who occupy the flanks, however, are often drawn from the Alpha, Bravo, Charlie, and Delta ranks, as a medium-tall height is acceptable, even if tall-tall is preferred.

At about six-foot, one-hundred-eighty pounds, Taheny was clearly on the smaller end of the acceptable CCG spectrum, but he'd proven his a worthy candidacy. Barring some unforeseen event, there was good reason to expect he'd be welcomed into the CCG platoon by mid-autumn.

Then, of course, an unforeseen event interfered.

Whatever it was that had seen CSM Winchester presenting Thurman and me with a weird either/or question, had seen Bravo Company leadership presenting Taheny with an unequivocal recall. Regardless of where the man was in his CCG training process, Bravo needed bodies—Taheny qualified as such.

"Did you have any say in the matter?"

"None. I was told to be in formation today at 1000hrs. Here I am."

"I'm sorry, Jamesy."

"Me, too. I was doing really well over there."

Thurman then put words to a sentiment we all shared, even if to varying degrees.

"It's good to have the three of us back under one roof."

"Agreed," I said, "whatever's next, I'm glad we'll be experiencing it together."

I adore the works of Alexandre Dumas, thus my numerous Three Musketeers references. Admittedly, I tended to overuse the comparison at times, and even double-booked it once too often for my own liking. Which is to say, I had employed it in reference to the incongruous trio comprised of myself, Billy P, and Robert "Squirrel" Williams, as well as when speaking of the trio comprised of myself, Thurman, and Taheny, which was characterized by far more in the way of congruity.

As it happened, the Squirrel left the Armed Forces early in 2003, and Billy P would not be joining us on whatever adventure awaited for reasons having to do with (a) the need for a rear detachment (Rear D) group, and (b) his rapidly approaching end-tour-of-service (ETS) date. So, I'd experience the months ahead with the latter musketeers, of whom there was, in fact, an honorary fourth.

My friend and roommate, Mike "Senator Fred" Thompson, had assumed the role of Fourth Musketeer and was a close member of our group. Like both Thurman and Taheny, Fred had worked in the Training Room, and was among those TOG soldiers who'd come to truly understand the Army. Just like those gentlemen, I had worked in a capacity quite removed from the standard duties of a given line soldier. Operations work had done for me what Training Room work had done for Thurman, Taheny, and Fred—we carried ourselves in the manner of know-it-all wankers. I expect we qualified as being something short of sufferable.

Though he had belonged to the Firing Party prior to his legendary board career, Thurman's talents were needed with the Marchers; he and Taheny would be platoon mates. I had originally assumed that this development was to Thurman's disliking, but a couple of factors kept it from being so. For one, Thurman was not attached to Third Platoon in the way I was to Second. Though prone to bouts of sentimentality and nostalgia, Thurman is governed by emotions to a lesser degree than am I. My own sense of longing for what once was is often characterized by a rather severe pathology.

Secondly, an excellent Marcher, Morgan, with whom Thurman had suffered through the rigors of Pre-Ranger Training some years earlier, had lobbied for his battle buddy to join First Platoon. Doing so meant parting ways with a platoon for which Thurman felt little in the way of overarching loyalty, while allowing him to stand alongside a remarkable soldier.

Fred was to remain in the Training Room, and I had apparently secured my Second Platoon assignment.

Captain Travers entered the formation area around 1012hrs and the platoons resumed their assembled and properly formed-up arrangement. The 1SG moved into position from wherever within the area he had been standing and provided his men with another few seconds to order themselves.

"Company, attention!"

THWUMP.

That sound—the sound of one-hundred right-foot rubber boot heels colliding with their left-foot rubber counterparts. Prior to that moment, I hadn't truly felt as though my return to Bravo was satisfactorily realized.

Now it was.

The 1SG saluted Captain Travers as the latter assumed his place.

"At ease!" spoke Captain Travers.

SCHWUUP.

That sound—the sound of two-hundred BDU-clad arms locking into place behind one-hundred backs. Yes, I was home.

Captain Travers could now speak, and did.

A few words acknowledging the uncertainty surrounding our situation were followed by a few words of understanding (paraphrased below).

"All right, men. There's going to be a lot coming down the pipe these next few weeks. Just bear with it as best you can. For now—Company, attention!"

THWUMP.

"Dismissed."

My intention is not to misrepresent the man's meaning when addressing his company on that slightly overcast morning; rather, I intend to convey that sense of vagueness which characterized his address, while rightly explaining the sense of uncertainty that followed its delivery.

We knew less than we had prior to the formation. Well, not really—we knew there would be "a lot" of, well, *something* "coming down the pipe" at some point. As to what that was, specifically … well, we didn't know.

"That was enlightening." Hooph was dismissive in his assessment as we headed into the barracks. "You were in S-3 last week. You don't have a clue what's going on?"

Having been in the operations shop, I should've known a bit more than the line guys. I did not. Except…

"There was talk of drawing desert equipment. I overheard the S-4 turds talking about ACUs and ordering new gear. I'd guess we have a deployment ahead of us."

"No shit, Mark. Of course we do. I'm talking about *where* and *when.*"

Was it that obvious to Hooph? Was it that obvious to *everyone*? It wasn't even that obvious to me. It seemed just as likely that we might be readying for some domestic security operation. A unit as unique as The Old Guard did not lend itself to intuitive operational forecasts.

I was summoned downstairs by a young private whose face I did not recognize.

"Specialist Mongilutz, Sergeant Boorman asked to see you in his office."

I acknowledged that information with a nod and found myself face-to-face with Boorman.

SFC Boorman was a man in his late-thirties, was perhaps two years removed from retirement, and had checked a lot of the correct boxes throughout his Army career. He'd been a drill sergeant, was a certified pathfinder (rather rare), and had seen about as many duty stations as I had seen months in uniform. He stood well over six-feet in height and possessed a somewhat burly build. He also seemed to be at psychological odds with the mental energy necessary to serve in the role of platoon sergeant. He meant well, a character trait I tend to value above much else.

"We're putting you in First Squad for now and will figure out what to do when you get your stripes pinned."

"Roger."

"Go find Sergeant Robertson. Let him know you're his newest report."
First Squad was about as recognizable as it wasn't. Which is to say, its
human make-up had changed by fifty-percent since June of the previous year.
Even by Army standards, that's considerable movement within a single squad
over the course of a year's time. For one, SSG Rivera had left the unit.

His replacement, SSG Robertson, was mostly unknown to me. Sgt. Brady
served as a team leader within First Squad and was, by that point, one of the
platoon's senior figures. Brady was a skilled carpenter and had an extensive
background in home construction. While I have only kind words to say about
all of those with whom I served during the Pentagon recovery effort, Brady
had demonstrated particularly impressive diligence throughout and was often
counted upon to direct complex, coordinated tasks where necessary. We
developed a close friendship in the months that followed, and I'd been proud
to attend the man's wedding, our professional reunion of sorts.

That feathers would be ruffled betwixt us during the months ahead …
well, that was almost solely a product of my own pride, nothing more.

For the time being, I was the newly returned Spec4(P) Mongilutz, and
something of a curiosity to many of the newer soldiers who couldn't make
sense of my *too* flippant tone in speaking with platoon and company leadership. I had imported much of my S-3 mentality into the line company ecosys-
tem. It would persist for a time, but not indefinitely.

Camaraderie is a compelling, potent aspect of the human condition. It's
also wont to take shape in ways often unforeseen. To be sure, shared suffering
is a universally reliable means of cultivating a sense of brotherhood between
those doing the sharing. I had scarce little in common with Roum, Naylor,
and Rohde prior to our Sand Hill days, but regard those men as family, and
struggle to envision a scenario in which I wouldn't offer my help to any of
them, should there be a need.

Later that afternoon, a list generated by the Training Room made its
way around the barracks. On it were three columns, one populated with an
alphabetical name-listing of all Bravo Company soldiers. The other two were
blank but featured "Boot Size" and "Blood Type" headings. Aside from organ-
izing my new off-post room wall locker, providing that information was all
I accomplished on my first day in Bravo Company (the Robinson run
notwithstanding).

As we were now working on the same schedule, Fred and I returned
home within minutes of one another. From that point on, we quite often carpooled to and from Fort Myer. Our other Bravo Company roommate, Matt
"Bacardi" Lemon, occasionally joined us, but preferred to drive himself.

"What the hell is going on, Fred? Blood type? Boot size?"

Fred was uncertain as to why that information had been requested, but shared a hint. "All I know is that we'll be drawing out a lot of shit this week and next. It isn't just boots."

"Okay, we're deploying." I had come around to Hooph's way of thinking.

"Yep, that's my guess. Just don't know where, or when."

"The only questions worth answering." I headed upstairs to the master bedroom while Fred descended into his basement lair. Fitting, as the Bravo Company Training Room was also a downstairs lair. The profession had, in Fred's case, chosen the man.

"By the way," Fred added, before we lost sight of one another, "your promotion orders came through. First of the month, buddy. Congratulations."

"Thanks, Fred. I left Bravo a private. Returning a sergeant is somehow validating."

"You ain't a sergeant yet, Mark."

Fred was right. I was not yet a sergeant.

XVII

"You boys been to Africa?"

Fred had not misspoken, nor had he been mistaken in suggesting that Bravo Company would be drawing far more than new combat boots.

Fort A.P. Hill was to become a home for Battlehard. Newly arrived soldiers aside, Bravo Company was closely acquainted with that sixty-year-old training center. Between annual EIB training, twice-annual rifle qualification, frequently scheduled crew-serve weapons firing, and the occasional land navigation or road march outing, Fort A.P. Hill was, for The Old Guard, well-trodden terrain.

What awaited us that autumn would eclipse all that had preceded.

No, it wouldn't so much "eclipse" whatever training exercises we had undertaken at A.P. Hill as re-create a good deal of it over an extended timeframe.

There were several ranges, to include qualifying with our newly issued M4 carbines (a shorter relation to the M16 rifle) and rendering several soldiers from each platoon proficient with the M249 (SAW) and the heavier M240B. My introduction to A.P. Hill three years prior had been during a visit to the SAW range. It was with some sense of nostalgia that I observed a dozen new soldiers detach themselves from the company for a day of doing precisely as I had done.

While the ranges were underway, there was new equipment arriving by the day. In some cases, it would be dropped off directly in the company quad/formation area. In one case, we were sent to Conmy Hall a platoon at a time to be fitted for new combat uniforms. Unlike our Vietnam era jungle-print BDUs (armies are always fighting the last war), these were desert-print DCUs, complete with tan combat boots.

Not visiting a range on a given day typically relegated one to assisting with unpacking, sorting, and administering of whatever gear had been placed at our doorstep. This included new assault packs, knee/elbow pads, combat goggles, advanced optical sights, and a bevy of equipment articles, which must surely have amounted to thousands of dollars per soldier.

Somewhere in all this frenzied activity, there was a company APFT. PT remained a top priority. For my part, I was grateful our platoon leader, Second Lieutenant Cesare, was committed to physical fitness as a way of life. We were of one mind in that respect.

One day, Second Platoon fell-in for morning formation alongside three eight-foot long logs. These are approximately equal in diameter to a standard telephone pole and are often used for "Log PT," or a PT session in which three to four soldiers position themselves beneath a log and perform synchronized overhead presses or bicep curls.

Cesare had something else in mind.

Rather than standing beneath the log's weight, we would *run* the better part of three miles beneath said log. Because the three logs collectively allowed for only a dozen or so soldiers to participate at a given time, we swapped out positions with our comrades every two-hundred yards.

I liked this Cesare guy.

Oddly enough, as I was exiting the quad encumbered under the weight of an eight-foot log, Captain Travers happened to notice me while presumably embarking upon a less-encumbered run of his own.

"Specialist Mongilutz! You're not in S-3 anymore, are you?"

He was rhetorically correct, I was not. I wondered if he realized (a) that I was under his command by choice, and (b) that I rather reveled in PT of the very sort in which I was participating.

I'd made the good captain's acquaintance seven months earlier, as many incoming and outgoing officers tend to take up temporary residence in the S-3 shop before moving on to wherever it is they are headed. It allows for their talents and experience to be employed in support of whatever operations might benefit from as much whilst they are around.

Travers had recognized in me a kindred spirit.

One of our first conversations had been on the subject of Francis Ford Coppola's film series, *The Godfather*. We debated which of the first two films was artistically superior, with my own case being made in support of *The Godfather II*. I should acknowledge that Captain Travers and I didn't establish anything in the way of close rapport during his S-3 stint. For one, said stint was too brief to allow for as much. Secondly, more than many other officers with whom I had worked, Travers took very seriously the officer/enlistee divide. And rightly so.

As Travers was readying to leave the shop, I inquired of him which company he was to command.

"Going to Bravo."

"Sir, please take good care of Battlehard. I miss those guys."

At this, Travers smiled and assured me the company was in good hands.

I probably found a moment to recall that exchange, even while happily struggling beneath the slippery, awkward mass of a telephone pole section. Or maybe not.

One thing was certain—everyone knew what they had in their possession and in what quantity.

Packing list layouts are central to the enlisted Army experience. Perhaps as central as is the proficient firing of one's assigned weapon system. They also carry with them a uniquely demoralizing quality when conducted repetitively and with scant little time separating one from the next. This might be said of many tasks, but it's true of packing layouts to a paramount degree.

Among those who had reported to Second Platoon during my S-3 tenure was a soldier from Indiana by the name of Ryan Fritsche. Though new to the unit (and to the Army), Fritsche had quickly earned for himself a place on the Full Honors casket team, was a well-liked figure within the company, and had become fast friends with many of those I had known best prior to leaving the company. We did not interact much during the early days of my Battlehard reunion, but I came to recognize the kid's worth almost immediately. He also allowed me use of his barracks room in preparing for packing list insanity.

We dumped rucks and bags with such regularity as to develop a certain muscle memory unique to the task. And we dumped as a company. Not that a single leader was helming the layout for one-hundred men. No, *all* squads were doing the same damned thing at *all* times of day.

I recall having to take unfamiliar routes when making my way from one section of the barracks to another, as packing list layouts were routinely blocking off entire hallways. Even stairwells, those sacred thoroughfares which allow mankind to ascend and descend via succession of low-height steps, were not safe from the great Layout Scourge of '03.

Had we been training for the purpose of performing rapid-fire, expertly administered packing list layouts wherever it was we were headed, Bravo Company was prepared to a degree which would've made our Old Guard forebears proud. Assuming, that is, that our Old Guard forebears would be impressed by packing lists and packing list activities.

When the time came for the platoons of Battlehard to collectively visit Fort A.P. Hill in the interest of companywide training, it was with some relief that we placed behind us the stuffy confines of those barracks.

Even so, the earlier references to camaraderie are not wholly out of place here. To be sure, our bonds would be strengthened more by what lay ahead in our shared adventure. But the wholesale misery that had seeped into the walls of our barracks throughout those packing list exercises did carry with it the unintended effect of nurturing newly planted seeds of platoon brotherhood.

Being as I was unknown to many of the First Squad soldiers, and had not worked with Brady in well over a year's time, it was the accumulated annoyances which stemmed from repetitiously laying out one's gear that would serve to acquaint (and re-acquaint) me with those men in the most advisable of manners—via shared irritation.

We weren't crashing into Normandy aboard Higgins boats, nor were we in any life-threatening danger of any significant sort. But, the seeds of camaraderie take root in ways often of their own choosing.

Trace elements of useful truth trickled out. Never too much at once; angels and ministers of grace defend us, we helpless (and hapless) soldiers, from clarifying knowledge of any sort.

The company's command group had long since abandoned any pretense that the newly arrived gear and ever-growing training schedule were direct preparations for an impending deployment. They were, however, quite happy to have us speculate amongst ourselves as to the location awaiting us. And as for the date? We operated under the sensible assumption that it'd be soon.

I'd broach the topic of our deployment location frequently with Fred, with little in the way of subtlety, only to be met with a decidedly uninformative answer. My rejoinder would occasionally manifest (in pouting fashion) as follows, "Little good it does one to have for his roommate a Training Room soldier."

Fred was reliably indifferent to my irritation.

I suppose it mattered little where we were headed when the time came. Bravo Company had plenty of tactical training immediately ahead of it, and whether it was North Korea or the Lunar surface, those training requirements needed to first be met in Virginia and Louisiana, respectively.

It is a complicated reality, finding oneself in a promotable (P) state of being.

It's weird.

Or it can be. Much of that depends upon the larger leadership framework into which one falls during that transitional period.

Had I been comfortably situated upon my S-3 perch while a Spec4(P), it wouldn't have been a matter at all, as most tended to regard Draftsmen as NCOs anyway. However, matters are rather different within a line platoon, an environment characterized by a necessary emphasis upon minor rank and time-in-grade disparities. And nowhere was that more true than in First Squad, Second Platoon.

Nowhere, that is, except within the other squads.

As a matter of physics, I could only be assigned to one squad at a time, that being First Squad, Second Platoon. And in said squad, small differences tended to matter greatly. Regardless of the deep-seated friendship Brady and I had enjoyed across the years, he was indeed a senior figure within the squad, within the platoon, even within the company, and he had little patience for the free-spiritedness with which I hadn't parted ways upon returning to Battlehard.

Which isn't to say that matters were tense, only that I found myself perplexed by the seeming inconsequence of my promotable status. Awaiting my promotion to E-5/Sergeant was merely a matter of paperwork processing and the passing of time. Yet during the interim, my untamed sarcasm led to my being treated little better than an experienced Spec4 ... which I suppose is what I was.

Still, I was largely unprepared for the austerity that characterized my time under Brady's charge. Reflecting on matters more closely throughout the months ahead, I concluded that the fault rested almost exclusively with myself. It simply didn't (and perhaps couldn't) seem so at the time. That (P) has the capacity to function as both bullseye and validating emblem. For my part, I couldn't wait for the graduation from promot*able* to promot*ed*.

Some few weeks following Captain Travers' vague addressing of his company on that slightly overcast September morning, Bravo Company set out in its near-entirety for Fort A.P. Hill. Ours would be a long stay, the training would be valuable, and the purpose for it all would remain unclear.

Battle Drill One Alpha.

Battle. Drill. One. Alpha.

Battle.

Drill.

One.

Alpha.

BD1A.

The men of Bravo Company would engage in a wide variety of training exercises throughout our autumn, 2003 stay. A wide variety, indeed. But it was Battle Drill One Alpha that would become the signature exercise of our pre-deployment (or at least pre–Polk) training cycle.

The drill is not complex in its design, but can be draining in its execution. Imagine two fire-teams situated around two-hundred meters from a nest of deadly hostiles. One of the two teams will spray towards said hostiles a steady helping of covering fire while the other runs on the outside flank towards the enemy's position. Once the flanking team is lined up with their target, that group's team leader will ignite a flare to signal the covering fire-team, who will then shift their fire forty-five degrees to the opposite side of the enemy's position. Once that shifting process is complete, the flanking team open fires on all visible targets while moving through the objective. When enemy activity has ceased because of capture or death, the covering team will, upon being signaled, run the battlefield's full length in order to join their flanking team comrades. Once reunited, the teams will secure that ground previously held by the hostiles, thereby concluding the battle drill.

We executed this drill time and time again. And I'd soon do so in the capacity of team leader.

It was SFC Boorman who summoned me on the perimeter of a live-fire range.

"Yes, Sergeant!" I responded while securing my gear and walking to join the man, who was accompanied by a staff sergeant who I knew only in passing. His name was Wilson, and it was he who addressed me as I approached.

"Hey, Mongilutz, you're gonna lead Second Squad's B-team on this next drill."

"Hi, Sergeant. Have we met?"

"Not really, no. But I know you're promotable, came from Second Squad, and I'm down a team leader. Do a good job on these next few drills and the team'll be yours."

I remember looking to the men SSG Wilson was asking me to lead and realized that half of them were unknown to me. There was one notable exception: Matt "Bacardi" Lemon belonged to that squad. We'd been roommates for the better part of a year. There was also PFC Garcia, who had reported to Bravo Company some two or three months prior to my leaving for HHC.

There was PFC Harding, a smart and thoughtful kid with a sense of patriotic zeal I invariably found uplifting. PV2 Reed, a soldier nearly ten years my senior who was married and had fathered several children. As it happened, I was younger than three of my four soldiers, and approximately equal in age to the remaining man. This would strike me as a bit incongruous. I was a junior leader (not yet pinned) and was being asked to lead a group of soldiers who each possessed sufficient facial hair to warrant a real shave every morning, as opposed to the imagined stubble I'd make-believe shear day after day.

"Okay, let's try this out. And, Mongilutz—"

"Sergeant?"

"Don't fuck this up."

"Tracking."

And I was.

Tracking, that is.

The role into which SSG Wilson had suddenly dropped me required that I order soldiers to advance towards an objective in a leap-frog capacity. Rather distinctive from BD1A, this was a simple "Cover me while I move" exercise. Two men provide suppressing fire while two others advance a dozen or so paces. Once those two have dropped into position, they provide fire while the others catch up. I'd order each pair to move in succession, and do so while running alongside one of the pairs.

"Fire One, move!" We were, as a platoon, using "Fire One" and "Fire Two" in distinguishing between each two-man sub-team.

In this case, it was Reed and Matt "Bacardi" Lemon, my friend and room-mate. I don't believe SFC Boorman and SSG Wilson realized Lemon and I were living under the same roof. Normally, fraternization rules would've pro-hibited as much from coming to pass. But as I wasn't yet an E-5, and as all indicators had one month earlier pointed to my being promoted while in HHC, neither I nor Lemon had made any effort to get in front of that potential problem.

"Fire Two, move!" and they moved. In this case, it was Harding and Gar-cia, the soldier who had reported to Bravo a month prior to my HHC draft notice. We hadn't known one another well, but I recalled his having been a family man … and motivated by that fact. There was no question of it— Garcia wanted very much to do well in the United States Army.

From what I could discern in observing he and Harding (Fire Two) advance ahead of Reed and "Bacardi" (Fire One), the motivation was palpable.

"Fire One, move!" and they moved. As that live-fire range was (is) per-haps two-hundred yards in length, each team was called upon to "move!" seven to eight times. The exercise begins and ends rather quickly, with each iteration enduring for three to four minutes, and seeming closer to half that. Thus, mass repetition is both achievable and advisable.

I'd been running in concert with this group, as was Second Platoon's unspoken (or was it spoken?) protocol, and was reveling in the armor-clad physicality of it all. Working in operations had surely been a high honor and an edifying experience, but I had subconsciously longed for the feeling of *suck* in which I now found myself.

We were nearing the range's endpoint, and I suddenly realized that I was being closely observed by SFC Boorman and SSG Wilson. These guys had every reason to question my tactical viability and leadership quality. Over a year in HHC, minimal field time throughout said year, and not yet a sergeant. Almost, but not yet. So, they must've wondered how this Spec4(P) would acquit himself when placed rather suddenly in the role.

"Fire Two, move!" And I moved. SFC Boorman and SSG Wilson moved, though they were ten or so paces to our "six." If I had concerned myself with anything at all in the seventeen seconds separating my being a First Squad soldier from my being an auditioning Second Squad team leader, it was with the physical fitness of my potential fire-team. I'd always kept myself in excel-lent condition, I had no way of knowing whether the same was true of these four soldiers. "Bacardi" was athletic and, therefore, the least of my concerns, but the other three…

They were moving rather well, in truth.

We'd grow faster as a team in the days and weeks ahead, but under the circumstances we were negotiating the terrain at a rate I found to be rather acceptable.

"Fire One, move!" and they moved to the range's endpoint, after which I ordered Fire Two to join them, which they (we) did mere seconds later. Breathing heavily, I was uncharacteristically smiling while speaking kind words to each soldier.

And then SSG Wilson did something similar.

"Mongilutz, that wasn't bad. Not too bad."

"You set the bar low, Sergeant. Not fucking up—it's an art I've strived to perfect," I said.

"Care to try again?"

"Well, I *do* have a lunch scheduled. But if we start now, I—"

"Shut the fuck up, Mongilutz. Get your ass back down there."

Second Squad's Bravo fire-team ran through the fire-range thrice more that afternoon, all while getting to know their prospective team leader. What better way to achieve that end? When we had completed our final iteration of the day, SFC Boorman formally approved (via informal means) my move from First Squad, Second Platoon to Second Squad, Second Platoon; in effect, he had provided me with my homecoming's final significant moment.

Later that evening, the team made its way back to the barracks and readied for a DFAC chow experience. As a majority of our meals were taken in the field, a dinner indoors was cause for high spirits. Morale was rather strong throughout those months of training, but even contented grunts welcomed creature comforts in whatever form they're offered. Hot (or luke-warm) cuisine served beneath a largely intact roof qualified as just such a comfort.

Prior to that fateful day, I had enjoyed most of my meals with First Squad soldiers or with Hooph. And given that the latter and I were now co-team leaders within the same squad, I might intuitively have seen fit to continue with that practice. Instead, I took it upon myself to become properly acquainted with the men I would be charged with leading throughout the coming months.

"Bacardi" served as a sort of conversational bridge where achieving that end was concerned. I had known Matt Lemon for well over two years' time, and as roommate for something short of half that time. He's among the most enduringly happy men I have in my day known, and exhibited that quality throughout our A.P. Hill stay, and thereafter.

"Hi, Lemon. Good work on the range."

"You, too." Lemon looked to Harding and Reed, both of whom were seated to his left. "Mark and I were casket bearers together, then became roommates after he went to sham in Drafting."

At this I smiled. "Keep the fraternization reveal in-house, guys, at least until we're overseas."

Both nodded. Being as I was not yet a sergeant, there was no need for anything overly formal. This was, I later learned, something of a flawed approach.

"Relax, guys, I'm your new team leader, not a commanding general."

Both laughed and seemed to appreciate my casual mentality.

"Good job today, Mongilutz." This was from Harding, the patriotic soul.

"Thank you, Harding. I appreciate your contribution to my successful audition."

And there it was. A beginning. Over the next few days, we would come to know one another's strengths and unique capabilities, as well as our blind spots and various vulnerabilities.

Reed was a lithe and capable man, a natural foot soldier through and through. But he was absentminded and prone to tardiness.

Harding was responsible in the extreme and sturdily built, but often found himself lost in thought at the expense of swift action.

Garcia is a bigger guy and often sought to shoulder heavier loads where possible, but he was often too eager by half. Had I been a more mature leader, we would've likely clashed less frequently. But I wasn't, and we did. The blame lay with me.

A strong kid and energetic in the extreme, "Bacardi" was a blessing of a soldier, even if he would, on occasion, fall asleep while pulling pointless tent guard duty.

I remained under a leadership microscope for the next four days, after which time both SFC Boorman and SSG Wilson regarded me as the platoon's newest fire-team leader. Wilson and I had discovered between us (along with Hooph) a good deal of common ground, largely with respect to science-fiction literature. Wilson tended to see himself as a Californian in many ways, though he had lived all over. He was a veteran of the Bosnian conflict, having deployed to that region some five years prior to his Old Guard assignment. Though he hadn't expected to deploy shortly after reporting to the Army's premier ceremonial unit, he certainly didn't object to the idea. Several soldiers and NCOs with whom he had served at another duty station were deployed in support of Operation Enduring Freedom. I don't expect Wilson was plagued by outright guilt for that reason, but the knowledge that he too would soon find himself overseas seemed to sit well with the man.

He was not alone. Hooph had experienced some time in Egypt with the 101st Airborne during the late-1990s, and was in some ways exhilarated by the prospect of once again adventuring abroad.

This subject could certainly amount to a rabbit hole of rather deep and wide dimensions. Every thoughtful soldier had internalized our impending mission in decidedly distinctive terms. Infantrymen are only uniform in outward appearance, as their commanders are often disappointed to realize. Many officers inhabit fantasyland scenarios in which their men are simpleminded patriots of a sort of canine quality—"What? We're going to the range? And it's raining? That's my favorite thing." Insert image of a wagging tail upon a human frame. In their defense, leading large groups of men is far more psychologically manageable when one presumes oneself to be inherently superior to said men.

Nevertheless, each Battlehard soldier had interpreted the impending deployment in ways wholly unique to their own circumstances, and unique to their politics, surprisingly.

Old Guard soldiers tend to regard themselves as being savvy and insightful as to the ways of the Army. There is something about the proximity to halls of power (White House, Pentagon, Capitol Building, Fort A.P. Hill DFAC—kidding. Nobody considers the Capitol Building to be a hall of power) that contributes to a sense of sophistication amongst many within the Regiment's ranks.

What this meant in relation to our impending deployment was a good deal of opining as to the geopolitical state of the world. Conservative soldiers adopted a "Fuck yeah—'bout time we get our asses over there" mentality. Liberals channeled the predictable, "Are we right and just in our every foreign adventure?" query. Moderates tended to reflect more closely than either camp and broadly concluded that the best we could do was to do our very best in whatever it was we did.

Our training continued and the previously mentioned collision with Battle Drill One Alpha materialized some seven days following my preliminary promotion to fire-team leader (preliminary because I was not yet pinned).

First-call was early.

It was earlier than usual, and they had *all* been early since our arrival to Fort A.P. Hill. We arose at 0500hrs. We donned our gear, and headed to the makeshift formation area immediately adjacent to our barracks.

The Virginia mornings were cold in October of 2003. We didn't experience freezing temperatures, but the mornings bit into one's flesh with their fanged, chill winds. As any infantryman will attest, counteracting the effect of cold winds is a matter of keeping one's organism in a state of motion for a sustained period. Once training was underway, the cold becomes something of an afterthought. By late-morning, the temperature generally reached something north of fifty degrees, ideal for a long day of battle drills.

Unfortunately, many early formations saw us standing about for ten-fifteen minutes' time, awaiting the arrival of a leadership figure. As the BD1A exercises were being undertaken at the platoon level, we were awaiting Lieutenant Cesare around 0600hrs. He arrived at 0615hrs. We weren't exactly suffering through the horrors of Bastogne, but a quarter-hour standing about in frigid climes tends to yield moody soldiers.

First World problems? No. Perhaps Second World. It isn't as though we men of the ceremonial cloth were unaccustomed to cold weather. The newly arrived soldiers notwithstanding, every Battlehard soul had endured in their day the misery of several sub-freezing funeral ceremonies. Standing atop a graveside mock-up while a chaplain (so often long of wind) puts voice to his spiritual musings is the centerpiece of every casket bearer's official job description. Doing so while one's toes succumb to chill-induced numbness, however—that's where we prove our mettle.

Whatever it was we experienced on those icy A.P. Hill morns surely amounted to no greater a hardship than anything to which we had been subjected within Arlington National Cemetery on virtually any given February day.

But soldiers are given to griping. And so we griped.

Fifteen minutes late?

"All right, men," Cesare began, "it's gonna be a long day. We got [Battle Drill] One Alpha today, and we'll be doing it through the night."

Momentary pause. Scanning of his soldiers' collective countenance.

"A *long* day."

It was.

God, how I did love it.

Either more so now than at the time, or less, I can't say with certainty. It was a truly good and worthy experience. Drafting had kept me from training of this sort for so long a time, I had forgotten how much I had forgotten. Even factoring in the strict PT standards to which I held myself throughout that year in the shop, I hadn't experienced such grueling training since Sand Hill.

Unlike the leapfrog drill into which I had been dropped less than a week prior, BD1A was the squad leader's show. Hooph and I played our part as team leaders, but it was SSG Wilson at the helm.

Not that it mattered much. We were each experiencing physical punishment of a bone-grinding sort, and we were intimately familiar with what the battle drill required. With perhaps one exception, any of us could've stood in for Wilson by midday; all of us by day's end.

We were a long way from day's end. The first iteration lay ahead. There would be many to come. And given his experience, I was happy the squad would act as a single entity under Wilson's leadership.

"Hoffman, you'll lay down suppressin' and run the gun team. Mongilutz, you'll take the flanking role. Make sure your guys are ready for a lot of this shit."

"Lemon said something about ballet rehearsal, Sergeant, but the others should be available until well after nightfall."

"Was he always this mouthy?" Wilson asked this of Hooph, who had known me since very early in my TOG tenure.

"You have *no* idea," Hooph said, his arms crossed.

"All right, well, Lemon's ballet aside, make sure your guys keep their mags (magazines) fed and their sights cleaned before each run."

I did exactly that, and was glad Wilson had mentioned it. This was, after all, a live-fire range.

A live-fire range we ran again...

...and again...

...and again.

As I sit before my keyboard this night (in a Starbucks), I struggle to fully inhabit the sensation of feeling completely drained of whatever energy my organism can fully house in a given day. To be sure, human beings before and since have suffered and endured more hardship than what the men of Battlehard suffered and endured in the leadup to our deployment; I would never argue otherwise.

But those were hard days, all the same.

"Let's go." This was SSG Wilson addressing my fire-team. Second Squad's gunners had opened fire on the enemy objective. As our imagined enemies were suppressed by a combination of M240B, M249, and M4 firepower, courtesy of Hooph and his men, SSG Wilson, myself, and my fire-team made our way towards the objective.

The run was almost exactly as familiar as it was exhausting. We had been on-site for twelve hours and had acquainted ourselves intimately with every step of the flanking path. Sprinting its length was psychologically akin to strolling through one's old neighborhood.

Well, not at all, in truth.

But the path's geography was certainly known to us in much the same way, subconsciously mapped beyond one's cognitive realization.

SSG Wilson sent up a flare, thereby signaling Hooph to shift the gun team's fire some forty-five degrees to the right as we trained our own fire on the enemy from a lateral position. Once Hooph's fire no longer posed a threat of turning "friendly" upon his fellow soldiers, we made our way through the objective, firing away at inanimate silhouettes standing in for the enemy.

A subsequent flare signaled Hooph's men (and Hooph himself) to rise from their firing position and race to join their squad mates on the now pacified objective.

Perspiration saturated our flesh, our clothing, our helmet lining, our gloves, et cetera. That very perspiration shifts wildly in its temperature, reinventing itself from warm to cold almost immediately upon cessation of one's physical activity.

It was a feeling of which I never grew tired, and one I came to enjoy. It was a feeling I hoped never to forget. It is a feeling I remember very well.

Imagine you are twenty-one years of age, just under six-feet in height, around one-hundred-eighty pounds in weight, and clad in armor and equipment amounting to around one-quarter your overall mass.

Now add an M203 weapon system (grenade launcher which affixes to the M4 carbine's barrel), a Kevlar helmet, and live rounds.

If your imagination is functioning adequately, you have just entered a state of being very similar to my own in October of 2003.

Now imagine you are running towards an enemy objective alongside six similarly clad men of varying heights and weights. Imagine the breath you draw escapes your lungs with every third step, thereby necessitating greedy subsequent draws. Imagine the bulky armor encumbering your upper body and rendering each drawing of breath slightly more difficult than its immediate predecessor.

Imagine you are laboring ardently to decrease your iteration completion time with each run through. Imagine you are a newly minted fire-team leader and under moderate/low-moderate scrutiny. Imagine you are a newly minted team leader whose soldiers do not know quite what to make of being led by a newly minted team leader.

Imagine that this realization routinely populates your mind not from the comfort of a Starbucks, but during each BD1A iteration ... of which there have been many ... and of which more are certain to follow.

And imagine you are running, and running, and growing stronger, and running ... and running.

And running.

God, those were good days. I cannot say with any certainty that I rightly recognized as much at the time. But I hope so. What a shame if I hadn't.

What a shame...

I *did* think of Ariel Denton at least once. She had populated my mental landscape far less frequently following my first full year in the Army's employ. On those rare occasions in which she did make an appearance, it was invariably accompanied by a feeling I hesitate to articulate via the written word for fear I will do it injustice.

Now imagine that the sun has fallen well below the horizon.

Darkness.

Darkness.

Darkness.

...

...

...

...

...now imagine you are readying for yet another BD1A run through.

"Let's go." This was SSG Wilson addressing my fire-team. Second Squad's gunners had opened fire on the enemy objective. As our imagined enemies were being suppressed by a combination of M240B, M249, and M4 firepower, courtesy of Hooph and his men, SSG Wilson, myself, and my fire-team made our way towards the objective.

It is a feeling I remember very well, even here, and now, in a Starbucks, some thirteen years later.

Imagine your muscle fibers are simply frayed to the utmost. Your lungs are wholly fatigued. Your vision blurs unless actively brought into focus. Your bones ache from the weight by which they have been burdened.

And imagine that very ache migrating from bone mass to psyche, and imagine it takes on a context of a decidedly favorable sort. No longer the painful ache of weary bones, but the yearning ache born of anticipating yet another run through of that battle drill whose every pounding step, fired shot, illuminating signal, and ragged breath you had come to know with profound intimacy.

Imagine lastly that you are twenty-one years of age…

…and imagine you once again feel invincible. It was a sensation I had not fully known since high school, though then that feeling had been predicated upon an *entirely* inflated self-image, rather than *almost* entirely inflated, as was the case four years hence.

When at last we had vanquished our foes of fog and wind for the final time, we gathered up the gear that had been sitting unattended for fourteen hours' time near the transportation pick-up point. Somewhere between noon and nightfall, my body had reset itself. It was as though it had simply found an energy reserve deep within itself and drawn upon it generously. This is to say that I was nothing even approaching exhausted, not until Second Squad, Second Platoon entered the barracks, dropped its collective body armor, and took a moment to simply *be*.

It was at that point that my eyelids found themselves tugged downwards by a force neither could resist, not even the left one … my dominant lid.

I will speak for the entirety of Second Squad in stating that we slept well and deeply that evening. First call did, once again, come early; but we rose rested, mostly, and looked ahead to whatever awaited.

We did a good deal of platoon PT while at A.P. Hill and visited numerous ranges. There was also a M.O.U.T. (Military Operations in Urban Terrain) stage, though we knew this to be merely preliminary. The authentic M.O.U.T. range awaited us some ways to the south.

But Battle Drill One Alpha was the centerpiece of Battlehard's Fort A.P. Hill pre-mobilization training plan. It did with us as best it could, and we did right by it as best we were able. Each man left that range feeling strong, feeling capable. It was as it should have been.

Of course, A.P. Hill represented but one phase of all that awaited Battlehard.

We returned from our Fort A.P. Hill excursion and knew further packing list nonsense awaited us. As space was almost always at a premium in our otherwise spacious barracks, those of us who lived off-post typically had a "go-to" on-post soldier whose room we would politely co-occupy when either readying for or concluding a packing list layout. In my case, it was often the room of Ryan Fritsche, a soldier who never once voiced a complaint of any sort; not on account of the layouts themselves, nor on account of necessarily sharing his limited real estate with yet another needy off-post soldier.

Never once.

This was something I came to observe more closely in Fritsche throughout the weeks and months ahead. Or, rather, it was *what I did not observe* that most struck me as being admirable, and worthy, and good, and rare. Fritsche, you see, was not given to channeling hostility, nor cynicism, nor frustration. In that regard, he was perhaps the best of us. I found this aspect of his person most noble.

* * *

When visiting Fort Polk nearly two years later, in the fall of 2003, I was in perfect health. For that much I was grateful, as the training that awaited us would be immeasurably valuable. Sitting idly by would not have done.

The good men of S-3 (my former colleagues) charged with Battlehard's pre-mobilization training calendar had kindly seen fit to afford the company some days of reprieve following our A.P. Hill excursion. These we spent well, by and large.

I distinctly recall having entered my beautiful Fairfax townhouse within two hours of returning to Fort Myer. There had been weapons to turn in and a brief formation, but most of the off-post soldiers were on the road an hour or so later.

If "Senator Fred" and "Bacardi" were home, I didn't see either. I walked upstairs to the master bedroom, showered, and considered the day ahead, the training to come, the impending deployment about which we still knew very little.

When exiting the shower, it occurred to me that, while I recognized the person inhabiting the mirror opposite me, I recognized him to a lesser extent than had been the case some weeks prior. I appeared curiously gaunt from the neck upwards, and fantastically muscular from the neck downwards. It was a bizarre incongruity, and one that occurs to me periodically even now. While I had maintained a good level of fitness for years, never prior to that time had my cheeks (generally cherubic in their form) appeared quite so sunken, nor had my abdominal musculature seemed ready to burst from its fleshly encasement. Battle Drill One Alpha had carved its Bravo Company practitioners into fighting specimens.

Following a couple of days spent in Fairfax, "Fred" and I carpooled back to Myer for a formation the purpose of which was a continued drip-feeding of information regarding the days and weeks ahead. We understood that we could expect another five days on Myer prior to our Fort Polk training, even if we weren't quite certain as to how those days would be spent.

But of course, there was packing to be done. And lists to be checked off. And items to be lain out.

There was more to our week of Myer time than mere packing lists, of course. There were also formations.

We packed, we formed up, we packed.

And when we formed up for the final time that week, it was immediately prior to our boarding buses for the airport. Fort Polk, it did await us.

I remember having left our beautiful Fairfax townhome very early the morning of our departure and wishing there were more daylight by which to appreciate the undeniably idyllic suburban residential setting in which we had been living for over a year's time.

But there was not. And so I left under a dark sky, and arrived to Myer thirty minutes later with only the faintest trace of the day's impending sunrise visible to the naked eye.

The flight to Louisiana was weird. For one, we were instructed to treat our weapons as carry-on items.

The hilarious image of an ultra-effeminate flight attendant struggling with the weight of an M240B while attempting to secure it in an overhead bin is worthy of recalling on at least a semi-annual basis.

The man had insisted we all keep our seats while he continued seeing to our carry-on weapons, crew-served or otherwise.

The flight was also weird in the way that any chartered flight is a bit weird.

Generally, when one boards a commercial aircraft, they do so in the company of dozens of perfect strangers. The effect is predictably one of uncomfortable silences and awkward, averted eye contact.

But when the flight is populated solely by fellow soldiers, most of whom you have known for two to three years' time, it's a far more comfortable and enjoyable travel experience. Throughout my late-twenties and early-thirties, I flew quite often for professional purposes. When traveling on personal time, I was often accompanied by a girlfriend (fiancée, on a few occasions; long story). But even the normalizing effect of routine jet setting, or that of flying in the company of a loved one does little to render air travel anything other than a tension-inducing necessity.

Not so on chartered flights.

The men of Battlehard were at ease (so to speak) throughout the duration of that airborne journey. We took every occasion to exchange verbal barbs, talked of what lay ahead, and appreciated the messy, elusive splendor of it all. It was rather splendid.

I recall us reaching Fort Polk proper late in the afternoon. Being well-practiced in the art of efficiently populating a set of temporary barracks, we men of Bravo Company quickly worked. We ate a meal in the neighboring DFAC and returned for an evening of much needed rest. The days to follow were to be decidedly full in their scheduled goings on.

There were ranges and shoothouses, MOUT drills and extraction runs, and there was PT. We would be putting to good use the conditioning A.P. Hill had bestowed upon us. The sensation of heavy weight resting upon one's shoulders tends to stick with most combat arms soldiers, whether theirs was peacetime service or wartime. Combat engineers, Special Forces operators, mortarmen, and infantry grunts: all are expected to be, at bare minimum, capable of bearing considerable burdens upon their backs, and for long stretches of time. I don't know that identifying this as a skill is necessarily accurate, but it certainly qualifies as a professional tolerance.

Throughout the Fort Polk chapter of our pre-mobilization training, that familiar feeling was very much with us most waking moments of every day.

First call came when it otherwise would've come had we been commencing with a Primary week back on Myer. I believe we awoke at 0600hrs for an 0630hrs formation.

It was possibly an hour of push-ups and partner-assisted leg-lifts that morning. The latter of these requires that one lay flat upon their back while a fellow soldier stands over one's head, their feet positioned on either side of one's head. It is the kicking man's responsibility to ensure (via active resistance) that his feet do not ultimately reach the earth below, thereby strengthening his abdominal musculature.

Coupled with push-ups, this was an excellent platoon-level PT session.

We showered, visited the DFAC, returned to the barracks, armored ourselves, and prepared for a day of suck.

And it sucked.

It was supposed to suck, and did.

We were a better company for enduring what we did—that which every mobilizing infantry company endures.

If Battle Drill One Alpha had been the tactical anthem of our A.P. Hill time, MOUT would be the DNA of our Fort Polk training regimen. MOUT (Military Operations in Urban Terrain) preparation(s) had assumed a new place of precedence within the military since shortly after the outset of Operation Iraqi Freedom. Bear in mind, basic training classes since the 1970s had emphasized woodland/jungle tactics and fieldcraft, with combat wisdom and lessons accumulated during the Vietnam War serving as the basis for as much.

Because much of the fighting in Iraq took place in and around urban environments, and as the surrounding desert landscape had scarce little in common with the jungles of Southeast Asia, U.S. Army Training and Doctrine Command (TRADOC) had been in the process of necessarily reevaluating its training/preparation manuals. By late-2003, the Army was working to metaphorically adjust its fire on that front. Battlehard's Fort Polk MOUT exercises were born directly of that adjustment.

Thus, Potemkin villages, houses, and streets line the Fort Polk landscape. These Potemkin fixtures are to simulate urban combat environments, and are of far sturdier construction than one might imagine. Hollywood famously fashions paper-thin buildings in service to filmmaking illusion. These are generally of a disposable nature, given their cheap construction and the limited degree to which actors and stuntmen subject their loadbearing limits to any significant stress.

Not so with the Potemkin infrastructure and numerous military installations around the country. These are required to withstand tremendous abuse and are hardy in their construction. Doors are kicked in, stone walls slammed against, staircases violently negotiated, floors rocked with the weight of falling bodies.

Battlehard came to closely know this side of Polk during the fall of 2003. There were other training items on the itinerary, but MOUT was granted top billing. And like its woodland/jungle counterpart, urban warfare requires a training system unique unto it. One structure can yield dozens of isolated combat actions, each carrying with it the same set of visibility obstacles along with the sheer geometry of tight turns and invisible murder holes.

MOUT, to say the least, is perilous business. I lay bare my infinite and undying respect for any soldier who has ever experienced the trauma that accompanies its lethal undertaking.

The men of Bravo Company did not yet have an understanding as to where we were headed. For all we knew, the environment awaiting us would be rife with urban combat challenges. Our leadership saw to it that we were acquainted with MOUT tenets and tactics.

Repetition be thy name.

By its very nature, MOUT training is a broad canvas upon which infinite plausible combat scenarios can be painted. One need not possess a particularly fertile imagination to conceptualize such scenarios, or to modify those used previously. They virtually write themselves. And most begin with a stack.

The stack.

To stack is to arrange oneself and one's men in line (typically three to five soldiers) immediately alongside an entryway, or at the turning point of a hallway/corridor.

Based upon the unit SOP, each man is to aim his weapon in a specific direction in a surveilling capacity prior to entering the room or passageway to be cleared. The point man immediately adjacent to the doorway will keep his weapon trained upon said doorway. To his rear will stand the team leader, whose weapon might be pointed over the point man's shoulder or perpendicular to the stack' position. Behind him will be either a SAW gunner or, a non–SAW gunner … also known as a rifleman. Either way, that man generally keeps his aim high and outward-facing (assuming an outdoor scenario) or level and to the rear of the stack. Lastly (assuming a four-man stack), the rear soldier will have his back to the team for the purpose of providing six o' clock cover.

And then…

BOOM!

Again, based upon the unit SOP, it might be either the point man or the man immediately behind the team leader, but one of the two will execute a breaching action. This often requires the kicking in of a door, the destroying of hinges via shotgun fire, or the swift turning of a sharp corner. The latter of these does not constitute the breaching of a solid object, but the breaching of something more abstract in its construct—the unknown.

BOOM begets further aggression, as the stack then populates a room, a corridor, a warehouse, et cetera with sufficient violence of action to overwhelm all those they may encounter, hostile or otherwise.

And there it is.

The stack. We men of Battlehard stacked daily. There were outdoor breaching scenarios, indoor multi-room-clearing scenarios, staircase ascending scenarios, staircase descending scenarios, entire house-clearing scenarios.

We stacked and cleared to the point of exhaustion on our second full day of training, until eventually, around 2100hrs, Captain Travers determined that our training had reached a point of diminishing returns. He was correct—it had. We returned to the barracks with an understanding that there was plenty of MOUT on the agenda in the days to come.

I would be remiss in not acknowledging the professional/historical significance of the compound in which our many Fort Polk days were spent: The Shughart-Gordon training complex.

Anyone familiar with Mark Bowden's paramount work of military non-fiction titled *Black Hawk Down*, or familiar with its film adaptation, or familiar more broadly with the events explored in those works, will likely know the story of Delta Force heroes and Medal of Honor Awardees Master Sergeant Gary Gordon and Sergeant First Class Randy Shughart.

The Battle of Mogadishu, which was waged in October of 1993, produced many heroes, summoned into existence incomprehensible valor, and regrettably yielded enormous tragedy and loss of an incomprehensibly painful sort.

No set of actions more fully embodied heroism, valor, tragedy, and loss than did those performed by Shughart and Gordon on that fateful day.

Suffice it to say that during the Battle of Mogadishu, Gary Gordon and Randy Shughart covered themselves in glory to a godlike degree, lost their lives in so doing, and stand alongside the greatest heroes in recorded history.

In their honor, Fort Polk's premier MOUT grounds are named Shughart-Gordon Training Complex, with "Training Complex" sometimes spelled out in strictly lower-case letters.

On the subject of honor, learning and practicing MOUT tactics in the Shughart-Gordon Training Complex was exactly that—an honor. We men of Bravo Company belonged to a unit whose shoulder tab featured the word "Honor" prominently, and were well acquainted with the notion of honor. We worked diligently to honor those men we laid to rest and were honored to be serving in and around the nation's capital.

Still, even with our unit's immersion in the project of honoring others, we found ourselves decidedly honored to be training in a complex bearing the names of those two men—two of the finest men ever to have worn Army green.

We learned a good deal during our time there. Some of what was covered did overlap with our A.P. Hill training, though much of it was new to us. A deeply respected combat authority from the Regiment was flown-in to educate the company in certain urban warfare tactics and principles. These included the covert approaching of a hostile township or cityscape, the aggressive breaching of blocked doorways and passages, the best means of evading fire in an otherwise vulnerable position (hint: get the fuck inside), and the covert withdrawal from a hostile township or cityscape.

With respect to the first of those listed, an exercise undertaken well after nightfall required that each platoon approach a collection of buildings quietly and in near total darkness. Somewhere along the way, no more than fifty yards from our objective, the point man encountered a lengthy and forbidding stretch of concertina wire ... a wire designed to prevent covert soldiers from approaching a given objective.

It was Hooph who quickly (and expertly) went to work with his wire cutters, and within a minute or so had opened a small section through which we might pass.

"Might" being the operative word. While most Second Squad soldiers passed through Hooph's adequate doorway, Matt "Bacardi" Lemon somehow managed to snag (there is no better word for it) one of his hands on a cruelly hooked section of concertina. And to say the least, "Bacardi" reacted in such a way as to hilariously compromise the silence we had, up to that point, collectively nurtured between us.

Hooph had closed the distance between himself and "Bacardi" while performing one of those peculiar whisper-shouts which most Old Guard NCOs come to master. Hooph had certainly mastered it.

Lemon quieted down while Hooph and one other, worked to free his hand from the unforgiving grip of that concertina barb. Once freed, Lemon resumed his approach alongside the squad as we made our way towards the objective…

…for the first time that evening. Repetition being essential to good performance, there were more to follow.

And the days that followed saw more of the same. Until, at last, our time at Fort Polk was complete.

Of course, it was not complete, not without yet another few hints as to what lay in store for the men of Battlehard … and where it was we could expect to find ourselves in a couple of weeks' time.

"Any of you men been to Africa?"

This question was put to us in wording along those lines by our platoon sergeant SFC Boorman. We were gathered in the lower bay of a two-floor barracks about an hour or so after dinner chow. I believe we had but a day or so remaining in Fort Polk.

A sort of half-chuckle circulated throughout the platoon, though none responded openly to Boorman's half-joking question.

"Well, you'll be there soon enough. We're going to the Horn. It's got Ethiopia and a place called Djibouti in it. Horn of Africa. Any questions?"

"Any clue what we'll be doing there?" This was from my longtime friend, Travis "Smitty" Smith.

"Not really, man, no. We'll probably know more soon, but all I can tell you right now is that we're heading to the Horn of Africa."

More unanswered questions followed, and that was enough for us. We had a firm understanding of where we were headed—the rest could wait.

A day later, we returned to Fort Myer after what had seemed like a short stay in Fort Polk, though it had, in truth, been rather long. We accomplished a good deal, slept little, and entered that tunnel vision phenomenon to which all humans are prone when subjected to intensive training episodes.

This yielded a sense of ours having been, as stated, a short stay in Fort Polk.

Our return to Myer was not unlike that earlier return following the Fort A.P. Hill trials. Nor was it quite like it. It was something in between. That same sense of camaraderie-born-of-weariness moved alongside each man, like a silent companion of light and shadow rather than of flesh and blood. We welcomed and cherished his familiar presence, but that familiarity had its limits, and it didn't render this return overly similar to its predecessor.

Something else loomed.

There was the knowledge that a mission awaited. A mission quite unlike anything Battlehard had expected to undertake. Some of the newly arrived soldiers found intriguing the notion that many of us senior Bravo souls had participated in the Pentagon recovery effort, and wondered if the impending deployment registered within our minds in anything like it.

The truth is it did not.

What had happened on September 11th, 2001 had happened on U.S. soil. Ours had been the response of home defenders. Yes, duty-wise it had amounted to a tremendous aberration for the Army's premier ceremonial unit; and yes, the work had thrust each man into a mindset wholly unlike anything we had inhabited prior to that day.

But we were within a mile or so of Myer through it all. War had come to our shores and we had responded accordingly. We carried on with the work that was our unique charge.

Then here we are. Or there we were, rather. Kids when the Pentagon had been attacked. Slightly older kids now, albeit with some rank to our name. The feeling in the air had scarce little in common with what we had felt in September and October of 2001.

We hoped we were ready.

And it's possible we were.

Strike that.

We were ready. As ready as was achievable within the space of two months' training time. It'd been a demanding ordeal—we were better for it. Better as a company, better as platoons, better as individuals.

Better, also, psychologically. Had we not stepped foot off Fort Myer following our return from Polk, I'd still consider those two months of training to have been time well spent. There is lesson in pain, lesson in stress, lesson in struggle. To varying degrees, the men of Battlehard had been subjected to each of these, as had countless thousands of our forebears throughout the annals of recorded history. There was something powerful about the realization of that ancestral connection.

Now if only we could find occasion to further solidify said connection. It seemed unlikely that the Horn of Africa would provide us with any real opportunity where achieving that end was concerned, but we'd leave that determination to the Horn.

For Bravo Co. of the 3rd United States Infantry "The Old Guard" was to be the first Regimental company to deploy since the Vietnam War had been underway some thirty years prior. There was significance in that fact, but we wouldn't be content with merely deploying. We sought to do good work wherever it was we were headed.

My hope, years later, is that we earned a victory of sorts in that regard.

XVIII

Wells and Volleyball

The Horn of Africa is a massive peninsula covering over seven-hundred-thousand square miles and comprising the countries of Djibouti, Eritrea, Ethiopia, and Somalia. It extends many miles into the Arabian Sea and is the African continent's easternmost projection. Well over one-hundred-million souls inhabit the Horn, making it about one-third as populous as these United States.

It is generally impoverished, but not entirely without exception. Ethiopia, in particular, is blessed with large tracts of arable land which yield potatoes, various cereals, sugarcane, and enormous quantities of coffee (the nation's chief export). For this reason, coffee is regarded as "black gold" by Ethiopians and others throughout Africa.

Ethiopian agriculture and strong economic growth aside, the Horn of Africa is home to enormous poverty of the sort one would be hard-pressed to find in the Western World. To be sure, countless Appalachian communities might seem to have more in common with the Horn than with, say, the Upper East Side, at least in certain respects.

That said, the comparison falls flat when one considers the infrastructural disparity between the First World and the Third. Roads, running water, electricity, and some degree of literacy are reliably present in the most backwater of American towns.

Not so in Djibouti. Not so in Somalia, And not so even in Ethiopia, the Horn's strongest nation state.

If any aspect of my time spent in the Horn and in Afghanistan continues to fascinate, perplex, and trouble me, it is that of having been confronted by rampant illiteracy and by the circumstances to which it both directly and indirectly contributes.

I reflect upon that often.

* * *

Bravo Company soldiers beset by wind-strewn dust in Djibouti. Notice the landscape's almost Martian–like quality (particularly when thusly filtered) (photograph by Spc. Eric M. McKeeby).

The flight had been long. Several flights, really. Eventually, and under the cover of night, the aircraft conveying Battlehard on its final leg landed at Djibouti-Ambouli International Airport.

Djibouti-Ambouli International Airport is home to Camp Lemonnier, the sole permanent U.S. military base in *all of Africa*. From Camp Lemonnier operated the Combined Joint Task Force—Horn of Africa (now USAFRICOM). As Djibouti's coastline comprises much of the strategically important Gulf of Tadjoura, and as the country sits rather near the Arabian Peninsula, it is a highly sensible choice for the situating of any such Western military base/task force.

Originally a French base (as its name implies), Lemonnier had been a launching pad for French Foreign Legion activity many years prior to 2002, the year in which the United States secured an agreement allowing its forces to operate from the camp in support of its broader anti-terrorism efforts. There would also be a humanitarian component, as is always the case when American forces take up residence in the Third World.

Long after my own time in Djibouti, I came to learn that much of what would ultimately constitute Lemonnier's command operations were literally offboarded from the USS *Mount Whitney*, a Navy *Blue Ridge* class command ship which is presently the Sixth Fleet's flagship. Apparently, the enormous *Mount Whitney* had been housing a base's worth of command personnel and equipment within its confines; enough of each to adequately populate Lemonnier in mid–2003.

It is amazing, is it not? The things we humans are capable of building and floating.

That transfer from sea to land took place months prior to Battlehard's arrival, so that by the time we stepped foot on Djiboutian soil, Lemonnier was very well operational and settled. True, we would be living in tents. But tents with structural reinforcement, wooden flooring, and electric wiring.

There were no cots anywhere in sight, as each soldier was assigned a sturdy bunk, and one never found oneself more than thirty paces from an ice-packed bottled water cooler. These took the form of waist-high wooden boxes in which scores of sealed water bottles were stored, and regularly replenished.

There were civilian trucks being driven by military folk, and military vehicles. There was a large gymnasium, a phone center, DFAC, and a medium-sized cantina. Yes, there was a cantina. It comes into play less than you might imagine, but more than at least a few soldiers might care to acknowledge.

There was also a large stretch of dirt immediately adjacent to the airstrip. This served as Battlehard's formation/PT area, as well as a rehearsal ground for the small unit tactics in which we would later engage.

Following our first night's rest in Djibouti, the jetlagged men of Bravo Company formed up on that lot to hear what Captain Travers had to say.

Though some ten days had passed since the conclusion of our Fort Polk training, that morning invited upon many of us a stronger sense of reflection than any we had recently known. It was as though the preceding week had allowed for memories of our recent tactical conditioning trials to firmly organize themselves within our minds.

I, as is my wont, reflected accordingly.

What had begun in September with my serving as a rifleman in First Squad, Second Platoon had ended with my serving as a fire-team leader in Second Squad, Second Platoon. By any reasonable standard, my men had performed well while preparing themselves in body and mind for our deployment.

They had accepted the assignment of a very young, recently promoted team leader, and worked hard to prove themselves tactically sound both individually and collectively.

Reed possessed enormous energy, a contagious sense of optimism, and was never heard complaining. He was the oldest member of my fire-team and Second Squad's second oldest soldier, being only a few years younger than SSG Wilson. The age difference carried with it an implication of maturity and perspective, both of which the man exemplified. He was the team's emotional anchor, though it was only in subsequent years that I'd come to fully understand and appreciate as much.

Harding was soft-spoken, a characteristic which misrepresented him to some degree; verbal gentility doesn't imply physical frailty. Harding evidenced as much by simply existing. He was sturdily built and had embraced the often-thankless role of SAW gunner with not one word of objection. If ever I took for granted any soldier's humble professionalism, it was in the case of Private Harding.

Garcia, like Reed, was a father and had joined the Army well into his twenties. He was motivated by family responsibility above all else and wanted, perhaps more overtly than most others in the platoon, to be a good soldier. His ambition was admirable in that he sought to make of the Army a lifelong career. I have come to learn that he did precisely that, and has thrived.

When it became known to platoon leadership that Bacardi and I were longtime off-post roommates, there'd been brief talk of re-assigning him to another team or squad. Fraternization is, after all, rather frowned upon within the U.S. Army. Ultimately, no action was taken. Instead, it was understood that I was to treat Lemon like any other soldier, despite our friendship and living arrangement. It didn't hurt that Lemon is an excellent soldier and a strong athlete. Either in observing us at A.P. Hill or during our Polk MOUT training, it was determined that our fraternal bonds were unlikely to manifest in any negative capacity. Bacardi demonstrated terrific field proficiency, weapons marksmanship, and general soldiering ability throughout the months preceding our deployment.

My thoughts in that first morning formation in Djibouti surely did not play out in so organized a manner. Instead, a vague realization of it all sort of circled through my mind as we awaited Captain Travers' arrival. I was pleased with my team and trusted them to a man. Of comparable importance was the extent to which I trusted my fellow team leader, Hooph, and our squad leader, SSG Wilson.

A strong fire-team, a longtime friend for a fellow team leader, and a kindred spirit for a squad leader. The men of Bravo Company were a largely bonded group and most teams/squads tended to exhibit the signs of brotherhood one might expect of siblings bound by consanguinity. Which is to say, mine was not a unique set of circumstances; nevertheless, I was quietly grateful for said circumstances. I loved my team … loved my squad. I was pleased to be standing on Djiboutian earth with them.

And then Captain Travers spoke.

Commanding officers differ widely from one to the next in their handling of this professional obligation. Personalities differ widely. Travers was given to leavening his addresses with rhetoric that seemed at once martial and evangelical. He did not take his position lightly, which is to his great credit.

He also enjoyed cinema.

During a conversation with the man a year earlier, while we were both in the shop (prior to his assuming command of Battlehard), we had enjoyed a round of film trivia one-upmanship. We both enjoyed the sparring match a good deal, to my recollection.

With that in mind, I wasn't in the least surprised when Travers first summoned a film analogy in laboring to rally his men. Or a second time. Nor a third.

Only once would I find surprising the man's penchant for borrowing silver screen passages and scenes in speaking to his men.

Our first company formation would be one of our few while overseas. If forced to put forth a number, I'd estimate we formed-up in full strength on no more than ten occasions during the deployment. Of course, none among us would have made that prediction.

Travers had concluded his address with words to the effect of, "You're doing God's work, men" before releasing us to our platoons for a round of PT, echoing a sentiment he had voiced stateside some weeks earlier. A brief run that morning, followed by showers and a visit to the sizable DFAC. Years later, while in one of Bagram, Afghanistan's two DFACs, I was distinctly reminded of Camp Lemonnier and found myself chuckling at the similarity. The Third World is decidedly less Third World–like within the confines of a contractor-built and contractor-run dining facility.

We even had an omelet guy. He was (is) Eastern European and did *excellent* work. During Second Platoon's many stretches away from Lemonnier, we tended to miss the omelets above most else. Of course, the enormous and well-equipped gymnasium ranked high in that regard, as did the cantina for those so inclined. As I had come to the Horn armed with several good books, I was essentially content wherever it was we laid our heads each night ... but those omelets—sublime.

As for the gymnasium, we also made do from site to site. Soldiers overseas do a good deal of weightlifting. This is true in HOA, in Afghanistan, and I have it on excellent authority that it is true in Iraq. For one, it's an ideal means of counteracting stress, boredom, and the excess calories present in all but the most barren of DFACs. Secondly, it provides a sense of returning home with something to show for the whole ordeal.

In many cases, a given soldier will set ambitious goals for himself. These might be strictly cosmetic in nature or might have to do with surpassing one's existing strength limitations.

One of the soldiers with whom I served in Afghanistan labored very diligently to maintain a bodybuilder-level physique throughout his yearlong deployment—and succeeded. It was a truly marvelous and impressive feat, given what I knew of the man's operation load.

All of this is to say that soldiers overseas (with few exceptions) lift early and often. Thus the Lemonnier gymnasium's enormous commitment of space and investment in equipment—lifting soldiers are contented soldiers.

So what were we men of Second Squad, Second Platoon to do upon reaching the well site?

Ours was a painfully simple mission: to provide tactical security for a small group of Army engineers presently drilling a well near Djibouti's oldest (though third largest) city—that of Tadjoura.

The Tadjourah Region (the "h" incidentally separates region from city) is one of Djibouti's six regions and sits northwest of the Djibouti-Ambouli Airport, and directly northwest of Camp Lemonnier. Of course, the region is separated from the airport by a large inlet, courtesy of the Gulf of Tadjoura, thereby necessitating a lengthy roundabout drive from one to the other.

We were but a couple of days in country when the word, so to speak, came down.

"Sergeant Mongilutz, Sergeant Hoffman." Wilson was reliably inconsistent in addressing his two team leaders. I was "Mark" as often as I was "Sergeant Mongilutz," while Hooph was either "Hoffman," "John," or "Sergeant Hoffman." Referring to us by rank and name suggested official business was at hand. Or that one of us had erred in some way.

"Okay, it looks like we're it. Second squad'll be the first of Bravo outside the wire."

Hooph nodded nonchalantly in that familiar way I had first come to know in December of 2000.

"We're going a little ways north. There's an engineering group diggin' a well. We're going to provide on-site security while they work and camp security while they sleep."

"Okay." This Hooph said as though being told that an appetizer order had been placed prior to his reaching the table. Apparent indifference is the man's most notable (and perhaps most likable) characteristic.

"It's three hours by Humvee, maybe more. We're to report by 1400hrs tomorrow, which means we'll have time for last minute preparation after breakfast chow. Even so, I'd rather have everything squared away before lights out tonight. That's mags checked, gear cleaned, food loaded up, all of it. We'll be there a week, so let's pack for two."

"Tracking." I had really taken to saying this around the time of my SK2K2 stint with Bob during our shared convalescence.

"Okay," Wilson continued, "take the day to do whatever you'd like. Gym time, chow, organize your AO (area of operation (bunk space)), whatever. But after dinner, get these guys ready for all of it.

Wilson paused momentarily as if thinking about something he had forgotten, then remembered.

"And make sure these guys get to the phone center to call home. We're not in the shit out here, but you never know. They probably have a sat (satellite) phone at the site; doesn't mean they'll be sharin' with us. Get your guys to the phone center."

Wilson was a good squad leader in that way. He had deployed some years prior and was thoughtful in his consideration of needs we and the men didn't know we had.

He was also right—we were not in the shit. The Horn was technically a conflict zone, I suppose, but it was nothing like Iraq; nothing like Afghanistan. It was sufficiently dangerous to warrant our being armed and vigilant, which says everything and nothing.

I can say with near-certainty that only Bacardi and Garcia made their way to the phone center that evening, despite my having urged Reed and Harding to do the same.

The following morning, we carried on in accordance with the company's vaguely defined routine. There was a fractured formation followed by PT and breakfast chow. As ours was the only squad headed out that morning, we ate with a little more purpose than did our platoon mates and returned quickly to the tent.

Following breakfast, Hooph's guys, to include the gun team, seemed far more active in their preparation than did my own. This activated within my psyche a trace element of paranoia, which was itself assuaged following the second round of clarifying questions I asked of each soldier.

"Magazines loaded? Canteens full? Gear clean? Clothing packed?"

"Roger, Sergeant."

This I heard no fewer than seventy times between my four men. They had made intelligent use of the prior day's evening hours. More so, it seemed, than had Hooph's men. This left me in the peculiar position of being seemingly disengaged from our squad's preparation process. There was little for me to do. The B fire-team was running smoothly.

When the Humvees (High Mobility Multipurpose Wheeled Vehicle; if ever there was a less necessary acronym) pulled up alongside our tents, we set to loading them with MRE boxes, bottles of water, spare ammunition, and the omelet guy.

Merely jesting. We were prohibited from asking the omelet guy to accompany us to the well site (though Bretty recalls having brought an omelet guy on an extended operation; perhaps the same one).

At 1000hrs, we were fully loaded and prepared for our northward journey. The Tadjourah Region, and its capital Tadjoura, awaited our arrival.

At around 1002hrs, something unexpected happened. Battlehard's 1SG approached the vehicle and signaled that I should lean my ear in for a spoken word message. This I did with a good deal of curiosity. This was, after all, the same First Sergeant who had (a) thrown a bit of trouble my way during the promotion board some months earlier, and (b) had made my return to Bravo Company anything but painless after said board.

With a hand on my body armor, the man whispered *directly* into my ear the following words: "Make sure these men do their weapon maintenance when y'all get where you goin.' You don't want Jessica Lynch bitin' us in the ass."

Jessica Lynch, as you will surely recall, was the lionized soldier who suffered severe battlefield injuries and was subsequently captured by enemy combatants during the early days of the Iraq War. It was generally understood that weapon system malfunctions had been a factor working against the convoy of which Lynch was a part.

"Tracking, First Sergeant."

Needless to say, I took the 1SG's words seriously and saw to it that my fire-team afforded their primary weapons at least a few moments of cursory maintenance within thirty minutes of our arrival.

But we had not yet arrived. There were miles to be covered and a very foreign, desolate country with which we would first become visually acquainted.

There is something otherworldly about Djibouti. I was keen to that fact soon after Second Squad had left behind the relative safety and amenities of Camp Lemonnier for the barren Djiboutian landscape.

Djibouti is small. It measures under nine thousand square miles, which makes it about the size of New Jersey.

But size alone does not make the country. What most plagues Djibouti is that nearly all its limited land is barren. Agriculture accounts for something like four percent of the country's economy. It is rock, dirt, thirst, impoverishment.

And it is inhabited by some of the world's poorest human beings. Though I should acknowledge that many of those we encountered throughout our travels were anything but poor in spirit. They haven't the luxury of cynicism, and the self-loathing that so often accompanies Western experience is entirely absent the Third World, at least among those with whom we interacted.

But we had not yet interacted with any Djiboutian citizens. We were on a long drive, and the desolate lands were taking root in our minds. In many respects, the emptiness of it all seemed to encourage introspection.

I was acutely aware of being in a leadership position beyond the relative safety of civilization.

And then we drove past the decaying carcass of a recently killed camel, its ribcage having been violently ruptured when struck by a vehicle (likely a

Humvee) moving at what must've been medium-high speed. The smell was thick, heavy, and made itself known approximately thirty yards out.

"You guys smell that shit?" Steele was smiling while asking that entirely unnecessary question. *Of course* we smelled the rotting animal. Steele was a natural jester in most respects, and given to compounding the gallows humor of a given situation with his cleaver-like wit.

Nobody responded, but I recall a few smiles and shaking of heads. What is a squad without its jokester?

We exchanged minutes for miles and reached the engineer's tiny camp ahead of schedule, having crossed into the Tadjourah region nearly an hour earlier. Though Djibouti is very small by most standards, Tadjourah covers over twenty-five-hundred square miles. Upon crossing into it from the southwest, one finds oneself some forty or so miles from Tadjoura itself. And the engineer's camp sat a little ways from the city.

The engineers had situated themselves in a weird place.

Reaching the camp did indeed require a good deal of elevation ascending, but it placed one in a sort of partially tipped bowl of a valley. On one side, we found ourselves enclosed by a small mountain/hill range, while on another we were confronted by a large, open expanse of nothingness. These accounted for over sixty-percent of the surrounding terrain. The remaining thirty-five or so was a broad overlook from which we could see far and wide into Djiboutian lands, and likely beyond.

Somehow a single squad seemed inadequate for the defense of such an area.

Not that it would matter. Nothing happened during our time there.

The engineers were a crusty bunch. Each NCO looked as though he had wedged sixty years of hard living into only a bit over half that time. A couple of the young lower-enlisted soldiers were apparently following suit.

They were a matter-of-fact bunch who did good work without exception. I liked them immediately.

Reed constructed a quality pull-up frame/bar with scarce little in the way of materials. I hadn't realized the former carpenter would take me seriously. But take me seriously he did.

"Not much in the way of exercise equipment here, is there?" I had put this question to nobody in particular.

"Unless you'd like to toss rocks around." Hooph was either serious or expertly feigning as much.

"Hmmm ... if only there were a carpenter in our midst." I cast a sly glance Reed's way, assuming he'd politely tell his fire-team leader to bugger off.

"Let me see what I can find." Reed dropped his gear near the tent we would know as home for a week's time and began looking around the nearby scrap pile.

Ten minutes later, he beckoned for the team to join him as he organized a few pieces of wood in something resembling a manifest blueprint.

Later that afternoon, we had a well-made bar-frame immediately adjacent to our tent. A polyvinyl chloride (PVC) pipe would stand in place of a steel bar. And though it flexed slightly with each repetition, it withstood the weight of every man throughout the entirety of our stay. I even took to performing sets while wearing my body armor, so confident was I in the pipe's considerable resilience.

I also developed a sunburn. A bad one. The Djiboutian winter had made a fool of me.

Our second day in camp, I had (stupidly) elected to exercise in PTs ... sans PT shirt. The temperature (about sixty degrees) was perfect for sustained physical exertion. I made the mistake of equating climate with sun exposure. It did not seem hot outside, not in the least. Therefore, I must not be subjecting my exposed skin to intense, unmitigated ultraviolet rays.

So very stupid.

Following forty minutes of push-ups, pull-ups, and sprinting, I returned to the tent to retrieve a bottle of water. What I hadn't expected was for the slightest touch to visit immense pain upon my flesh.

It was the tent flap. Merely brushing against it forced me to confront the miserable reality that mine was wholly toasted epidermal tissue.

Lemon took notice prior to the others doing so.

"Holy shit, Sergeant Mongilutz, you're straight-up red."

I was exactly that. My back more than elsewhere had assumed the color of a ripe red apple. Elsewhere I was pink, but my upper back had been effectively dyed crimson.

It was Bacardi who, morning and night, applied a generous helping of aloe vera to the wounded flesh of my back for the next three days. By the fourth, the redness had given way to a deep bronze color which would stay with me (to varying degrees) throughout the deployment.

As for the job, it was as simple as advertised. One fire-team would each day accompany the engineers to their dig, while the other performed campsite perimeter security. The latter we would also maintain through all hours of the night.

These, I might add, were cold nights. Not terribly so. Just cold enough to warrant additional layers of clothing. Kern would even cocoon himself in his "wooby" (read: poncho liner) while performing guard duty. Being as he was the squad's best marksman, I would've preferred he not be swaddled like a wee little baby while seeing to the security of his sleeping brothers; but he was confident in his ability to immediately cast aside the liner.

"Are you seeing what I see, Kern?"

I did not look to Kern when asking this question, and with good reason.

On that nearly pitch-black night, just after 1100hrs, I had shone my daymaker flashlight towards the nearby mountainside upon hearing a sound of rustled stone and falling debris.

"Baboons? *Baboons.*"

It was the eyes.

We could certainly make out the distinctive morphology of those tiny primates, which we later learned were of the *P. hamadryas* species, but it was those glowing eyes that most struck the two of us in that moment. So very numerous were they. It was as though the mountainside had come to life in the form of a firefly hive, or something equally fantastical.

There was an ease and a grace to their fluid traversing of that mountainside which defied either gravity or our feeble human vision. Either way, it was surely a sight to behold.

"Where do you suppose they're off to?" I asked Kern, as though he knew.

"Baboon Land, probably."

"Wanker."

This last jibe I voiced in the tone of someone dazed by violent trauma. My eyes remained fixed on that massive troop (over one-hundred, we estimated) of baboons as they moved in and out of our dancing daymakers, eyes gleaming and vanishing as each elusive creature looked our way with equal parts curiosity and irritation before continuing their journey.

Being a hunter by training and upbringing, Kern was likely feeling mildly trigger happy in that moment. But self-restraint (and my own presence) subdued the man's instincts.

If only we had been armed with a camera...

There's little else to say about our well site guard duty. We spent both Christmas and New Year's Eve/Day there, and enjoyed the company of several officers, including the good Captain Travers, on the latter holiday. They came bearing hot chow and kind words. It was memorable in the way that any such unusual Christmas is.

And then we returned to Camp Lemonnier. Our first foray beyond the wire now complete, there was work to do elsewhere, and mission-specific training to undertake.

T.R.A.P. (Tactical Recovery of Aircraft and Personnel).

Here I am trespassing upon the terrain of the United States Marine Corps, as T.R.A.P. missions are a fixture within their training/operational framework.

But if I trespass literarily, it is only for having trained in the art of T.R.A.P. upon invitation from the good Marines with whom we cohabitated while in Lemonnier.

T.R.A.P. missions were to be a cornerstone of our time in country. Or readying ourselves for such missions should they materialize on our watch.

In principle, the T.R.A.P. is as straightforward a mission as one could hope to know. In execution, they can be rather taxing.

For those unaccustomed to long-distance rotorcraft travel, they can also push one to one's motion sickness limits. At least the first time out, as they did with me.

I'd come to know the taste of vomit rather closely during our inaugural T.R.A.P. dry run. Never again thereafter, though our platoon leader had hoped very much to see me reenact that first spell of severe nausea. It was bloody awful. I vomited until nothing remained within.

To say I was a bit apprehensive when readying for my second outing would be putting things quite mildly.

But nothing came of it. My flesh and blood had acquainted itself with the rhythms of tactical helicopter travel and mercifully exacted nothing more of itself in the way of vomiting tribute.

T.R.A.P. runs see teams of infantrymen (or combat-trained personnel of one category or another) making their way to aviation crash sites in what is largely a rescue capacity. Second Platoon had been educated by a trio of Marines in tactical/intelligence considerations inherent in any such operation, to include: (a) safeguarding of a crash-site's perimeter, (b) retrieval of personnel (regardless of their condition), and (c) the recovery or (if necessary) destruction of sensitive materials, equipment, et cetera.

Training runs for such missions, however, are often preceded by several hours spent in the rear of a rotorcraft. In our case, a CH-53E Super Stallion. The reason being that pilots are often in need of logged flight time. Towing human cargo while logging those hours matters to them not in the least. Not even if one member of said cargo has exhausted a lifetime supply of vomit throughout the perfunctory flight.

Still, innumerable soldiers across time and space have had it much worse. Even in a state of self-pity I was cognizant of as much.

Upon at last reaching our training ground, following an hour of flight time, Second Squad performed to standard in every detail. We established a perimeter, retrieved our "personnel" and materials, and made a cautious return to the aircraft. For those who had not spent the better part of forty minutes' time confronting whatever it was they had eaten for breakfast that morning, the dry run was a veritable cake walk. For those of us who *had* confronted whatever it was we ate for breakfast (and we numbered around five-six), the cake walk was complicated by horrific nausea and the general feeling of weakness that follows any round of brutal vomiting.

Still, we ploughed ahead as was expected and concealed the rubber-kneed sensation by which we were beset.

The airsickness continued to wreak its havoc during the return flight, for which reason I thought of my bunk and little else. I did not eat, I drank little water, I showered only briefly—I yearned for rest upon a firm, unmoving surface.

Among the last of my thoughts that evening was the realization that we were expected to repeat that exercise several more times across the coming weeks.

England's greatest naval hero, Horatio Nelson, suffered from seasickness throughout the entirety of his legendary maritime career. Whatever courage the man exhibited during battle, his willingness to brave the incessant sensation of nausea for decades on end is comparably remarkable.

My own did not return. At least not on rotorcraft. A half-dozen or so training exercises of that sort and not once was I beset by nausea or the like. Small miracles, and what have you.

That was our first month in the Horn of Africa. The well, the gymnasium, the DFAC, T.R.A.P training—place the latter three on a three-week loop and you'll have an idea of how it was we went about acclimating to what was a weird deployment.

The Old Guard in Africa. Weird indeed.

"We're up for Ethiopia, guys." Wilson was addressing the squad one afternoon following that day's second trip to the gymnasium.

"What's goin' on down there?" Steele inquired for the good of the order.

"First Platoon set up camp in Hurso. Third followed. Second is moving in once they leave. We'll be teaching Ethiopian soldiers to shoot, and some other shit."

"Seriously?" Steele was incredulous.

Wilson replied affirmative through a very heavy sigh. Steele had taxed the man's patience time and again, though usually in the interest of building morale via laughter.

"It's gonna be a long stay, guys, and there's not a lot down there. No running water, no gym, no DFAC. Pack whatever you think you'll need for a month or so. Might be shorter, but it's up in the air. Okay?"

"Tracking, Sergeant," I said.

"All right. We'll be flying down in about thirty-six hours. Oh, and make sure you get to the phone center. I want you talking to whoever gives a shit about you. I think they have a sat phone in Hurso, but it'll be a limited usage situation. Call your wives, moms, girlfriends, whatever."

And all did. Reed and Harding, who had passed up their chance to do exactly that prior to our week at the well site, visited the phone center immediately after dinner. I joined them both.

Harding and I had discovered a mutual interest in history and shared many a conversation on the topic. Between him, Hooph, and Wilson, I wanted for nothing in the way of exchanging ideas while overseas.

The following day was a medium-busy ordeal consisting of morning PT, breakfast, packing, lunch, gymnasium, dinner, phone center, packing, and lights out.

Early the next morning, Second Platoon split itself up between two helicopters and flew the two-hundred miles southwest to Hurso. The flight seemed rather long, though it was little more than ninety minutes in duration.

A number of our Bravo brothers who had arrived much earlier were there at the tarmac to drive us (in civilian vehicles) to what, earlier that month, had been formally named Camp United, north of Dire Dawa.

Camp United is maybe two acres in total area, or was in 2003–2004. I understand the camp has since been shuttered. It was enclosed by a combination of concertina wire (Watch out, Lemon) and short stretches of fencing. A single guard tower had been constructed within the wire and, being twice the height of a man, offered excellent visibility of the surrounding lands. Centered within the enclosure were a half-dozen tents which served as our makeshift barracks. A set of pull-up and dip bars had been emplaced by a group of useful First Platoon soldiers who had also constructed a covered dining area with the help of a contractor.

There was also a decent volleyball court which our First Platoon predecessors had taken the time to carve out.

I have many memories of my time in Hurso/Camp United. Most readily comes to mind when I reflect upon Second Platoon's several stretches in that camp are the many meals we shared beneath that dining area.

Second Platoon's three squads had interacted very little with one another since having reached the Horn. That all changed during our first Hurso stint. Suddenly, we were once again a unified platoon, complete with a shared mission.

Squad cohesion still went a long way, and most soldiers tended to interact with sub-sects of their respective squads. Even so, there was a strong sense of heightened morale amongst we men of Second Platoon once the reunification had come to pass. And it was good to see those First Squad guys with whom I had briefly trained prior to assuming leadership of my own fire-team. I sought out Fritsche at one point and asked after his wellbeing. As was invariably the case, he spoke in terms either neutral or positive. Though it was almost certainly not the case, I hope to have to learned from his example. But, then, we are so rarely the people we hope to be.

And we played our share of volleyball.

We settled in quickly, generated a campsite work rotation, agreed upon a guard duty schedule, and otherwise familiarized ourselves with our temporary home.

But then, *all* homes are, in the long run I suppose, temporary.

A couple of days later, we made our way the short distance over to Camp

Hurso, wherein the Ethiopian National Defense Forces conduct their combat training.

Whereas we had casually moseyed over to the compound, the Ethiopian contingent with whom we'd be working jogged in a tight formation which recalled so many images of Benning.

We men of Second Platoon stood in the center of a carved-out area not unlike those used in A.P. Hill's EIB lanes. Within minutes of our arrival, we were enclosed on three sides by the contingent who had arrested their jogging and, in ordered fashion, marched into the outdoor lecture area.

Our interpreter, Taddese, spoke to a man who was the contingent's commanding officer. After which he turned to SSG Wilson.

"Okay, Sergeant," Taddese began, his accent heavy, but not so much so as to compromise his making himself understood, "they are ready to learn what you are here to teach them. Go ahead. I will say as you say, and they will know your meaning."

To my surprise, Wilson appeared pleasantly nervous. He was not overwhelmed, but the task of addressing the Ethiopians on the subject of land navigation was yielding a giddiness within the man.

He began: "You have a beautiful country!"

Wilson was correct. Ethiopia is beautiful. Stunningly so. It is so very much a far a cry from the Djiboutian lands we'd been coming to know in recent weeks as to create a sense of incongruity when coupling one nation with the next.

The country is florally vibrant. To be sure, there are relatively dry, arid regions. But large areas are densely treed, experience healthy rainfall, house rich soils, and are replete with wide-ranging fauna. If ever there was an Eden, it modeled itself upon the natural splendor that is Ethiopia.

The country is life itself. It is not merely beautiful, it is the reason that word exists at all.

It is also home to an army of gracious and kind soldiers. When they aren't firing shots in anger towards an enemy, that is.

Wilson had elected to open with an observation which was either (a) known very well to his audience, or (b) of little consequence to them. They seemed, to a one, confused upon registering Taddese's translation.

To his credit, Wilson realized as much and quickly moved on.

"We're here to teach you land navigation, and we're looking forward to working with you."

Taddese dutifully translated, during which time every Ethiopian eye present was on the man. Once he had finished, all eyes returned to Wilson ... who turned first to Taddese, then to me and to Hooph.

"This is Sergeant Hoffman and Sergeant Mongilutz. They're going to be teaching you the basics of land navigation."

Caught somewhat by surprise, I smiled and waved. Hooph waved, his smiles being reserved for moments of genuine amusement rather than feigned enthusiasm.

Immediately following that awkward wave, I noticed that every Ethiopian eye present was on *me*. Following Wilson's briefing, I inquired of Taddese, "Why do you suppose the soldiers were staring at me?"

"Blue eyes," he explained, "very rare here. They don't see them often."

Ah, yes—that. My eyes are pale blue in color. People occasionally remark on them, most commonly out of plain curiosity.

"Are you wearing contact lenses?"

"I am not, no."

"Oh. Your eyes are like an icy blue."

"They were a gift. Thank you."

Conversations of that sort have played out since I was very young. I could understand why the Ethiopian soldiers found my eyes rather odd. I was also uncomfortable with the attention, and responded in a manner taken straight from Steele's playbook.

I made a bizarre bird call which had everyone around me (except for Hooph) laughing. The decoy measure had plenty of replay value, and I would employ it daily as our Ethiopian friends/hosts reached the training ground. Doing so took all attention off the immutable characteristic of my eye color and allowed for that age-old human mechanism of humor to transcend that age-old barrier of foreign language. We laughed together, American and Ethiopian, and reveled in the experience.

We taught those guys to use a map and compass. The lessons 1SG Triton had imparted upon me I was honored to impart upon soldiers of Ethiopia. They listened, learned, and maintained positive control of their weapons while moving from point to point. In all, those days amounted to a paramount transaction between teacher and taught, one upon which I find myself reflecting fondly well over a decade hence.

At some point during our first month in Hurso, Taddese delivered to we men of Second Platoon a formal invitation to dine with a number of senior Ethiopian military figures and academy cadets. We accepted and two evenings later found ourselves enjoying a feast of flavorful local food. On the menu were various lamb and rice dishes, a poultry cut I never did identify, several delicious soups, a variety of sliced fruits, and Fanta. Yes, *actual* Fanta. They served both orange and grape Fanta.

And as we were but a stone's throw from Harar, from where coffee is said to have originated, there was, indeed, plenty of coffee. I rather enjoyed the local preparation method, which yielded a tart, dense taste.

We were treated as honored guests and were most gracious in our bearing. It was a delightful occasion.

The remaining weeks saw us establish a loose routine. Duties rotated from squad to squad, but no two days were dissimilar from one another. A staple of our routine was a good deal of volleyball, which provided a secondary form of PT. Often finishing the day's lesson (marksmanship, land navigation) by 1400hrs, that left us with many hours of daylight to do two things: (1) the aforementioned volleyball, and (2) cook and eat.

In fairness, the culinary work fell to a select few soldiers from throughout the three squads; specifically, those inclined towards the culinary arts. These were led by Travis Steele, a soldier whose talents ranged from music and comedy to butchery and stew cooking.

It was, I believe, during the latter half of our second week in-country that Patters and a few others, having grown tired of MREs and Harvest Bars, purchased a goat from one of the locals. The price was something obscenely low—perhaps five USD—and the meat was very welcome.

While most of the platoon cycled through games of volleyball (Harding and I read in between), Steele and a few guys from First and Third Squad butchered our livestock, cut meat sections sufficiently small for a stew recipe, sliced vegetables, and prepared a broth.

Shortly after nightfall, Steele bellowed out to his platoon mates: "Soup's on!" Indicating he and his culinary henchmen had completed their work.

My god, were we in their debt.

The stew was divine. Even correcting for the fact that we had been subsisting on MREs since the feast ten days earlier, I can say with certainty that what Steele achieved in realizing that stew was something bordering on miraculous.

Everything told, we probably enjoyed a meal of that sort no fewer than seven times. Each was the best meal any of us had ever known, equaled only by the previous and the next.

During that first Hurso stint, the squads made a handful of trips into the nearby town of Dire Dawa. These were visits of a touristic nature, our being armed notwithstanding.

Fewer than ten miles from Hurso and populated by well over a half-million souls, the century-old city of Dire Dawa is cosmopolitan by Horn standards and notable for its bustling commercial scene. Markets, restaurants, hotels, cars—Dire Dawa is an Ethiopian splendor, to be sure.

Our driver and cultural guide, "KT," typically drove to the same intersection and set us loose with warnings to be mindful of thieves and the like. Food poisoning followed a few of us back from that initial excursion, myself and Garcia included, the latter of whom had elected to order a milk shake … in Ethiopia.

Food poisoning was, it happens, the least consequential Dire Dawa after-effect to visit itself upon the Platoon during that first stretch.

A week or so later we packed our gear/clothing, loaded up a few vehicles, said farewell to Hurso (for the first time), made our way to a nearby airstrip, boarded a C-130 turboprop, and made the twenty-minute return flight to Djibouti.

That evening, I received an unexpected visit from Jamesy. Having seen very little of Senator Fred, Bretty, and Jamesy throughout the deployment, this was a truly welcome crossing of paths. I remember the circumstances more clearly than the conversation; we spoke for a good long while alongside a pull-up bar, a pull-up bar I used throughout the conversation, as my aim was to exceed one-hundred repetitions prior to lights out.

Jamesy and I parted ways, not realizing that we wouldn't see one another again for several months' time.

A short time later, while walking to the DFAC in a state of supreme hunger (the gymnasium had preceded the meal), my friend and roommate Travis Smith, of Third Squad, approached me with a question I could not have anticipated.

"Hey, Mark, didn't you work for SFC Taylor up in S-3?"

Looking quizzically upon my friend and colleague of over three years' time, I responded as though stepping into a trap. "I did, yes."

"Did you hear he's coming to Djibouti? He's our new 1SG."

"I hadn't. Are you having a laugh?"

"Serious, man." And on and on this played out again and again that day and into the next, as soldiers from throughout the company approached me with variations on Smith's question.

Within hours of my exchange with Smith, I had visited the phone center and called Scott's mobile. It would've been prior to first call Eastern Standard Time when Scott answered.

"This is Scott."

In a semi-whisper, I inquired of my friend, former boss, and the toughest soldier I had yet known. "Scott, it's Mark. Is there truth to it? You're to be our 1SG?"

"That's right, bud. I'm heading out in a couple of days."

"What the hell is going on?"

"Well, bud, I don't quite know."

None of us did, as it turned out.

Nor would we ever know the story in its entirety.

XIX

Out of Africa

It was all so mysterious. We had deployed with a 1SG. The very same 1SG who had been present during my promotion board. The very same 1SG who had curtly welcomed me back into Bravo Company. The very same 1SG who had referenced Jessica Lynch prior to Second Squad's Tadjoura mission.

The very same 1SG who was no longer a part of Battlehard.

There had been tension within the upper echelons of Bravo Company's command group. Matters had deteriorated beyond all reprieve while Second Platoon was in Hurso. By the time of our return, Battlehard was without a 1SG.

At least without an in-country 1SG.

For one had been assigned.

Scott Taylor—my friend and former boss.

Though he is disinclined towards acknowledging as much, I have it on excellent authority that CSM Winchester had handpicked Taylor for the role. And with good reason.

Though The Old Guard possessed deep benches of leadership and soldiering talent at that time, Taylor outclassed the majority of the unit's senior NCOs, and most of its officers. Winchester knew the man's worth and knew he could be counted upon to do good work wherever it was he was assigned, be it Arlington, Virginia or Camp Lemonnier, Djibouti.

Camp Lemonnier, Djibouti it was.

The company was far from fully assembled when 1SG Taylor called us to attention for what was his first time while serving in that capacity. Something like fifty-percent of Battlehard was on mission at the time. One of the platoons was operating with a Navy SEAL team (literally at sea with a carrier group), while others were in Tadjoura, or in the Mediterranean.

Those of us present on Lemonnier appreciated the novelty of an unexpected change in 1SG leadership.

Taylor spoke to us briefly. It was more or less a "Keep doin' what you're doing" and "Don't fuck up" sort of speech. Perfectly appropriate under the circumstances.

After the fact, Scott and I none too subtly connected not twenty feet from Second Platoon's tent and spoke like the old friends we were. Several Bravo Company passersby seemed confused as to why a buck sergeant was casually conversing with our newly arrived 1SG, and one with a reputation for leadership ferocity, but at least a few knew of our having worked side-by-side in S-3.

"What do you think so far, Scott?"

"It's fuckin' hot, bud. I like the gym, though."

"I expected you would. If you make time for nothing else, at least take advantage of the excellent weight-sets."

"Will do. How you doin' over here? Everything goin' all right?"

Scott had been shrewdly gathering intelligence on the state of the company since prior to his arrival. He had spoken with me (Second Platoon), with his former Echo Company soldier Burhoe (Third Platoon), and with Jamesy (First Platoon) in hopes of piecing together a comprehensive understanding of where it was his unique leadership qualities should best be brought to bear.

"Fine, mostly. There've been a few leadership challenges, but I've likely been one of them myself. I've not made things easy for Wilson."

Scott grinned knowingly, paternally, "That mouth of yours?"

I smiled sheepishly. "Indeed."

"Well, keep it together a while longer. I'm sure he knows you're a good kid."

"Do *you* know I'm a good kid?"

"Smartass—I wouldn't have let you leave the shop if I didn't."

"And here we are—reunited on the far side of the world."

"Life's unpredictable, bud. Are you guys going anywhere soon?"

"We're up for another month in Hurso, but that's at least three weeks out. Possibly more. The LT mentioned a few small-scale missions; single fire-teams, and what have you."

"Yeah, I saw some of that coming down. Keep me posted of where you're at."

"Of course."

"And you haven't seen Taheny?"

"Not for a while, no."

"I've been talking to him and Burhoe. Between those guys and you, it's like I've been here all along."

"You chose a good trio of observers. Plus, you've Fred in the Training Room. You might also connect with Thurman. He always has a good sense of the situation."

Scott nodded. "He does. Smart kid. Sucked losing you both at once."

"Thank the CSM for that much."

"I did. Then he sent my ass here."

From that point forth, I saw little of Scott while in Djibouti. He would make a brief stop in Hurso a month or so later, but we crossed paths rather infrequently following those early days. He was needed everywhere, and Second Squad found itself tasked with a host of minor security details on a near-daily basis prior to our next Ethiopian safari.

On a couple of occasions, we were assigned to guard a medical team as they performed physical evaluations for local Djiboutians, administering treatments both cursory and comprehensive on many. These were regarded as miracle workers by Djiboutian citizens and American soldiers alike. If the American presence in Djibouti can be said to have yielded any good at all, it was in the works of those physicians and medical professionals.

We accompanied a Marine SSG on a weird outing, the details of which were rather opaque. As far as could be discerned, we were a presence-of-force for the man while he made his way to various Djiboutian military outposts. At one such outpost, we were treated to a dinner of meatball spaghetti and, yes, Fanta. It was grenadine flavored, and therefore delicious. Such a weird outing.

For nearly a week's time, we provided site security for a group of Army engineers who were operating in a carpentry capacity. Their mission was the building of a large schoolhouse. I found myself marveling at their work. So small a group of men, so sizable and well-made a structure. Truly excellent craftsmen. Our part was embarrassingly easy, if irrefutably essential. Those excellent makers could concentrate solely on their work, while we riflemen kept our eyes on the roads, on the horizon, on all who passed by.

We also continued with our exercise regimen. Harding was fond of cycling and spent a good deal of time spinning furiously atop a stationary bicycle. Reed had a boxing background and befriended a similarly inclined Marine Corps officer; the two trained together on a few occasions. Garcia had goals both cosmetic and strength-focused; he worked rather hard in his pursuit of both. "Bacardi" has always preferred athletic events to the weightlifting/calisthenics grind. Even so, he was often seen lifting in the company of Second Platoon men from one squad or another. My own pull-up fixation had matured into an unmitigated obsession. Commonly preceded by a mid-distance, fast-paced run, I would then perform pull-ups by the dozens. By deployment's end, my back and shoulders had assumed sizes disproportionate to my larger anatomy.

Our return to Ethiopia materialized as suddenly as had the initial trip. We were instructed to ready ourselves for yet another long stay and to expect a departure date/time of tomorrow morning.

Though it defied comprehension, our return to Camp United, and to Hurso more broadly, carried with it the sensation of a warm homecoming.

For reasons probably stemming from the presence of so many high-ranking officers, Camp Lemonnier had failed to assume a similar quality.

In Hurso, we operated with not inconsiderable autonomy. It was as though aspects of my S-3 experience had fused with Robert Altman's 1970 motion picture *M*A*S*H*. Also, our interactions with the Ethiopian soldiers were a source of much joy throughout the platoon.

Steele had promised to further perfect his stew recipe. That was in and of itself worth the flight down. As for the return journey...

* * *

Volleyball is popular in Ethiopia. It is popular in many parts of Africa, but very much so in Ethiopia. As the Fates (those mischievous creatures) would have it, a semi-professional Ethiopian volleyball team was training out of Hurso during our time in-country. If our liaising officers were to be believed, this group was training for Olympic glory. Its members were also required to maintain some degree of soldiering proficiency, or so it had been explained to us.

Regardless of the details, the fact remains that a well-trained team of volleyball players were bunking very near Camp United and had extended to Second Platoon an invitation to play an exhibition match.

"We're damn good, I'd say," said one soldier, who continued, "I mean, we've played for a month straight. We're all in good shape. We know team-work. I think we could hold our own."

"I agree," contributed another soldier. "You give a few solid soldiers a month to practice anything and they're gonna come out bein' competent. I'm not saying we're pros or anything, but we know what we're doing."

"There's likely some truth to it," I said. "It isn't as though we'll be facing them without ever having played the game. And we are in excellent physical condition. It could be a good showing."

The platoon being largely in agreement, we accepted the challenge and reported to Hurso's nearby volleyball court the following afternoon.

Twenty-one to three.

We lost by eighteen points.

As for our three points, they had been clumsily achieved. The ball being pushed desperately over the net, only to fall in ugly fashion to the sand below.

We knew upon arriving what would come of our efforts. It was Hoffmann (not to be mistaken for Hooph;) who turned to us after viewing the Ethiopian team's warm-up regimen, and said in a rather serious tone, "I think ya'll are gonna get tore-up."

A truer prediction might never before have been articulated by any Second Platoon soldier.

They moved as one. Every action, no matter how inconspicuous, seemed to have stemmed from the collective efforts of every player. They were fluidity itself, and their organization was paramount.

We must have looked very much like amateurs. Which, of course, we were, our delusions notwithstanding.

Of the twenty-one points scored by our elite opponents, well over half were of the cinematic, full-force spike variety. At one point, I noticed one of our own players assume a look of abject terror as the ball was punched in the general direction of his head. The scene would've been comical had it not been so damned awful. Or is it the other way around?

On second thought, it was both. It was comedy gold, certainly for the spectators, and an awful display of no-contest athletics. We were over-matched.

Still, I was happy we had played. One of the platoon's most ardent weightlifters, a kindhearted man named Russell, inquired of the Ethiopian volleyball team, "Would you guys like to do a push-up contest?"

They politely (and wisely) declined.

We feasted on yet another stew and bread dinner that evening and carried on with our routine for weeks thereafter. The routine included camp maintenance, the worst part of which required that we systematically and in time-consuming manner burn human waste … as in feces. While large areas of Ethiopia are home to complex plumbing systems, Camp United had no such luxury. Soldiers defecated in burn barrels situated beneath wooden toilet holes. Once these had reached *capacity*, they were dragged into the sunlight to have the *contents* doused in kerosene and burned to ash. Thorough completion of this task required a patient *stirring* of the *contents* with a lengthy section of rebar.

In service to morale, team leaders did not exempt themselves from this most challenging of duties.

Volleyball, the burning of human feces, the training of Ethiopian soldiers, exercise—between these and a few other goings-on, the days turned quickly to weeks, weeks into a month, and then…

"All right, guys, we got a few more weeks of this and some stuff back in Lemonnier," Lieutenant Cesare had called a platoon meeting one afternoon. "After that, we're done. It's back to the States."

It had all gone very quickly. Lemonnier, Tadjoura, Lemonnier, Ethiopia, Lemonnier, various Djiboutian locations, Ethiopia—we had certainly kept busy. Being committed to challenging his men, Cesare had also seen to it that Second Platoon visited a French Foreign Legion compound during one of those rare afternoons in which we were all gathered on Lemonnier. The trip was organized around our completion of a Legion obstacle course.

How I do wish we had one of these on Myer, I recall thinking. The course was superb. It was challenging. It was worthy.

Djibouti, having come under French influence in the late-19th century, has maintained a French presence into the present. French is also one of several official and prominently spoken languages, Somali and Arabic being the others.

The country is also about ninety-five percent Islamic in terms of religious faith. Ethiopia, for comparison's sake, is over sixty-percent Christian (split between Ethiopian Orthodoxy and Pentay Protestantism) and about thirty-percent Islamic. The Horn of Africa is a rather divided land in that regard.

Things came together rather strangely towards the end of that strange deployment. I describe it as "strange" only because, having deployed again some years later, the HOA adventure was, well, strange. And, anyway, it was rather strange.

"We don't have air out of here." Wilson was speaking in a heavy, bleak tone. "And we don't have shit to make a real convoy."

"So, are we walking back?" Hooph seemed half-serious. "We could probably make it back in a week or so, but we'd have to leave a lot of gear behind."

Mike was either irritated with the question or with his resignation to the alternative. "We're not walking back. We've got to work with "KT" to hire a few civilian drivers. U.S. dollars buy anything down here; they'll drive us back."

How fitting it was that my final TOG-HOA trek would be with Second Squad, Second Platoon. It was the squad/platoon to which I had been in late-2000 assigned mere hours after learning I would not be reporting to Alpha Company. It was the squad in which I had served under Bradley's formative leadership. It was the squad in which I served as a casket bearer across countless burials. It was the squad with which I had reported to the Pentagon following that dreadful attack nearly three years prior. It was the squad to which I had reluctantly said goodbye when pulled up to HHC. It was the squad to which I had always felt I still belonged while in S-3. And it was the squad to which I would ultimately return as an E-5/sergeant upon informing CSM Winchester of my desire to be with Bravo Company.

And it was with Second Squad, Second Platoon that I would return to Camp Lemonnier across two-hundred miles of roads, dirt pathways, and half-formed trails—and in a miserably dilapidated van, no less.

I would not have had it any other way.

We had done a very thorough job, Hooph and I, in readying the men for our departure. Our packing list layout experience ensured that no sensitive items or otherwise important equipment pieces were left behind. We swept the tents' plywood floors, emptied trash bins, packed food and water for the journey, conducted communications checks, and otherwise prepared for the long road ahead.

And when the vans drove into the camp, we wondered if it had all been for not.

There were two vans, both in poor states of repair. One of the two appeared to be hanging together via the adhesive power of saliva-activated chewing gum. The other looked much the same, with one troubling exception—its tire-set consisted solely of spares. Or, if not actual spares, they would've comported with the Western world's spare tire dimensions.

"You mentioned something about our returning to Lemonnier on foot, didn't you, Hooph?" I was not entirely serious in asking that question. I was not entirely *unserious.*

"Nah. We have too much shit to haul back with us. Let's try our luck with these guys."

"By all means," I said while walking towards the tent. "So long as we brace ourselves for the possibility of having to push those machines up any hills we might encounter."

"It's only two-hundred miles, Mark. We'll make it."

It was apparent that we would be exceeding each vehicle's weight/space capacity. Between bags, rucks, weapons cases, communications equipment, and men, we had likely burdened each rickety van with over one metric ton of mass. I'd estimate that was nearly double what would have been deemed acceptable by anyone who knows about such things; like, say, an engineer.

As our departure finally came to pass just after sunset, and as we had spent many an hour packing and cleaning—

Did I mention Bacardi was pierced in the foot by an aggressive scorpion?

It was a bizarre scene.

Per Wilson, it was like something straight from the pages of Heinlen's *Starship Troopers.* Well, at least in appearance, not in size.

"Shiiiiitttt!" Lemon dropped to the floor, clutching his poisoned foot and sliding away from an assailant approximately one-tenth of one-percent his size. And who could blame the man? That arachnid (of the Scorpiones order) was in no mood for negotiating—it meant Lemon harm and was continuing to move towards him.

Patters captured the clawed warrior using a water bottle and some cardboard. We would keep Lemon's assailant as a pet for some days thereafter; until, that is, another horrid creature came into our possession—a sizable camel spider (solifugae).

So, naturally, a contest was arranged. A small box was found; this would serve as the ring. Both scorpion and solifugae were placed (carefully) in said ring. The fight ensued. It seemed rather one-sided initially, with the solifugae clearly possessing more in the way of strength and agility. Nevertheless, the scorpion patiently stung away while being otherwise overpowered, so that by the time its abdomen had been violently torn open and its animating life energy extinguished, enough poison was coursing through its killer's hideous form to have felled a far larger creature.

Within minutes, both were dead. It seems predator-vs.-predator matches bode well for neither combatant in the uninhibited arena that is the natural world.

All of that had occurred some weeks prior to our return trip, by which time Lemon's foot had healed.

The vans were packed in a sardine-like manner. The men were exhausted from what had been a far more draining Hurso excursion than had been the case our first time 'round. We had also been supplied far less generously, relying very much on Steele and his crew for nightly nourishment. He had even cultivated several relationships with local goat herders, thereby securing favorable pricing for our semi-regular livestock purchases. Second Platoon had established another such relationship with a local bread baker. The baker's hovel being a small stone house situated remotely (fairy tale-style) within the wilderness.

Though it was with some sadness that we said farewell to Hurso for the last time, our return to Lemonnier was nothing if not a bit overdue. Already very lean, I had somehow managed to lose five pounds during our second stint and appeared somewhat starved to most eyes.

I also refused to sleep or in any way afford myself any comfort during our five-hour return trip. For one, I did not trust the roads. Secondly, I scarcely trusted our vehicles. And last, we had made it through the deployment without so much as a training injury befalling anyone within the squad. If any misfortune was to visit itself upon our cohort, it would be during this final stretch of time and space.

Thus, I positioned myself in that narrow strip between the van's front seats and watched the dirty yards turn to dusty miles through scarcely blinking eyes. If I seemed paranoid it is because I was paranoid. We had entered the final hours of what had been our sacred Regiment's first overseas mission in three decades' time. Things had taken shape for us rather favorably, and Second Platoon had represented the unit rather well.

"Provided we can negotiate this last stretch without incident..."

Words to that effect circled through my mind like a murder of crows flying overhead on a forbiddingly dark morning; their presence known, their forms unclear.

Mile upon mile. A deep hole swallowing in its entirety a hapless tire while pushing a weak suspension to the upper limits of its low damage tolerance. A comically narrow hillside road seeming anything but comical in that moment. A sound emanating from the engine which suggested anything other than a healthy engine.

This was far from the worst fate ever to have befallen an infantry squad. *Very far* indeed. It was simply as dangerous as it was, which was enough to warrant my being concerned for the wellbeing of my men.

I watched the road, the (probably broken) fuel gauge, the horizon, the driver's eyes for any sign of fatigue—all of it.

And then ... well, and then it was there, and in plain sight.

Beneath heavy eyelids, I could clearly make out the massive HESCO barriers behind which the hearth and home of Lemonnier does sit. It was past nightfall, but the camp is suitably well-illuminated as to render it visible to the naked eye, even under the cover of night.

I smiled and made appreciative eye contact with our hired driver and patted him on the shoulder. Knowing full well he could not understand me, I nevertheless said, "We've nearly arrived, sir, keep us on the road for another moment."

He smiled in such a way as to suggest my meaning had resonated.

Upon reaching the well-guarded front gate, Wilson, Hooph, and I exited our vans to present identification. There was little hassle in securing re-entry for ourselves, particularly given that we had hired as drivers a pair of foreign nationals.

I recall we were required to walk the remaining distance from front gate to Second Platoon tent. We did not object. The distance was far less than the two-hundred miles we had just covered.

Around this time, I strangely remembered a one-night stand Pennartz had arranged for me during my S-3 year. The pretty girl and I had got on well, though she expressed considerable irritation at my having lost interest in the, ahem, "connection" during our third go 'round. It wasn't so much *that* as it was my eye having caught a film airing on a nearby television set. I hadn't yet seen the film and was intrigued by one of its expertly rendered scenes.

The strangest thing to have populated my mind in that moment.

And we were returned.

Everything was going on.

The overwhelming majority of Battlehard had returned ahead of Second Squad, Second Platoon, to include our sister squads. Ours had been the final group to return from beyond the wire prior to the company's return flight.

And, indeed, *everything* was going on.

Packing, mostly. Everything was being packed in preparation for our return.

I had received a care package from my aunt while in Hurso. God knows how long it had been seated atop my bunk, but there it was. Candy, Hostess products, letters from my cousins. Unfortunately, we were boarding a return flight in something like twenty hours and space was limited. I quickly parceled out all food items; some of the MPs who had deployed with Battlehard in a supporting capacity were happy to absorb the Hostess goods, while my own guys took the candy.

Thank you, dear aunt.

Exiting the shower early the next morning, I was surprised at how thin I had become while in Hurso. Gaunt, indeed.

No time to dwell on such things. We had to move, and quickly.

We packed and cleaned for perhaps two unbroken hours before heading to the DFAC for our final Camp Lemonnier lunch.

I then went to find Scott and was successful in my efforts.

"Scott."

"What's up, bud? You packed and ready?"

"I am. Listen, I'm getting out within sixty days or so of our return."

"Yeah, I know. You sure I can't talk you into re-upping?"

"Very unlikely." This was familiar conversational terrain. "But I'm thinking of staying in the area. How would you and the family like a boarder?"

As though I had just requested a second helping of mashed potatoes, Scott replied, "You wanna do that, bud?"

"Seems sensible. Yes."

"All right, that should be doable."

"Well, that takes care of that. Thanks, Scott."

"You got it, bud. Now go get your shit ready. We're wheels up in hours."

He was correct. We were wheels up in hours.

I had re-connected briefly with the "Musketeers" after having seen very little of them since arriving in-country late the previous fall.

Bretty and Mike "Senator Fred" Thompson had sought me out in Second Platoon's tent. I had spoken with them while performing my final sets of pull-ups on that bar I had come to know so well.

Jamesy and I were again ships passing in the night. But it mattered little. I knew we would remain in touch once returned to U.S. soil.

And then, after what had at times seemed like a brief jaunt throughout the Horn, and at others like an endless Third World slog, we boarded our aircraft and prepared for that interminable Middle East -United States flight which many a soldier has come to know so closely.

My mind being the reflective instrument that it is, I reflected.

I reflected upon the preceding months. I reflected upon the days immediately leading up to my Battlehard return, a return I was sublimely grateful to have realized with Bretty, my dearest of friends. I reflected upon the arduous training which had forged unbreakable bonds throughout the ranks of Bravo Company. I reflected upon my unexpected training ground promotion from First Squad Spec4(P) grunt to Second Squad Spec4(P) fire-team leader. I reflected upon my official promotion from Spec4(P) to E-5/Sergeant and of the part Scott Taylor, the finest soldier I had known in the Regiment, had played in preparing me for line company leadership.

And I reflected upon all we had seen and experienced in the tragically beautiful Horn of Africa. We had seen humanity at its economic worst and its spiritual best. We had seen the pain that accompanies endemic impoverishment and the hope that endures through it all. We had formed friendships that transcended spoken language; indeed, friendships that thrived in its absence. And we had come to appreciate the human experience in a way few of us could have accurately anticipated. No degree of prescience can reliably anticipate the wonder that is heartfelt cross-cultural connection.

And when my reflecting process had yielded, leaving in its wake that sense of clarity and context for which the function presumably exists, I slept.

And dreamt.

Probably of a future whose face I did not yet recognize.

XX

A Brief TOG Return
and a Morose Out-Processing

A stranger in a familiar land.

If there is a string of words more suitable for describing my feelings upon returning to the Washington, D.C., metropolitan area, they have not yet organized themselves in my mind.

A stranger in a familiar land.

And so I was.

It's a feeling known to almost anyone who has experienced the phenomenon of returning to the First World having just departed the Third (or the Second).

CIVILIZATION.

It overwhelms the senses.

Densely packed freeways, monolithic shopping centers, monolithic monoliths (particularly in D.C.), wealth of the sort that is ubiquitous in any developed nation—these combine to render one acutely aware of their decided absence in much of the world.

Such as, for instance, in the Horn of Africa ... from whose lands Battlehard had, only moments ago, just returned. For the most part, our eyes blazed with wonder at sights we had always known, but whose magnificence we never rightly (nor fully) appreciated.

The airport terminal was itself sufficient to prime this involuntary response, but it was the brief bus ride to Fort Myer whose sights most forcefully collided with our collective sense of astonishment—astonishment at the prosperity which we had, to a one, reflexively taken for granted since childhood. We had been blind to First World opulence in the way a marine lifeform might be blind to the ocean in which it swims. Which is to say, very.

It was good to be back, indeed, but we wouldn't soon forget the East African lands with which we had become closely acquainted, nor the resilient peoples who know those lands as home.

We had returned in body, but a piece of Battlehard would forever be intertwined with that vitality by which cultures both Ethiopian and Djiboutian are animated.

Forever intertwined.

Conmy Hall had changed not at all since our departure. I could see the floor had been painted the deep blue that is its trademark. Whether it was on our account or because of a recently conducted indoor ceremony, I never thought to ask.

The Regiment had spared no expense in welcoming us back into its embrace. There were several tables of food, there was a handsomely produced banner, and there was at least one high-ranking figure for every five Bravo Company soldiers. One of these had sought me out for some light ribbing.

"Hey, Mongilutz."

I knew the voice very well. It belonged to my former mentor Sergeant Major Hunter, who was still running the shop.

Anticipating a harmless joke, I responded warmly, "Sergeant Major, it's very good to see you."

"Hey, they didn't let you drive when you were over there, did they?" This was in direct reference to my Pentagon parking lot crash.

"Huh-huh. I'm afraid so, Sergeant Major, though there were no buses within miles of us; or rather, none capable of damaging our vehicles."

"That's good. I was more worried about that than you getting shot at."

He then inquired as to Bretty's whereabouts.

Thurman and SGM Hunter had grown close while the former was accumulating an endless collection of Board victories. He was a beloved figure within the Regiment's upper echelons, and had been guided in his ascent by the wise counsel of SGM Hunter.

"He's digging into that cartoonishly large submarine sandwich, Sergeant Major," I replied, while pointing in Thurman's general direction. Always a slender man, Bretty was nevertheless known to possess a healthy appetite. He certainly worked hard to warrant as much.

Having spoken with Sergeant Major Hunter, the author of my S-3 fate, and shaken the hands of several field-grade officers, I quietly made my exit from the gathering. I appreciated all that had been done in preparation for Battlehard's return to Fort Myer ... but far greater than said appreciation was a need to be alone with my thoughts.

For my time with the 3rd United States Infantry Regiment was rapidly nearing its end, yet somehow mine was the heavy heart of one whose work was far from complete. It was as though I had had left so much undone, as though I could have done so much more.

Would it ever have been enough? Anything?

I did not know then.

I do not know now.

What was known was that there was a release formation scheduled, the attendance for which was, like all company formations, mandatory.

Having afforded myself the better part of an hour in wrestling with those thoughts which plague me still, I joined Second Squad, Second Platoon in the company formation area and awaited the arrival of Capt—

"Oh, look at that, he's already arrived."

The routine played out as always it had. We were called to attention. We were placed at ease. A safety briefing was articulated. We were called to attention. We were released. But the days that followed, well, they were less familiar.

Soldiers nearing the end of their enlistments have the option of signing out well ahead of their official ETS date, provided they have accumulated adequate leave days to allow their doing so. To do so is to take one's Terminal Leave. In other words, one may effectively subtract one day of their remaining enlistment for every one day of leave they've stored for the occasion. In my case, I had stored sixty days for the occasion, which is also the maximum number of permitted Terminal Leave days.

I would not be signing out just yet. A contract extension to which I had agreed while overseas (thereby ensuring my ETS date wouldn't come to pass during our HOA tour) would keep me on active duty for another month, or thereabouts, the conclusion of which would then see me signing out on Terminal Leave.

I never again performed a casket mission, and I visited the shop strictly in the context of a social call. Futrell—dear Futrell—was there, and I owed him a visit.

As for why my skills and talents were employed in neither of the capacities in which they had been employed in prior years is very simple: Battlehard, in its near-entirety, signed out on well-deserved post-deployment leave. I would have done the very same, of course, had my ETS date not been fast approaching.

Instead, I was assigned to oversee or participate in several work details in and around the company while very nearly every person with whom I had deployed was away.

There was a notable parallel to this state of affairs. After all, I had reported to the unit on a holiday and walked the halls of a virtually empty barracks for three days' time. This was, to some degree, reminiscent of that peculiar Thanksgiving weekend.

Quiet.

Quiet

Quiet

...

But I would not slip away from the unit so quietly into the night. For

Captain Travers had arranged a small ceremony of sorts (it is, after all, The Old Guard) to honor a few soldiers who had performed splendidly while overseas, and to bid farewell those of us whose time with the Regiment was nearing its end.

We numbered around twenty and stood in a long line on Summerall Field. The afternoon was mild, unseasonably so, the sky a rich blue. If ever there were a schematic detailing just how such a ceremony should be outfitted weather-wise, that day surely satisfied its every detail.

Travers waxed eloquent about the service we lined-up soldiers had performed throughout our respective enlistments and wished us all well in whatever endeavors awaited us in the days and years to come. Some of us were pinned medals, others received certificates, all received handshakes.

We were also invited to address the company in turn, which was common enough for soldiers soon to leave the Regiment, though I had never before seen the tradition carried out as such—what, with the lot of us standing in a can-can array, speaking one after the other from right to left.

I was somewhere towards the middle and followed a soldier (herein unnamed) whose speech went, in its entirety, as follows: "I'm out this bitch!"

Travers, to his credit, merely laughed and shrugged in a "What am I gonna do?" sort of manner.

My own words leaned towards the … well, they took shape how you might imagine they took shape: "At times, I find myself wondering if I ever should have been a soldier in the first place."

Ebner, that kindred spirit and marvelous friend, laughed upon hearing what was only the first sentence of my longwinded adieu.

"Which is not to say that I in any way regret my having enlisted, nor my time spent in these ranks. I have come to understand how much effort and sacrifice is necessary for the safeguarding of our nation's borders."

Ebner no longer laughed, but instead nodded knowingly.

"If I take nothing else with me upon leaving behind this way of life, I intend very much to take and guard and share that knowledge. It's been an honor serving with you, Bravo Company. I wish you all the very best."

Someone shouted out a muscular "Hooah!" at that point, which brought a rare smile to my face.

I also said something about my intention of becoming a teacher and joked about that day on Summerall being my last ceremony, or some such inanity. And though I did work as a writing tutor while in college, I have taught only intermittently since that breezy, blue-skied afternoon. A college course I taught in the spring of 2014 was met with mostly positive student reviews, though one did formally complain about my liberal (though tongue-in-cheek) use of the term "wanker" while lecturing. I've long been fond of British slang and the like.

The formation ended abruptly with Captain Travers dismissing us then and there. What followed was a clustered migration back to the barracks, as the off-post soldiers were eager for a change into civilian clothes and the barracks rats were eager for whatever video game system awaited their activating touch.

Despite the mass of aggregated bodies and the haste with which said mass was moving, I managed to track down the Musketeers prior to our reaching the barracks.

They all agreed to meet, and perhaps five minutes later we had gathered in a forty-square-foot staircase area which led directly to the building's rear exit. Much to my surprise and lasting gratitude, Garcia had, moments prior, tracked me down for a somber handshake and a sincere voicing of well-wishes. An element of conflict had occasionally plagued our professional relationship, and I had dreaded the prospect of leaving a burnt bridge in my wake. That dread was laid to rest then and there as Garcia spoke kind words and wished me the very best in life. I echoed as much in return.

And when he had gone, it was merely myself and the Musketeers.

"Fred, I realize you find the notion exceedingly dorky, but..."

Fred was already shaking his head, "Nope, Mark, not doing it."

"All for one—"

"Nope."

"Let's go, Thompson. Bretty and Jamesy are of a mind with me."

"I ain't doin' it, Mark."

"Fred. It's non-optional."

"Yes, it is, and I ain't doin' it."

"Fred."

With a heaving sigh, Fred, for what was the first and last time, hurriedly provided the rejoinder.

"—and one for all."

Not long after that moment of brilliant levity had come to pass, I commissioned four mounted rapiers, one for us each. Jamesy's read "Athos," Bretty's "Aramis," Fred's "Porthos," and my own "D'Artagnan." Upon receiving his blade, Fred left me a kind voicemail in which he articulated a feeling of sincere gratitude for the thought. The honor was mine.

Otherwise, that was it.

Never again were the four of us united in one place. Jamesy and I have seen one another on perhaps a dozen occasions since that day, while Bretty and I have maintained intermittent phone/e-mail contact. Oddly enough, he and I were initially the closest of the group, even if time and geography would wedge themselves between that friendship. We recently reestablished a connection and are actively discussing the prospect of an overdue reunion.

With Mike "Senator Fred" Thompson I lost contact outright mere weeks after leaving the Regiment. Close friends for three years, roommates for nearly half that time, we simply fell out of touch. Miraculously (or so it seemed at the time) we did track one another down via social media in the fall of 2016 and have plans to attend an automotive race.

As for 2004, however...

Jamesy and Fred had a bit of time remaining in uniform, having joined after both me and Thurman, the latter of whom had accompanied me on several of our out-processing appointments (and there are *many*).

A day or so later, I joined my platoon mates in visiting a country bar whose karaoke attraction was managed by the multitalented Travis Steele. Matt "Bacardi" Lemon recalled a pact into which I had reluctantly entered prior to our reaching Djibouti. In effect, I had committed myself to consuming a shot of alcohol upon returning to these United States. It was Travis "Smitty" Smith who made certain mine was a particularly strong concoction. What I remember most about the immediate aftereffect was that I felt rather unwell. Having adhered closely to my teetotaling ways since that evening, I occasionally summon the experience to mind in pursuit of a mild laugh.

Jamesy and Fred were, of course, enjoying their post-deployment leave, while Brett was busy preparing for his post-enlistment life. I have never (before or since) known anyone to so strategically plot their life trajectory in the manner of one Brett Thurman.

That I was characteristically morose at this point should come as no surprise. On one occasion, mere days prior to signing out on Terminal Leave, I drove to Fort Myer in civilian athletic attire for the express purpose of carrying out an exercise regimen Jamesy and I had engineered some months prior to the deployment. It was a brief run from Sheridan Avenue out the Iwo Jima gate, 'round the memorial itself, back through the gate, and up CIF Hill before heading to the Caisson stables for twenty minutes spent climbing the fast-rope.

While I had intended to sprint full-speed up that hill, mere steps into the incline I slowed my pace considerably and likely placed myself in the mind of that eighteen-year-old kid who, nearly four years earlier, had struggled so stubbornly to keep pace with the human greyhound that is Mike McGuinness. I would surely have enjoyed greater success in my efforts by that point, but it was of no concern to me. What mattered was the journey which had, in certain respects, seen its first step taken on that chilly fall morning.

But not in *every* respect.

Benning had, after all, played its part. So, too, had my beloved Washington.

It all flooded back as I made my way up that hill. That beautiful hill. That painful hill. That worthy hill. That damned hill.

There was that fantastical woodland which runs adjacent to the neighborhood in which I experienced most of my youth.

There were my loving parents, sister, and grandparents.

There was the World War II veteran and former POW who had taught me the values of self-respect and discipline.

There was Geoff, that hyper-analytical creature; and there was Andy, that born logician. Those two, perhaps more than any educator I would ever know, taught me how to think and how to learn.

There was the loss of my virginity to a seasoned woman of eighteen years and the homecoming dance that had wholly overhauled my self-image.

There was the vanity born of hollow gymnasium muscle. How inadequate it would prove mere months later.

There was 30th AG and the misery of the administrative.

There was Charlie Company, 2/54—Sand Hill's toughest battalion, and the home of Drill Sergeant Spencer, whose reputation I had uncannily come to know while still in the Sea-Tac Airport.

There were the flutter kicks, the push-ups, the miles of forced marching, the thousands of rounds shot, the suck, the struggle, the pain, the enormous joy of small pleasures.

There was the Bayonet, and there was Roum guiding his brothers home in that last mile.

There was the comic wit of Mann, the effortless charisma of Rohde, and the marvelous soldiery of Naylor. I thought of those guys and hoped with my every fiber that they were, indeed, doing well.

There was Airborne School, the holdover for which nearly saw me disqualified on account of a fluke APFT shortfall. Funny, I had scored well over one-hundred-percent on nearly every APFT since, but that close call at 2/58 … it haunted me.

There was falling from a plane.

There was the twenty-day HRAP program which had reacquainted me with my beloved Washington and the hidden gem that is Marysville.

There was my midnight reporting to Regimental Staff Duty.

There was the Thanksgiving weekend of 2000 and those days spent exploring the wonders of our nation's capital.

There was the very real threat of my being assigned to Alpha Company. Thank you once again, Nelson. Truly.

All of this had preceded that first run with McGuinness and the Headquarters Platoon, but none of it had quite made clear just what sort of standard I would need to set for myself in order that I might be a useful and worthy Old Guard soldier.

And was I?

Sometimes, yes.

Other times...

I had too often placed pride above reason when blessed with the good leadership of Sergeant Bradley.

I had allowed haste to overcome patience when first pursuing my Expert Infantryman's Badge.

I had thought myself invincible the following summer, and paid a high price for that hubris on Summerall Field.

And then the Pentagon was attacked on September 11th, 2001. I do not know how it is one goes about assessing their contribution to such a recovery effort but I do know that it never feels as though it was enough. Never.

I felt much the same upon returning from the Horn of Africa.

Is it ever enough? It is never enough. The ever-spinning wheel—a question asked, a question answered.

S-3 had made for a good year, even if it was rather civilian in its construct. Perhaps *because* of that fact. We Draftsmen had been entrusted with outsized responsibility and abused our station rarely. I had worked tirelessly to earn Scott's trust and respect; the friendship had materialized rather incidentally, I suppose. I had accumulated sufficient standing to warrant my promotion board invitation, and had cultivated enough of a reputation to be, in the CSM's mind, a known quantity.

The Draftsmen had come to know Washington, D.C., as our professional playground, with White House trips accounting for enough of our time to render familiar our faces to at least a couple of Secret Service professionals.

And when the question of returning to Battlehard had been presented, well, it was no question at all. The company was my home, even if every day spent in the shop had been worthwhile.

I thought of Hooph and of Brady, of Williams and Palmer, of the Bash Brothers, of Dussard and Bradley, of Lemon and Wilson, of Smith and Slyder—I thought of those extraordinary souls alongside whom I had played my small part in honoring our nation's fallen warriors.

And I considered the human project. The very nature of life itself. I considered pursuits noble and impure alike, and wondered if anything separated one from the next in the grand scheme.

Or the scheme, anyway.

I could not say with certainty, but I had my suspicions that nobility is inherent in all existence, and is something worth embodying as best as one is able.

The 3rd United States Infantry is as good a vessel as any other where achieving that embodiment is concerned, and almost certainly superior to most. As for whether I had myself proven worthy of it, I simply don't know. I know that I tried, and I know that, often enough, I failed. Perhaps there is dignity in effort alone; perhaps there is not. Perhaps...

To all those whose journey with that storied and sacred Regiment has not yet begun, I wish you nothing but paramount success, meaningful connection with what is truly an important mission, and memories of a most blessed and enduring sort.

A few months later, I made the impulsive decision to leave the Virginia area entirely. I would make a new start for myself out west. Saying goodbye to Scott proved rather difficult. I had been raised by good parents (a patient mother and a generous stepfather), and I am in their debt for as much. But Scott had himself become a surrogate father figure across those two years' time.

I was possibly the best I ever was or ever will be while striving to equal the standard of Old Guard excellence. The power of youth to vitalize a body is in many weighs counterbalanced by its power to diminish comprehension of the intrinsically valuable. If only the exchange had amounted to a more equitable transaction. If only a great many things.

Travis, my future brother-in-law and friend of ten years, flew to the D.C. area to make with me the two-thousand-mile westward drive to Phoenix, Arizona.

As we placed Arlington and Alexandria and Myer and D.C. in our rearview mirror, I looked silently to the road ahead. I don't know with certainty what it was I thinking in that moment…

…but it's very possible her name was Ariel Denton.

Epilogue

It's been a short thirteen years since I headed west to Phoenix, AZ. Days, weeks, and months have piled one into the next at a rate that would have seemed unthinkable during childhood and adolescence.

Arizona has been good to me. I've earned a few degrees, worked in the corporate sector, screwed up a few relationships, authored two works of fiction, and now work as a contract writer.

I also owned a couple of motorcycles because, well, why on earth not? My next purchase along those lines will likely be of the purely electric sort. Send me your suggestions to the contrary, if you'd like.

And, as mentioned in the text, I did return to the Army for a little over a year's time. In the spring of 2007, I switched my Inactive Ready Reserve status to that of an Active Reservist, and did so in order to join an MI Battalion headed for a tour in Afghanistan.

Why?

I genuinely missed the haircut, I suppose.

Rubbish.

In truth, it was guilt. Nothing more. I simply felt guilty enjoying the life of a degree-seeking civilian whilst so many soldiers—many of whom I had served and trained alongside—braved the stew of violence lethally simmering in combat zones across the world. I wanted to contribute.

And I saved a few shekels on shampoo that year.

As for those men alongside whom I was fortunate enough to serve...

Several of those whose names appear in these pages would go on to serve in a career capacity. Among them were my friends John "Hooph" Hoffman and Timothy Pennartz, the latter of whom retired shortly prior to my penning the first page of this work. Hooph is in Germany at the moment, though by the time this work goes into print he, too, may have retired. He's nearly reached twenty years in uniform.

Weird.

I was blessed with many a good friendship during my TOG years, and knew to appreciate as much even at the time. But with John Hoffman I enjoyed a decidedly unique brotherhood. From mentor to team leader in the space of a year's time, and a fellow team leader upon my return to Battlehard from the shop. Through it all, we were friends bound by common interests and a fondness for the literary world's more esoteric of entries. When at last Hooph retires, I wish him a life of endless reading, cycling, and overall fulfillment.

I have reestablished contact with Tim Pennartz, who telephoned me within minutes of my sending him what I imagined was a longshot LinkedIn message. It was a particularly enjoyable and uplifting conversation. He is enjoying the life of a family man and is settling into a good, happy, and well-earned retirement.

Matt "Bacardi" Lemon ultimately made a career of it and paid a price in terms of bodily health. He was medically retired around the fifteen-year mark and now busies himself with caring for a sizable family. We caught up with one another after I began writing the book. It was as though not a single day had passed since last we spoke. He is as sincere a conversationalist as ever the world has known.

Chris Bradley contacted me almost immediately upon learning of the book project. We had not seen one another in fourteen years' time, for which reason (among others) I found myself terrifically moved by the conversation that followed. He works as a K9 handler, is a father, and set himself to learning the banjo.

Matthew Mann (Matt-Mann) would go on to earn a Bachelor of Science in the field Criminal Justice. Working initially for ICE, Mann would subsequently attain his CDL and pursue work as a full-time truck driver. He is also the father of six children (three biological, three via his having re-married). Mann and I reminisced about our shared Sand Hill experience several months past. He's happy and at peace with it all. May he know only prosperity.

Monte Swapp lives in Utah and works in the field of information technology. He is an avid bicyclist, a skilled gamer, a committed vegan, and loves his pets.

My dear friend Dennis Brady, that excellent soldier, is also a military careerist and has done marvelously well for himself in the twelve years since last we saw one another. There has been talk of a phone conversation at some point.

The saga of Bob "Squirrel" Williams and Bill "Billy P" Palmer never really ended. Their brawl in the Daman's parking lot on that crisp Veterans Day of 2001 played out several times more in the years that followed, but their friendship was somehow strengthened through it all.

I moved in with Bob for around six months' time upon reaching Arizona on Halloween Day of 2004. Of all those with whom I served during those first four years, I have seen the most of my dear friend Bob. He works in a sales capacity for Federal Express and has largely prospered in that profession. Marriage and fatherhood have reshaped him considerably, though the SK2K2 memories (including that misguided Valentine's Day prank) still hold a special place in his heart.

Billy P, the wittiest of us all, remained in the D.C. area for some time after leaving the Regiment in mid–2004. We spent a good deal of time with one another during the month or so that separated my own Old Guard departure from my Arizona relocation. When speaking with Bill, we discussed at great length that somewhat aimless month and agreed that it had amounted to time *very* well spent. I miss those days, though they scarcely felt real while unfolding. The time immediately following one's departure from the Armed Forces tends to resemble a hazy dream, of sorts.

Jamie Nelson and I reconnected after having not seen one another in very nearly fifteen years' time. I thanked him for ensuring mine would be a Bravo Company assignment while with the Regiment. He insisted he had merely been trying to help out a fellow soldier. Soon to be married, Nelson seems rightfully happy and at peace.

Scott Taylor retired a couple of years following our return from the Horn of Africa. He had served his country marvelously well across two decades and deserved the joyous family life that had already begun to embrace him prior to his career's conclusion. He found a suitable contracting job and has pursued one layer of higher education after another, seemingly without once coming up for air. Scott, if you are reading this, I implore you to relax— you've earned as much. More so than any human I have in my day known.

Matt Genkinger, the excellent Colors marcher and my friend from very early on, also remained in the D.C. metropolitan area after leaving the Army. He was among the very first to express his ardent support and enthusiasm for this project, an expression for which I am immeasurably grateful. Genk was among the best First Platoon would ever produce during my time with the Regiment.

Roy Gabriel has done exceedingly well for himself, a fact which truthfully came as no surprise to me. He is a hardworking and intelligent man with a strong entrepreneurial spirit. I remain honored for our having served together.

William Roum, my Sand Hill/Airborne comrade and fellow TOG new report, has struck a fine balance between adventure and family. He is a combat veteran and career defense contractor with a loving wife and children. Of all those with whom I muscled through the rigors of Benning's OSUT program, it is for Roum that I am most happy.

Or, rather, he's tied for first.

Douglas Rohde and Joseph Naylor have gone on to lead full, accomplished, and productive lives. Whatever OSUT would have amounted to in their absence, it would surely have been a lesser experience. If we soldiers are fated to once again experience Sand Hill in some existence born of reincarnation, I hope very much to do so alongside those brilliant souls.

Brian Hett, the excellent Firing Party soldier of singular quality (and former roommate of Bob and Bill), left the Regiment in 2003 and went on to earn a pair of B.S. degrees; one in accounting, one in finance. He reenlisted shortly thereafter and is still serving his country in that capacity. Wherever it is he finds himself assigned, that unit is undoubtedly better for his presence.

The three sergeants major (Butts, Hunter, and Winchester) I would, through sheer happenstance, come to know rather closely as a lower-enlisted soldier, have moved on to prosperous civilian sector lives.

Aubrey Butts lives in southern Virginia and earned a doctorate degree some years past; I made contact with him after coming across his son's Facebook profile. I am grateful to my sister for having created that social media account on my behalf.

Todd Hunter retired from the U.S. Army and remained in the D.C. area. He has occasionally run into Taylor and Thurman, and is predictably enjoying great success in his civilian pursuits. Intelligence and diligence couple well together in any pursuit; Todd offers evidence in support of that contention.

Hank Winchester left the Army after having given that organization everything he had to give. There may well be retired soldiers who've walked more difficult paths than that experienced by Winchester, but I've never met one personally. Like his friend and protégé Scott Taylor, Winchester also entered the defense industry's civilian chapter. From what I understand, he came to enjoy the work, by and large.

As for the Musketeers, we've not yet reunited, though plans towards that end are in the making.

In early 2005, James "Jamesy" Taheny returned to the Bay Area with the love of his life and soon after began pursuing a degree in civil engineering. He has enjoyed an active and fulfilling decade and brought into being a daughter upon whose raising he is eminently focused. I should note, in the fall of 2011 I was honored to stand in Jamesy's wedding ... and doubly honored to have broken from a script authored by his bride. My own words were superior to those assigned me.

Michael "Senator Fred" Thompson left the Army in late-2004. A lifelong racing enthusiast, he has spent a good deal of time on dirt tracks and attending races whenever his busy professional schedule allows. At present, the Texas native is living in Houston with his wife and children. Dr. Pepper is still a fixture within the man's diet.

Brett "Bretty" Thurman, first of the Musketeers with whom I was acquainted, off-post roommate during the 9/11 attacks and for over six months thereafter, excellent soldier, respected professional, and as brilliant a friend as one could ever hope to know, ended up in the D.C. area upon leaving the Regiment, with several years in Chicago taking up a middle stretch. He has earned a pair of degrees (or more) and is presently working for the State Department.

Those Taken Too Soon

Staff Sergeant Ryan Fritsche was killed in July of 2007 while deployed to Afghanistan in support of Operation Enduring Freedom. I learned of his death shortly before a deployment of my own and was saddened in the extreme. The loss of Fritsche immediately rendered the world a poorer place and left a great many holes in a great many hearts. We had not been close, and I had not seen the kid since mid–2004, but I had never forgotten his quality, his sincerity, his worth, his virtue. In a world beset by artificial sanctimony and rank moral posturing, the absence of a truly good soul like that of Ryan Fritsche is particularly acute. He was, quite possibly, the very best of us.

Staff Sergeant Jake VanMeter died on March 8th, 2010, in Schweinfurt, Germany. Only 27 years of age, VanMeter had spent nearly a decade in uniform when he was taken from his family, friends, and loved ones. More so than nearly anyone I had known before or have since met, VanMeter possessed the ability to find hidden humor in nearly every given situation. He could always be counted upon to have those nearest him reduced to a joyful state of laughter. His loss was hard on all who knew him, even those of us who had regrettably fallen out of touch with the man, a consummate soldier if ever there was one.

Index

275